On Women Turning 60

Embracing the Age of Fulfillment

On Women Turning 60

Embracing the Age of Fulfillment

Interviews and Photography by

Cathleen Rountree

Foreword by Carolyn G. Heilbrun

Three Rivers Press
New York

Published by Three Rivers Press, a division of Crown Publishers, Inc.,
201 East 50th Street, New York, New York 10022.
Member of the Crown Publishing Group.

Originally published in hardcover by Harmony Books,
a division of Crown Publishers, Inc., in 1997.

First paperback edition printed in 1998.

Random House, Inc. New York, Toronto, London, Sydney, Auckland
www.randomhouse.com
Three Rivers Press and colophon are trademarks of Crown Publishers, Inc.

Printed in the United States of America

Design by Deborah Kerner

Library of Congress Cataloging in Publication Data

Rountree, Cathleen.
On women turning 60: embracing the age of fulfillment/
interviews and photography by Cathleen Rountree; foreword by
Carolyn Heilbrun.—1st ed.
p.   cm.
1. Aged women—Interviews.   2. Aged women—Psychology.   I.
Title.
HQ1061.R593   1997
305.26—dc21   97-5889
CIP

ISBN 0-609-80228-3
10   9   8   7   6   5   4   3   2   1
First Paperback Edition

With gratitude and affection,
this book is dedicated to
Ellen Levine
Deena Metzger
and
Gloria Steinem

In memory of
Nabeela George

Contents

It takes so much effort to hold on to the illusion of youth, to keep the fear of age at bay, that in doing so we could fail to recognize the new qualities and strengths that might emerge.

—BETTY FRIEDAN,
The Fountain of Age

Paradoxical as it may seem, to believe in youth is to look backward; to look forward we must believe in age.

—DOROTHY L. SAYERS,
Dorothy L. Sayers,
James Barbazon

Carolyn G. Heilbrun

When Cathleen Rountree asked me to join the group of distinguished women she was interviewing for *On Women Turning 60,* I demurred, partly because I was about to turn past sixty, but mostly because I was myself writing a book about my sixties and beyond. Cathleen kindly allowed me to write a foreword, a privilege for which I am grateful since it permitted me to read these stories of women in their sixties in advance of their publication; this gives me a sense of belonging in this book, which I most emphatically wish to do.

The last part of the book's title, the subtitle, is *Embracing the Age of Fulfillment,* and that description of the sixties is illuminated by every woman's account of her seventh decade. They are not all alike, these women, not at all, but each has faced her sixties with a sense of adventure, not defeat, despair, or self-pity. When I say they are different, I mean they think differently on many issues, but they are all alike in welcoming age as the adventure it is if we will make it so. Some have done with romance, some are still relishing it, with the added satisfaction that you don't have to hope it will last forever; to put it another way, forever is not, in one's sixties, that long a time—a satisfying thought. Some go in for cosmetic surgery in a mild way (chiefly eyelids); others relax with evident triumph into relishing whatever wrinkles or sags they have earned. Some have long marriages, some ex-husbands, some are with women; many have children, others, without regret, do not. There is, in short, no stereotype here, though there is a pattern.

Ann Richards, recently governor of Texas and a woman known for her pithy observations, remarks that, past fifty, "you don't have to pretend anymore," which is perhaps the theme of this book. I am, each woman in her individual way declares, myself at last, what I want to be, not what society, or culture, or the media, or anyone thinks I should be. Ann Richards also knows that "women are constantly reinventing themselves," a process for which this book is ample evidence. Although all the women treat the subject of men delicately, they are all clearly aware that men are less likely to reinvent themselves, but those who have stuck around to accompany their women into their sixties have been remarkably agreeable to the results of female reinvention. I suspect that men like those in these long relationships have been too little noticed, let alone celebrated, by our society; perhaps they are what used to be, though never without some skepticism, called gentlemen. They are, above all, gentle, little given to arrogance or unwarranted assertions of their male privileges.

Most of the women have been married to the more usual run of men—that is, those more easily identified as American males—and Rose Styron, married to William, has one of the best clarifications I have read of what makes a long marriage endure: "The easiest thing in the world would have been for us to separate, and I'm sure we both thought of it many times. You decide again every decade or every morning, are you going to go on with this or are you going to run away and do something else? But if you don't separate, then you tend to go deeper, to know each other better, to know your own needs and his. You make your compromises, and I guess you're glad the other person is still around."

If the interviews presented here can be in any way sorted into groups, the most obvious distinction, perhaps, is between those who speak primarily of life in their sixties and those who tell the stories of their lives. I myself prefer those who, while offering a gesture or two of explanation provided by the past, speak mainly of their present time of questions and fulfillment. But that is simply to express my own preference, not to make any sort of judgment.

These women are largely in agreement about the blessing, in one's seventh decade, of women friends, many of them younger and therefore likely to hang around a while. All the women are feminists, although a few might prefer not to be so-called, or if so, not too loudly. Fay Weldon, who recognizes that what she writes is going to be feminist, puts the matter with her usual acerbic elegance:

"Of course it is no fun being a feminist! Being a feminist is the opposite of fun. That means, if you are going to be a proper feminist, you need to live by your principles, and this is impossible. . . . It's no fun; I recommend it to nobody." But of course, as with romance, she recommends it to everyone.

Many of these women are writers, one way or another, and for each of them, I daresay, work is what matters: work is the center, the meaning, of life. But if writing is the work, it is not as regular in its manifestations as we might like it to be. In my book on the last decades of life, I mention Käthe Kollwitz and her recognition that with work at the center of our lives, we must still wait for the tide to rise. And the tide *will* rise. Ursula Le Guin, one of my favorite writers and people, puts this with her usual modesty and acumen and offers us, by the way, since she herself is so wonderful and productive a writer, infinite comfort: "I try to write regularly in the mornings, but I can't write all the time. There are vast periods of time when I don't have a story to write, so I have to make work for myself. I keep writing, but I may just do correspondence. On the other hand, if I don't have a story to write, what am I doing sitting in my office? Chewing my fingernails, probably."

It has been said that one of the defects of many literature courses in our universities is that they are devoted to the works of "dead white males." That is a phrase that is both useful and disturbing: disturbing because it is dismissive of great genius, useful because it reminds us that not all writers worth studying are necessarily dead, or white, or male. We are, in this collection, wonderfully able to announce that the writers are not dead, or male, or all white. They are women who have in common the accumulation of years, the courage of hard-earned wisdom, and a devotion to social causes or to art and who are redolent with the sort of bravery that is simultaneously ordinary and unique.

Which is to say that our sixties, too, can be fulfilling and not the stuff of repetition and despair; that each of us, no matter who we are or were, can reinvent ourselves—not as youths, but as creatures little known in our culture, secretly triumphant, and each day more ourselves.

On Women Turning 60

Embracing the Age of Fulfillment

Introduction

SOMEWHERE IN THE BACK OF MY MIND,
THERE IS THE NOTION THAT [WOMEN IN THEIR SIXTIES]
ARE WHAT AMERICANS CALL "OVER THE HILL." RATHER,
I FEEL THAT I'M NOT EVEN HALFWAY UP AND
I'M GOING TO KEEP CLIMBING STRONG.
—RIANE EISLER

WHEN I WAS APPROACHING SIXTY . . . [THAT]
ROUND NUMBER 6-0 MEANT "OVER THE HILL,"
"YOUTH GONE," "OUT TO PASTURE" . . . MY FEAR WAS
THAT . . . I WOULD HAVE TO THINK ABOUT DECLINE AND
REORDERING MY LIFE AND CHANGING MY PRIORITIES
AND STAYING HOME, AND I DON'T WANT TO DO ANY
OF THOSE THINGS.
—ROSE STYRON

When I first started thinking about women in their sixties, I was surprised about how many of whom I thought, Oh, she *can't* be in her sixties. How *vital* and dynamic these women are! Like most individuals in Western culture, I, too, had fallen prey to the myth (as Riane Eisler, Rose Styron, and others articulate in this book) that for a woman in her sixties her "youth is gone," that she is "over the hill" and needs to be put "out to pasture." I was dismayed to discover that I myself held this stereotype about women in their sixties. *On Women Turning 60: Embracing the Age of Fulfillment* shatters the fallacy of "over the hill" once and for all. And good riddance!

On Women Turning 60: Embracing the Age of Fulfillment is a collection of interviews with women from diverse cultural, geographic, economic, and professional circumstances and assorted lifestyles. This book presents dedicated women between the ages of sixty and seventy who share passionate concerns about their lives and pioneering visions for the world. By developing their intrinsic inner authority, the following women have devised their own "initiations" into a productive later life or third age. *On Women Turning 60* explores the effects on women's lives of aging, meaningful work, relationship, feminism, creativity, and spirituality, in a deeply personal manner. It offers women in their later years a variety of role models to contemplate and hold as positive internal images. It gives the reader a feeling of pride and strength in her maturity and provides alternative ways of viewing herself and of moving through her remaining years.

Although I am "only" forty-eight (Einstein was right: everything—including age—*is* relative), I have cloistered my own fears of aging. Undoubtedly this apprehension has been the fundamental motivating factor for my ten-year-long study on the subject of women and aging. My previous books on the subject—*On Women Turning 40: Coming into Our Fullness* and *On Women Turning 50: Celebrating Midlife Discoveries*—along with my nationwide workshops for women in midlife, have acted as an analgesic on my anxiety about aging. Perhaps the singular most affecting benefit I have received from my work is the opportunity to confront these demons of dread head-on and unmask them for what they are: a fiction. In so doing, I then have the privilege of sharing my revelations with you, the readers of this book.

Who are women in their sixties? Women over sixty-five are the fastest-growing segment of the U.S. population. They are our mothers or grandmothers, our sisters, our aunts, our neighbors, teachers, and friends. They are ourselves, either now or later. This book offers insights into the sixty-something woman's consciousness: her joys and sorrows, her aspirations and compromises, her liberties and responsibilities, her visions and restraints. It can help us to understand these women and eventually ourselves at their age. These women are role models and trailblazers who are helping to free society from its handicap and constraints of ageism; from the epithet of "over the hill." The women in this book are guides for how to "grow" older rather than to "get" old. They offer us the wisdom of their years, and it behooves us to acknowledge them.

While writing *On Women Turning 60,* I came across a film that beautifully elucidated this myth of "over the hill." Appropriately titled *Over the Hill,* it starred Oscar winner Olympia Dukakis as a widow named Alma. It begins at her sixtieth birthday party in her new basement apartment in Bar Harbor, Maine. The apartment has recently been remodeled by Alma's well-meaning son, Steven, in order to accommodate her. Alma has been coerced into selling the home in which she had lived with her husband and raised her two children, because now that she is a single woman, "the family" feels that it is too large for her to keep up on her own and that, as "an older woman," she would be "much better off" living with them. Unfortunately, Alma (which means "bountiful" or "nourishing" in Latin and "soul" in Spanish) is not consulted about what *she* wants for herself. Rather, she is made to feel that her "youth is gone," that she is "over the hill" and needs to be put "out to pasture."

Alma looks bewildered, and her submissive body language indicates that she has resigned herself to the future of invisibility that is allocated to all "old" women. She appears, at first, to accept her fate. But as Steven hands her a birthday cake that, like a portentous fiery Medusa's head, blazes with five dozen candles, Alma, without a word, walks calmly and purposefully upstairs and, after opening the front door, heaves the cake out on its face into the snow as if she were exorcising a demon. She is, of course, the demon of compliance, of fearful acquiescence, the demon of self-doubt and defeat. The look on Alma's face is one of triumph mixed with the glee of an eleven-year-old who has just disobeyed her parents for the first time and affirms to herself incredulously, "I did it!"

The palpable rage toward family, life circumstances, age, fate, and herself that led to the action of this fictional character is genuine and recognizable to every woman who is accused of, or sees herself as, being "over the hill."

Alma runs away from "home." She buys a souped-up 1959 Chevy Bel Air from her granddaughter's boyfriend and drives off "over the hill," into the bush, and on her way to Melbourne, where she plans to "loop the loop" by making a complete circuit around the Australian continent. "Travel broadens the behind," she impishly tells her stunned daughter as she revs the throttle. This double entendre on the phrase "over the hill" brings a second, more constructive, and hopeful meaning into play. Rather than washed up, wasted, and of no use, "over the hill" becomes synonymous with independence, adventure, determination, and new horizons, vistas, and perspectives. As Alma, in her duckbill cap and black mirror wraparound eye shades, heads into the Australian outback alone, we root for her, we're proud of her, and we identify with her spirited demonstration of defiance.

Ironically, *Over the Hill* was directed by George Miller, the man who helped Mel Gibson sweep to worldwide recognition in the macho films *Mad Max* and *Road Warrior*. In its way, *Over the Hill* is a feminist *Road Warrior*. It is about a sixty-year-old budding Amazon who meets her fears of the unknown full face and assumes responsibility (probably for the first time, the film suggests) for her own life.

We watch as an initially naive Alma is briefly terrorized by a band of desert hooligans, then rescued and pleasingly seduced by an eccentric retired dentist who refers to himself as "a middle-class gypsy." After a series of escapades suitable for an Amazon, Alma, at last (in the words of Ursula Le Guin), "becomes pregnant with herself."

After a lifetime of taking care of others, Alma, the nourisher, learns how to nurture herself. Alma/soul enters the world of soul making. As a result of her experiences, she is rewarded with the self-confidence to live her own life and the courage to *choose* what that life will be. She refuses to accept anyone else's prescription for her life. Alma discovers that, far from being "over the hill" in the negative sense, her life is filled with potential for growth, adventure, love, friendship, sex, and, above all, independence. She has recognized and embraced the age of fulfillment.

Because several women I interviewed for this book spoke to me about their fears of being considered by others as "over the hill"—and their ultimate refusal to view *themselves* as such—this film had a special resonance for me. The women I met, like the fictional character Alma, have struggled with feelings of self-doubt and insecurity in regard to their age. As a sixtieth birthday gift to herself, my friend Susanne Short embraced her fulfillment by embracing the world: she circumnavigated the globe in a nine-week journey. "I started thinking of all the things and places I wanted to do and visit and experience before I get too old," she told me. Susanne visited Buddhist monasteries and temples, Islamic mosques, and Christian shrines in Russia and the Gobi Desert, Mongolia, Bali, and China. "It was like fulfilling a dream that I thought I might not ever get to do," she said, smiling, filled with memories.

Women in their sixties—not yet old, but no longer young—often find it to be an almost awkward decade; as Carolyn Heilbrun perceptively told me, "It can be a time of feeling very alive without any particular external evidence of it." According to Susanne Short, "The sixties are such an in-between time of life; it takes some adjusting to being in this interim. I don't feel old—I think of old as being seventy-five or eighty—and young is certainly younger than I am. One starts to think about life in terms of time left and what to do with it."

Unlike menopause in the fifties and cronehood in the seventies, no traditional designations exist for the sixties, and with the official age of retirement inching closer to seventy, there are few limits. Ms. Heilbrun exemplifies this decade in the title of her latest book: *The Last Gift of Time.* I think she is accurate. The women I interviewed primarily looked forward to their sixties and, indeed, felt them to be a gift. Because it is a decade without definition, no one—young or old—seems to have any expectations of what people in their sixties are like or should be doing. As Sue Hubbell wrote in her *New York Times Magazine* article "A Gift Decade," "Our sixties are like a decade-long February 29, a ten-year leap second. I think we are getting away with something: an extra time before old age and after life's middle."

Women in their sixties such as Susanne are older, yes, but not—thank you very much—*old.* As women phase out of midlife into their sixties, they often enjoy what Margaret Mead referred to as a postmenopausal zest. They enter what the French call the Third Age and what I designate as "the third third" of life. In fact, aided by a vigorous life of the mind, the creative powers of many women are only now *beginning* to peak. As sixty-four-year-old British novelist Fay Weldon optimistically told me in regard to her creativity: "There's always more where that came from!" At sixty-three, former Texas governor Ann Richards believes that she has "at least twenty *good* years left." And at sixty-five, author and futurist Riane Eisler counts on working another *thirty* years. "Over the hill"? Hardly.

After sixty, there is often an increased level of self-confidence and personal authority, a deepening trust of the inner process, and an ability to be present in, pay attention to, and appreciate the "now." An older woman can have as much vitality, passion, and focus as a younger woman half her age, and in many cases even more. I have seen them. I *know* them. And, heaven forbid, there is still sex—in variance to what Francine Du Plessix Gray cagily regards as "the quaint taboos that still shroud the association of carnality and old age"—even if it is "only" "sex with one," as quilter Virginia Harris, sixty, who is single, calls it.

Is it true that memory diminishes with age, as the current theory would have us believe and therefore fear? Not according to tympanist Elayne Jones, sixty-eight, who remembers hundreds of scores to operas and symphonies as well as the names of people and places she knew and visited either yesterday or more than fifty years ago. A number of women did make reference to their "poor memories," but a recent study in Italy shows that the reason for the apparent decline of memory in the elderly may be *loss of self-confidence* (italics mine). The latest research indicates that while the human brain may lose some of its speed and capacity with age, this decrease is offset by other aspects of intelligence that are honed by practice and function best in later life. Unsurprisingly, it was noted that our mental attitude influences the brain. An upbeat, cheerful outlook improves brain function at *any* age.

What are women in their sixties doing with their lives? The women I met are teaching other women to "fly" on low-flying trapezes and to "walk tall" on stilts; rewriting school curriculums; working with rape victims in Bosnia; educating the world about chimpanzees and other wildlife; mentoring the young; raising funds for elders; performing in symphony orchestras; directing plays; writing poetry and novels; acting in films; singing in concerts; lobbying for rights in Washington, D.C.; traveling the globe on behalf of world peace; making quilts; analyzing handwriting; and (would you believe?) learning to surf. Nothing seems impossible to these women.

Few can imagine themselves retiring: "I expect to die, but I don't plan to retire," Margaret Mead once stated. "I'll drop dead first!" was sixty-seven-year-old graphologist June Canoles's adamant assertion. Both Ann Richards and Elayne Jones look forward in later life to buying seaside properties, respectively, on the Gulf Coast and in Barbados. Rose Styron, sixty-three, who is addicted to travel, expects to be hiking off into the sunset as long as her body can carry her. Primatologist Jane Goodall, sixty-three, whose mother and father are ninety-four and ninety-six, says dryly, "Nobody dies in my family." She therefore expects her hearty ancestry to transport her through at least another three decades. However, poet Nellie Wong, sixty-three, who began working at sixteen, looks forward to retiring in two years, when she can devote herself more to her writing and the political causes she fosters. She says she will also enjoy "going to the movies at a senior discount."

Because the world of the arts—literature, cinema, theater, dance, music, opera—are alive for us with sociological relevance, we look to them as a mirror of the zeitgeist and as paradigms for ourselves in our own lives. The arts assist us in viewing ourselves as we are or as we wish to become. They provide a context in which we can observe what society is thinking about us and itself. In contemporary art forms we are seeing more constructive and enthusiastic role models of women in their sixties. In 1995, off Broadway, I saw a superb production starring two sixty-something actresses, Vanessa Redgrave and Eileen Atkins (who also adapted the play): *Vita and Virginia,* the story of the intense love affair between writer Virginia Woolf and novelist Vita Sackville-West. In the film *Unhook the Stars,* Gena Rowlands, sixty-six, plays a lonely widow in her sixties who begins to partake of life and laughter once more through her friendship with a small neighborhood boy. In this movie she also dates a much younger man, a truck driver, played by Gerard Depardieu. Talk about fulfillment! The 1994 film *The Summer House* starred a radiant and vivacious Jeanne Moreau. Mademoiselle Moreau, then in her mid-sixties, portrayed a wise but obviously still sexy older woman who, with true panache, helped save her niece from a fate worse than death: a loveless marriage. And Marilyn French, who is now in her sixties and is the author of the best-selling feminist novel *The Women's Room,* has written a new novel called *My Summer with George* about an aging heroine, an adamantly erotic romance novelist who finds herself, once again, ambushed by love. In this book, Ms. French challenges convention and pungently raises the possibility of a full romantic life for a woman in her sixties.

Vanity plays less of a role in the lives of women in their sixties than it does for women in their forties and fifties. Women in their sixties grasp that, as Betty Friedan wrote, "[it] takes so much effort to hold on to the illusion of youth, to keep the fear of age at bay." It was a real relief to discover that most of these women no longer *worry* about how they look. They *care* about looking their best, but not to the exclusion of more pressing matters like writing novels or directing plays or working for world peace or gardening or quilting or stilt walking or spending time with grandchildren or friends or just going out in nature for a walk. I wondered if this is because women now in their sixties are the last generation to be spared the compulsively addictive concern with how their bodies and faces age. (The next generation down and subsequent generations of baby boomers have come to be obsessed with their looks.) Or does this ease with the basic process of aging come naturally to us at a certain point in our daily routine, when we more readily redirect our attentions into other areas?

Of course, some women become even more militant about their looks as they try to beat back the years. In this attempt they may have face lifts or dye their hair or painfully adhere to an insistent and merciless regime of diets and exercise.

Louise Erdrich calls these women "Valiant Looks Warriors, hardworking, airbrushed grandmas, who refuse to go gently or at all." I know what she means. A few weeks ago I saw a well-known actress, who is *only* fifty (funny how *young* fifty now seems, isn't it?), on *Charlie Rose*. She looked as though it hurt to smile! True, she didn't have any wrinkles, but what price beauty? I'll take the late Italian actress—haggard, earthy, love-besotted—Anna Magnani, who said to her director Federico Fellini, "Don't retouch my wrinkles, it took me so long to get them." Germane to this is George Bernard Shaw's statement comparing the French actress Sarah Bernhardt, who apparently wore gobs of makeup, with another Italian actress, Eleonora Duse, who wore relatively little: "I prefer the Italian because her wrinkles are the credentials of humanity."

Still, cosmetic surgery or not (as each woman must decide for herself), there is the need for what one woman called "higher maintenance," as she good-humoredly grumbled about having to take twenty minutes in front of a mirror each morning in her sixties as opposed to the five it had always taken her when she was younger.

Consistent with the wish to make less of a fuss with physical presentation, there seems to be an undercurrent of desire to simplify: "Just keep it simple," was a stipulation I heard from a number of women. And Jungian analyst Marion Woodman, at sixty-eight, is following that advice by cleaning out years' worth of her files of notes, boxes of pictures, and closets of old clothes. "I'm getting life down to the essence," she said with a wise smile.

This sentiment was echoed by others. Writer Ursula Le Guin referred to this essence as soul making. According to her, this concept is built into the Hindu view of human life in which, after a certain age, "when a woman gets older, she drops most of her plates and concentrates on learning to be alone. She focuses on her spiritual powers." Dancer Luly Santangelo, sixty, calls this the "distillation process," when a woman becomes "more economic with her energy." By the time they reach their sixties, women know who they are, what is important to them, and how they wish to spend (or not spend) their time. There is what could be called a wise distribution of energy. In a recent telephone conversation I had with writer Barbara Grizzuti Harrison, who is sixty, she humorously signed off by saying, "Well, I've got to get back to doing nothing." Women in their sixties are gutsy, dauntless, and emboldened to be exactly who they are and to say exactly what they think and feel.

Unquestionably I believe this growing concern with a spiritual life during the seventh decade is directly related to an increased cognizance of one's mortality, a recognition of finitude. As Virginia Harris, sixty, explained, "We know that our destination is death." The eventuality of death is very real to these women. But, rather than holding them hostage in a paralyzed state of fear, it seems to add an intensity to their lives. They become more committed to living fully in the present moment and less concerned with either their past or their future.

This heightened awareness seems to have less to do with an actual fear of death than with the dread of an incapacitating illness, either physical, mental, or emotional. Matilda Cuomo spoke to me at length about her involvement with raising funds for breast cancer research after losing twenty-one friends to this disease, which has reached epidemic proportions. Three of the women in this book have survived cancer. And Nabeela George, a woman who had lived with the crippling effects of polio since she was eleven months old, was diagnosed with breast cancer two weeks prior to my interviewing her for this book. Three months later she was dead. I have chosen to include her, as I feel that her inspiring story merits telling, but also because the sobering fact is, women can and do die in their sixties. In a society that seels unrelentingly to avoid the reality of death, we need inspiring forerunners who move through this passage with courage, heart, and tranquillity and who teach us how to die.

The seemingly eternally youthful Audrey Hepburn died at the age of sixty-four; Jackie Onassis, who appeared to be at her peak of happiness in terms of a satisfying career, a meaningful romantic relationship, and a joyous involvement with her grandchildren, was just sixty-three. Who among us did not take for granted that these icons of beauty and success would endure forever? During the course of writing this book, the beloved former Democratic congresswoman from Texas, Barbara Jordan, succumbed to complications from multiple sclerosis at the age of sixty. Illness and mortality seem synonymous with aging. But it can be helpful to view the impermanence of life as a gift or a wake-up call to the present moment and the appreciation and fulfillment of the time left.

Financial security is another major concern of aging women—and should be. One in five women over sixty-five lives in poverty. "If you are a woman," writes one economist, "you have a sixty percent shot at being poor in old age." Even Ann Richards revealed to me that the rather unlikely possibility of her becoming a bag lady is her "greatest fear." Two of the women in this book, for lack of funds, do not carry health insurance. They told me that because they "cannot afford to get sick," they take special care planning and following their diet and exercise programs.

It is hard to believe that well-known women, who many of us "grew up" with, are now in their sixties. Think of the "sex kitten" of the 1950s, Brigitte Bardot, who is now an ardent animal rights activist. To give you a vivid picture of the spirit of aliveness that can exist at sixty, following is only a partial list of the names of the most recognizable women in their early, mid-, and late sixties: Elizabeth Taylor, Joanne Woodward, Shirley MacLaine, Anne Bancroft, Gena Rowlands, Ellen Burstyn, Barbara Walters, Ruby Dee, Eartha Kitt, Rita Moreno, Julie Andrews, Carol Burnett, Debbie Reynolds, Mary Tyler Moore, Claire Bloom, Gloria Steinem, Helen Frankenthaler, Kate Millet, Cicely Tyson, Trish Brown, Olympia Dukakis, Toni Morrison, Jeanne Moreau, Adrienne Rich, Sophia Loren, Edna O'Brien, Yoko Ono, Maya Angelou, Della Reese, Dianne Feinstein, Vanessa Redgrave, Joan Didion, Eleanor Coppola, and Jill Ker Conway. If these women's lives, which are representative of lives filled with creative expression, are possibilities of what we have to look forward to in our sixties, what are we afraid of?!

Far from being "over the hill," the women just mentioned and those on the following pages offer us a hopeful yet realistic look at the possibilities that await us as we "grow" rather than "get" older. We should celebrate our aging process, be thankful for our life, and embrace the decade of the sixties as the age of fulfillment that it represents. Instead of being (as performance artist Rachel Rosenthal, sixty-nine, expressed it) "bamboozled by the completely denigrating views of chronological time and what it means," views commonly held by our society, we must respect and enjoy ourselves and each other as older women for the receptacles of knowledge, experience, and wisdom that we are and for the sheer amount of time we have spent on the planet.

The women in *On Women Turning 60: Embracing the Age of Fulfillment* are altering the image of age. They are champions—heroines, if you will—at the forefront of change: changing a society obsessed with the fantasies of maintaining youth to one driven by the realities and *potentialities* of age. In the words of Dorothy L. Sayers, they "believe in age." And they truly embrace the age of fulfillment.

Sixty years bring with them the privilege of discernment and vision: a capacity to behold, in the blink of an eye, the sweeping panorama of a life fully lived. This perspective lends itself to the metaphor of the tapestry. "I see now," said Marion Woodman, "how all the threads have miraculously come together. All are woven into the single tapestry that is my life and work." Every woman I interviewed spoke, in her own eloquent way, about the meshing of her life experiences; how she now better than ever before understands, and more easily accepts, the integration of her life into a whole; how she has come full circle and "over the hill" into the age of fulfillment.

CATHLEEN ROUNTREE
Aptos, California
January 28, 1997

That's one of the nice things about becoming sixty: you really know whether you're a success because you've done it. When I look at my children and my grandchildren and my husband and my house and my garden and my friends and my dog . . . If this isn't success, I'm in the wrong biz.

— MARY TRAVERS

Mary Travers

Of all the possibilities that could have transpired during my interview with Mary Travers, a midnight skinny-dip in her backyard swimming pool was not one that had occurred to me. But there we were—two full-bodied women, aging nymphs: steam rising from this seventy-eight-degree fountain of age; dodging the alien-looking menace that doubled as a pool vacuum; our illuminated, round faces mirroring the full moon; discussing matters personal, political, and otherwise. All this in between savoring sounds of silence.

Mary Travers (the "Mary" in Peter, Paul and Mary) had her first singing lesson at the age of six with a teacher from the Caribbean islands. By the time she was a tall, willowy high school student, she already knew and was recording with the undisputed father of folk music, Pete Seeger. Having been raised in New York City's Greenwich Village, Mary already had the distinct advantage of being in the right place at the right time. In the late 1950s and early 1960s, Greenwich Village was the home of the burgeoning modern American folk music scene. And in 1961, after the premiere of Peter, Paul and Mary at the Village's seminal folk club, the Bitter End, a legacy of music—which by definition is a music of activism and hope—was born.

Thirty-seven years later Mary still sings and tours with her partners, Peter Yarrow and Noel Paul Stookey. Remaining true to the tradition of folk music, which is a commitment to the struggles for social justice, the group has ardently supported the causes of civil rights (for which they marched tirelessly, and accompanied Dr. Martin Luther King Jr. in Selma and Washington, D.C.), the anti–Vietnam War crusade, support for the non-intervention efforts in Central

America, the anti-apartheid cause in South Africa, the emigration struggle of Soviet Jews, and on behalf of the homeless. After eight gold and five platinum albums, countless Top 40 hits, and nearly four decades of performing, Peter, Paul and Mary continue to execute at least forty concerts a year.

Mary retains the same 1960s hairstyle that three generations of fans have come to associate with her: long and straight, flaxen, with a frame of bangs. She easily and spontaneously skips in and out of decades, her mind sharp with colorful details, personal anecdotes of living legends, and alive with a sense of humor and irony. At sixty years old, Mary continues to be a spokeswoman for a counterculture that has been assimilated into the conventional. But her passion for causes and justice infuses her life and keeps her aware of current events and social issues.

It seems clear that wisdom has become a close personal friend. Not reticent about speaking her mind, Mary offered many obviously deeply considered words of advice to other women, one of the richest of which is for older people to make younger friends. "Pick up some young ones," Mary said with the sense of humor that characterizes her, "because when you get closer to the finish line, it's very helpful to have people you have an emotional relationship with who are not dying or dead." This mention is particularly poignant in light of the fact that Mary's own mother, at the relatively young age of seventy-eight, is suffering from dementia and, thus, was recently moved by Mary into a nursing home.

She speaks with gusto and vigor, and is at times boisterous, pounding on the table or using an expletive to make a point. Her voice articulates subtle and sensitive distinctions. This one might expect of a singer whose vocal phrasing is her method of expressing all manner of emotions, but the listener is still surprised.

Mary and her husband, Ethan, live in a picturesque early-eighteenth-century remodeled cottage in Redding, Connecticut. Three-quarters of the two-story house retains the small, low-ceilinged rooms of the period, while the addition of "the barn" (their description), a structure that serves as a combination dining and living room, adds a dimension of spaciousness. The medium-size boulders culled from the excavated land on which the new addition rests compose one long side of the room. This wall of stone together with the opposite wall of windows, which offers the vista of an encircling English cottage garden, and the high-beam ceiling above give the space a genial and rustic quality.

Comfort is number one to Mary and Ethan, and their hospitality extends to all who cross their threshold, including the four-legged. True to Mary's word, Peaches, an adopted SPCA dog, is allowed on the couch, bed, and the plaid overstuffed chairs in the kitchen alcove that serves as an informal dining nook.

The afternoon that we scheduled to share spontaneously turned into a marvelous twenty-four-hour event when they invited me to have dinner and spend the night. Throughout the time that we shared, our discussions crisscrossed myriad subjects that interest us both: popular culture, all types of music, vanity, love and marriage, racism in the United States, literature and cinema, food, food, food, gardening, politics, and, of course, turning sixty.

The Singing Activist

❖

Probably the most vibrant influence on me was my mother. My mother started work as a newspaper reporter in Albany when she was seventeen. I was born in Louisville, Kentucky—not raised there, just spent my early childhood there. I was the equivalent of an army brat, only I was a newspaper brat. Both my mother and father were newspaper reporters, so I had exposure to the arts from a very young age.

My parents separated when I was about three, and my mother and I came to New York City. The Second World War was storming, and my father became a merchant seaman. When the ship came back to the States he got off for a week and then left on another ship. So I really didn't see much of him at all during the whole war, although my parents remained friends. But I grew up surrounded by people in the arts, labor lawyers, constitutional lawyers, labor organizers, sculptors, who were all politically left oriented.

So, unlike my contemporaries, I had nothing to reject when the 1960s came around. They were rejecting wall-to-wall carpeting. We didn't have wall-to-wall carpeting. We had some very tattered old Persian rugs, some with holes in them. I remember at the march on Selma-Montgomery, Dennis Hopper had his camera and he was taking pictures wildly. My mother was marching with me and he said to me, "That's your mother? How hip!" And I said to myself, Yes indeed. I'd always thought she was hip. I *didn't* always think she was my friend, but I always thought she was hip. She was brilliant: a good writer, ethical and strong, quite a superior person.

I spent most of my childhood in Manhattan, in Greenwich Village. I went to small, slightly left-of-center private schools. When I was in the first grade I had my first music teacher, who was a woman named Charity Bailey. She was from the Caribbean islands and taught folk music. When I was older, my mother used to take me to the Village Vanguard club on Sundays, where people like Harry Belafonte and Josh White, all the folk singers, would appear.

Harry is still a good person. I've known him off and on—not well, but I've certainly done enough marches with the man. It's wonderful to see how some people age. He's totally gotten better as a human being. I'm wondering if this has to do with aging. But when he was younger so much of his personality was kind of a sexual persona that it was distracting from who he really was. So I think he's better now. Not that he isn't sexy, because he still is. There are very few women of any age who would say to Harry Belafonte, "You cannot park your shoes under my bed." But it's not the only thing now. He's acquired a lot of wisdom in his years.

I certainly never thought of myself as a sexpot. Other people may have, but I wasn't in a business that promoted that image. I remember the first year of performing, the guys were constantly taking the neck of their guitars and poking me in the back to remind me to stand up straight. I was five feet ten. Imagine being five feet ten in high school when all the boys came up to your waist and you were trying to disappear. So it took me longer to be who I am than it might have taken somebody else. But on the other hand, maybe not, because the business itself, and fame, tend to obscure the question of self-image quite a bit.

Fame came to me very young. I was only twenty-three. There were two considerations that helped me to hold my center during the rush of those years. One is that I already had a child, Erika, when I started singing in Peter, Paul and Mary. As my father would have said, "Having a child is a sea anchor." A sea anchor is used when your boat is in deeper water than an anchor can go. In order to stop the drift of the boat—mind you, we're talking about small boats—you throw a triangular canvas wind sock into the water. It fills up with water and drags the boat to prevent it from drifting so fast.

So children, at least for me, became great reality checks, great sea anchors. Because, so what if you were met by a thousand people at the airport? The baby has to go to the pediatrician and I've got to buy her new shoes—you know how kids' feet are? One moment the shoes fit, the next moment they don't. I mean, literally, on Tuesday they fit; on Wednesday they no longer fit! These are real concerns. Having a thousand people meet you at the airport is unimportant in the big scope of things.

And the other inducement was my mother. In style there is also content. I'll give you an example of what I mean. At one point, Peter, Paul and Mary had bought an airplane because we were doing so many small college concerts and we couldn't get from one small college to the next by commercial airlines, but if we flew all night in our own plane, we could. So we purchased a Lockheed Lodestar. One evening I was at my mother's house for a dinner party and I started to tell a story—"Well, we were coming in on our plane the other day"—and my mother went on one of her diatribes and she said, "Mary, it's not in good taste to talk about things that are so out of the realm of other people's lives."

"Yes, Mother."

My mother did not contribute to my inflation! She was the kind of woman who would say things like "Be careful of compromise, Mary. There's a very thin line between compromise and accomplice." So between my two daughters, Erika and Alicia, and my mother, they didn't leave me a lot of room to get screwy in. That makes it especially hard now with my mother having dementia, because that wonderful mind is gone. It's very difficult. The symptoms started five years ago and they've gotten worse. She just keeps having little strokes.

I have to admit, it frightens me about my own life. But, you know, I think that's one of the gifts that your parents give you, if you're lucky. You're able to watch their anxieties before you actually have them in your own experience. So when my mother decided to build a room onto her house because she was fore-seeing not wanting to climb up ship-carpenter stairs at a very sharp angle, I said, "Gee, that sounds like an interesting process. I like that. Yeah, let's build a room." When my mother first started talking about pension plans, it was like a wake-up call to me. Oh, yes, I'd best do that.

When my daughter takes her children to see my mother in the nursing home, there's a little self-interest in that for me. If you want your children to treat you well, you'd better treat your parents well. You have to set an example and let them know what is *expected*. Children need to know what's expected of them, and I think the desire to be decent can get perverted by many things. We all start out wanting life to be fair. But we can run off the track sometimes. So it's nice that my daughter goes with my grandchildren to see their great-grandmother. And something wonderful happens when they go. They become sort of generic grand-children for the whole ward; they're *everybody's* grandchildren. And with demen-tia patients, they *really* are everybody's grandchildren because these people have a vague understanding that they have a grandchild, but they wouldn't recognize their own anyway. So they're just thrilled.

Is it fair that my mother is in this condition? Justice is a concept I have been thinking about for a *long* time. If we were to use a computer to find how many words in the dictionary describe negative items as opposed to how many words describe positive items, I think the negatives would win. Goodness is not some-thing people talk about. You call up your friend on the phone and ask, "How are you?" They're more likely to tell you what's wrong with their life than what's wonderful about it. I think part of it has to do with envy. You don't want to say, "Oh, everything's fabulous," when you know your friend's life is falling apart. Some people are embarrassed by good fortune.

But that doesn't answer your question. There is not as much justice as we would like there to be. But that has nothing to do with whether or not you should try to work for it. I remember a quote from a rabbinic scholar—and I'm para-phrasing—"It wasn't your duty to finish the task; it was only your duty not to neglect it." I guess that's what people of goodwill try to do; that's their job. They don't divorce themselves from the suffering of others because they need that reality check.

I don't think we should discourage young people from thinking they can solve the world's problems. Because, even though they may not reach *their* goal, they certainly will far exceed our concept of what's obtainable. So I'd rather go with their idealism and at the end support them when they're feeling a little crushed and they say, "But I didn't get it all done." Well, if it was easy, it would have been done already. People have been worrying about justice, equality, peace, poverty, for at least five thousand years. So our own singular lifetimes are such a drop in the bucket.

You know, I've seen a lot of change in the last thirty-five years, but I'm looking at it very optimistically. When I was a sophomore in high school in 1952, I went to an interracial school in Greenwich Village. At that time, if my class had wanted to go to Washington, D.C., for a school trip, we would have been unable to eat together—blacks and whites—at the lunch counter in our nation's capital. Well, I think we've made a little progress. In 1952 black men were being *lynched* in this country.

Many people were appalled by the recent church burnings in the South. The interesting thing is that the burnings have unified white and black, Christians and Jews, in a very concerted effort to maintain their religious freedoms and their basic civil rights. The fact of the matter is that most of the civil rights legislation in this country started in black churches, so it's a setback, but it's not major. We have a *big* racial problem in this country. Can we eliminate racism in our own time? Of course not. If it were so easy, Serbs would not be killing Croatians.

So we can't look at it in the short term. You'll win battles, you'll lose battles, you'll feel like you're taking steps backward. Maintenance is everything. It's like your garden. Every year it's a struggle. Some years are bad; some years are glorious. Some years it rains too much and everything's got mold on it. Other years you have a drought and you're out there breaking your back watering.

I jokingly say to people, "If you really don't want to worry about aging, just don't put your glasses on when you look in the mirror. You'll look exactly the same as you did in your twenties or thirties! You won't see any wrinkles." But, seriously, there are aspects of aging I don't like. I don't like the fact that my feet hurt, that my knees are bad, that I've got a torn rotator cuff that acts up in my shoulder. These are boring things. Do they stop me from doing what I want to do? No. Do I get down on the ground sometimes and can't figure how to get back up? Ha! Yes. Are these things important? Not yet.

Wrinkles; some wrinkles are okay. I'd love to get rid of all this upper-eyelid fold. And I might, someday. That's about all the cosmetic surgery I can ever envision doing, though. I don't want to get involved with face lifts. Please, that's too much. The rest of it can go the way it's gonna go. I think you have to take a real hard look at vanity at a certain point, and say, "Am I gonna buy into this?" Or am I gonna say, "Screw this"?

At whatever weight you are, you are. Yes, I'd like to lose some more weight. Is it paramount? No. Does my husband love me anyway? Yes. If losing weight meant I had to give up butter for the rest of my life, would I? No way! Some people in show business can have cocaine as their drug of choice; I have butter. If some doctor said to me, "You're gonna drop dead, Mary, 'cause you're eating butter," boy, I'd have a problem because I like butter. I *love* milk. And I don't want to know about two percent.

When I'm on the road and I'm really tired and a little frazzled, as we're coming away from the theater, I often ask the driver to stop at a filling station on the way to the hotel. I run in and buy one of those half-pint chocolate milks, which I take up to my hotel room and drink. Then I go to sleep. It takes care of all the acid of the day and tastes so good, so I don't want to give up my milk and sugar.

Here on the East Coast there is an acceptance that age is a natural process. This attitude is more European because its roots are more European. There's the appreciation that an old tree is a good tree, is an interesting tree; same for old houses, lichen on stones—there's a sense of history. You go to Boston or to Philadelphia and that's where the history of the United States began. So here history is significant. On the East Coast you find a plethora of eighteenth-, even seventeenth-century antiques. There's a feeling of tradition and time. It's less subjective.

I used to say there is really a difference in the function of show business on the East and West Coasts. For years the Russian Tea Room in New York City was like the Polo Lounge in L.A.—but with a major difference. If a guy was in a play and it was a big hit, sure, he'd get a great table at either, but if the next play he did was bad, he'd still get the good table in New York; in L.A., he'd be relegated to the back of the bus at the Polo Lounge. The concept of theater in the East is "There will be another play" and "If he was good once, he'll be good again."

Age! What can you do about it? If you can't do anything about it, why not look on the up side of what it does bring you? It is true, though, I find it a little unsettling when people say to me—and I hear it very often these days—"I've grown up on your music," and you're looking at a face that is clearly forty, you know, and you say, sarcastically, "Thank you very *much!*" Or some tall, good-looking guy in his thirties says to me, "Oh, I've loved you all my life," and he *has.* That's a little disconcerting. But I like my age, I like where I am in my life. I've never been happier. I'm not worried about the future. I love my husband. My kids are great. I live in a beautiful place, in a beautiful house. So, this is the best time in my life.

I realize there will be annoying things that may happen in the future as less and less of my body works at perfection. But, last night, I was at a wedding for Peter Yarrow's daughter Bethany. Her grandfather on her mother's side, Mac McCarthy, is the brother of Gene McCarthy, the politician and now elder states-man. So Mac was there, Gene was there, and their sister was there. Their sister is *ninety-two years old.* She's walking around as spry as could be, every faculty in-tact. She even remembered a conversation we'd had at the 1968 Democratic Convention in Chicago. So, in a funny way, barring major health issues—major ones—part of growing old has got to be about *attitude.*

Ethan and I went to the grocery store the other day and bumped into an old friend of my mother's who has cancer—now in remission. He's probably eighty-three and very cheerful. The only time he's not cheerful is when he talks about the friends he's lost. And, I've already figured out, once again my mother has shown me the way: Have younger friends; don't make your whole circle of friends just people of your own age group. Pick up some young ones, because when you get closer to the finish line, it's very helpful to have people you have an emotional relationship with who are not dying or dead. It's very sad for people who live a long time because their entire memory bank is gone.

We all feel that loss in little ways. Sometimes I'll mention a political figure or I'll say something about Henry Wallace. The kids will look at me and say, "Who?" Or I'll mention the name of Franklin Roosevelt's dog. Now, that *does* put you in some frames of reference that you are going to lose. I mean, *you'll* have them, but nobody else will know what you're talking about, except someone from the same vintage.

It's odd when it happens, because you realize there's a whole area of pursuits that young people don't do. Like read! They might see some of the movie classics, but there are many literary classics they don't read. And a lot of those books will make it into the twenty-first century to be read only by a few elitists of society. That has to do with our Information Age, the Computer Age. Everything is so quick; attention spans are so short now.

Computers are wonderful things and they're here to stay, God knows. I have a girlfriend who's real good at dealing with computers. I called her up and said, "Come to the country and program all my little whosey-whatsis." She asked me, "What do you want the computer to do?" I said, "Nothing but word processing and spell-check. Forget about everything else. I don't want to know about it." Well, she did. So I have a stupid computer, but I love it.

But I have a feeling that the twenty-first century, or at least the first couple years of it, will see an incredible surge in intimacy, in humanism, in family and family values—not family values as a cliché, but the reinvention, if you will, of family. I jokingly say that my children aren't allowed to move more than a hundred miles away from me. I think I'm probably not alone in feeling this way. Perhaps one of the reasons that children are staying home longer and coming back is not just economics. If you destroy community, as we have, certainly in the big cities, then you need to reinvent something to take its place, because human beings are not isolated animals. We're pack animals. So we made this incredible explosion in the sixties, seventies, and eighties. Now, in the nineties, I see the concept of family trying to reorganize itself. I think it's good.

I believe the actual nucleus of mother and child, father and child, whether the parents are divorced, separated, or whatever, has restrengthened because we don't want to be out there by ourselves. And I don't blame us. I certainly don't. I feel bad for people who don't have children. Who's going to take care of them? So family needs to be reinvented. Sometimes, in answer to the big question of justice, you have to reinvent justice, too. You have to reinvent it and you have to reinvent the family. It's fundamental to what kind of world we're going to have. People need to learn to care for each other through thick and thin. It's a very scary world out there.

I feel lucky to have such a good marriage now. I think the problem contemporary marriages have is that people tend not to work through the difficult times. They see their unhappiness, but they don't want to see the way out of it; in fact, they are not sure there *is* a way out—and for some people, there isn't. For them, divorce should be an option. But I have a feeling that people don't work quite as hard as they could.

To work at a relationship means that you have to really understand where the other person is coming from. You have to be able to put yourself in the other guy's shoes and figure out, What do I think is really important to my partner? What does he need from me? What does he need from the world? Are we really in conflict? I've got a maxim for that. My husband and I say, "We could do that." You know the situation when one person says, "Let's tear this apart," and the other partner says, "What are you—crazy?" And they get into an argument. We have "We could do that," which allows us to put a buffer statement in between the idea and really having to deal with the idea. It's worked for us.

This is my fourth marriage. I've never been together with anybody this long. After ten years of knowing Ethan, I married him because I wanted to be married all the way through. I wanted to make a real commitment, one you don't get out of, one you see through. By the time I was fifty-five, when we got married, I think I was more ready for marriage, more capable of it, than I had been when I was younger. I knew what I wanted. When you're very young, you can't know what you want, because you don't know who you are. I think as you discover who you really are, and discover what you really want, you begin to learn what's important.

Is ambition important? Is social status important? Is money important? Is intelligence important? Is a sense of humor important? Is ethics important? Is general all-around kindness important? You know, there's a laundry list of things.

On my list were kindness, ethics, excitement about life. Someone with whom you could read a book and say, "You gotta read this." And he would! Someone you could learn with. But, fundamentally, it was the fact that he is probably the best person I've ever met in my life. He's fabulous. When things at work are not the way I want them and I get a little sticky—ready to bite somebody's head off—he's always the one who says, "Well, maybe they're not feeling well." Or "Maybe *they're* in pain or distracted." And by the time he's finished massaging my temper, I've lost the killer instinct and I'm ready to think about it. So he's really fair. And the few times he's not, then I do for him what he does for me.

He was incredible, *incredible*, when I had my hysterectomy about ten years ago. To make a long story short, I'd gotten a massive staph infection when I was in the hospital—it was one of those hospital horror stories, I mean, sort of an Andy Warhol kind of thing. After the operation, I was really thirsty and drinking a lot of water, but I couldn't pee. At first they didn't know what was wrong. Finally they discover it's a staph infection and take all the stitches out, leaving this crater in my belly. Now the wound has to heal from the bottom up, not from the top down.

After ten days the doctor says to Ethan, "Get her outta here; she's not gonna get well here, but meanwhile let me show you how to clean this thing." Well, there is a myth that if you scratch every Jewish boy, you find a Jewish doctor. This is not true. My husband doesn't wanna know about blood. In fact, he's a little wussy about those things, so he leans over the doctor's shoulder and he says, "Oh, my God, if I were a surgeon, I'd be a vegetarian." However, he rose to the occasion and he cleaned out that wound three times a day every day until I went on the road. He was great. That's a kind of love, you know. He always says that it was love on both our sides. I trusted him to do it, and he loved me enough to do it. There was a wonderful bonding. Sometimes bad things and difficult times can be so important in a relationship if they're met the proper way. If the best part of you reaches out.

That's how I work with the guys. I may be pissed with them beyond reason. They might be making me crazy. But what we try to do—and ninety percent of the time succeed in doing—is this: we don't sing to the person we just lost our temper with, we sing to the person we believe they could be. So we're singing to this idealized person, this perfect person, and very often by the end of the show, they *are* that perfect person.

As far as performing in the group for nearly forty years goes, about half the program, every year, is new. We always have control over our own solo section. We each do two songs of our own choosing, and then there are four or five new songs we do every year, which keeps it from being repetitive. In the act of trying to make the new songs jell, you're on your toes already for the old songs. Also, the old songs are ones that you're really required to keep. They are the songs that have a greater significance. You read the newspaper and sing "Blowing in the Wind." Which verse would you like to apply to today's news? "How many years must a people exist before they're allowed to be free? How many ears must one man have before he can hear people cry?" There's a contemporary interpretation that's constantly going on with that song. It's always relevant. It's always new. It's always making you think about something; you're bringing the gestalt of the day to the song, and that puts a little different spin on it.

When I became successful in the world's terms, it was a "we" are successful; it was very hard to separate myself out in that. This awareness was really helpful: "Don't get so inflated here. You're not doin' this by yourself." If you feel good about yourself, you say, "Well, they couldn't do it without me." On the days that you *don't* feel so good about yourself, you say, "Well, if it weren't for him . . . He's the driving force."

So, what is a success? I *am* a success. It's hard to know you're a success when you're in the middle of it. That's one of the nice things about becoming sixty: you really know whether you're a success because you've *done* it. When I look at my children and my grandchildren and my husband and my house and my garden and my friends and my dog—shit! If this isn't success, I'm in the wrong biz. No kidding, I mean, this is good stuff.

I do love living in the country now. I loved New York for years; it's too much of a hassle at this point. That may be due to age. I don't want the fight anymore. I like the sense of community I have here in Connecticut. I like to go into the grocery store and shoot the bull with the guy ringing up my groceries. I love going up to the grocer and saying, "You know what you oughta carry? Order it for me."

I think the next ten years are just gonna be super. I'm going to finally stop procrastinating about writing a book. I don't think I want to write about Peter, Paul and Mary. First of all, you can't write about a relationship in which you are still in the middle, not unless you want to leave the relationship. I don't want to write about the awards Peter and Paul and myself have received; I'm not interested in that. I wouldn't mind writing about some aspects of the time in which I've lived, because it certainly was an exciting time. I'm not interested in one of those tell-all books. I don't read biographies and autobiographies very much. I'm not into gossip. Any fool can write that, and then they never speak to their partners again. If you love people, you love them, and whatever garbage is going on with them is your garbage, too.

I think people's attitude toward aging is going to go through a massive change, especially in the next twenty years, because the baby boomers are all getting older. Just as they were a huge influence on the culture in the 1960s, they will be a big influence on the culture in the new century. A positive influence, because they are not going into that "dark night, gently." They're gonna want to go out with some creature comforts, regardless of what the Republicans want.

Throughout your life, you have little samplers—remember the old sampler? Little embroidered sayings that you tell yourself. If I had a sampler over my desk, it would be something that Bette Davis said: "Growing old ain't for sissies!"

I remember a wonderful scene when Lena Horne did her one-woman show a few years ago. She was wearing an incredible, sexy dress that was cut very much on the bias so everything showed. At one point she looked at the audience, made a very provocative pose, and said, "If you can't get trampy now, when?" I liked that. She must have been in her sixties then. As one gets right down to sixty, why not? If you can't be who you really wanna be *now*, then you're really in trouble. That goes along with "Growing old ain't for sissies!"

$\mathcal{D}$on't think about your birthdays; they're not a bit important. It's how you feel that matters. Don't spend time looking back over mistakes you might have made; just think ahead in a positive way and believe, implicitly, that every day you live makes a difference because you impact the world around you and you have a choice as to what sort of impact you want to make. Do you want to use that day to try to make the world a better place, or don't you care?

— JANE GOODALL

Jane Goodall

ONLY IF WE UNDERSTAND CAN WE CARE;

ONLY IF WE CARE WILL WE HELP;

ONLY IF WE HELP SHALL THEY BE SAVED.

—JANE GOODALL

I did a double take: was that *the* Jane Goodall in a television advertisement for Home Box Office, sitting in close proximity to wild chimpanzees who seemed to be lip-synching famous lines from movies like *The Godfather* and *Animal House* in voices imitative of Marlon Brando and John Belushi? Well, there is only *one* Jane Goodall, and it was she. A few weeks later when we met and I shyly asked her to set the record straight, she said, "Entertainment chimps are often cruelly treated. It dawned on me that there was a way to show how animals can be used in advertising in a nonexploitive manner." Besides, she added, "the HBO thing is hilarious. If you can make someone laugh, you can make the world a better place."

And with that Jane summed up her driving passion: to make the world a better place. "Dr. Jane," as she sometimes refers to herself with a rather self-effacing dignity, an English ethologist, is the world's foremost authority on chimpanzees. For more than thirty-five years she has studied the humanlike primates in their natural habitat in the Gombe Stream Game Reserve in Tanzania, East Africa. Her observations of chimpanzees' behavior have shed significant new light on the study of prehistoric humans and their evolutionary development.

Jane Goodall was reared in London in early childhood and in Bournemouth, on the southern coast of England, where, at the Birches, "a lovely red brick house, with a big garden surrounded by a tall hedge that shuts out the world," a few minutes' walk from the sea of the English Channel, she spent her later childhood and adolescence. She grew up in an extended matriarchal family of her maternal grandmother, aunts, and a sister. Her father, Mortimer Goodall, having gone to serve in the Second World War, was eventually separated and divorced from Jane's mother, Vanne.

Encouraged by Vanne, Jane began a lifelong fascination with animals at an early age. As a curious four-year-old she spent hours cramped in a henhouse, waiting patiently to observe a hen lay an egg. This was her first scientific observation of animal behavior. The children's stories of Tarzan and Dr. Dolittle and *The Jungle Book* were her special favorites. They planted the seeds of enchantment that would eventually take her to Africa.

After leaving school at eighteen, Jane worked as a secretary at Oxford University; as an assistant, doing music selection and some editing, at a documentary film company in London; and as a waitress at a large coastal hotel near the Birches, until she had saved enough money to go to Africa. When an old school friend, who had moved to Kenya with her parents, invited Jane to join them, she was thrilled and ready.

Within a few months of her arrival, she met Dr. Louis Leakey, the famed anthropologist and paleontologist who was curator of the National Museum of Natural History in Nairobi, Kenya. Jane immediately became Leakey's secretary at the museum, assisted him in digging fossilized remains of prehistoric creatures at Olduvai Gorge, and made a study for him of the vervet monkeys on an island in Lake Victoria.

Leakey was also curious about the evolutionary implications that might be found in the behavior of the chimpanzees, who are closer to humans in their intelligence than are gorillas. Although she had no formal university degrees, Jane's patience and persistent desire to understand animals prompted Leakey to choose her for this pioneering study. He believed that a mind "uncluttered by academia" would yield a fresh perspective. Leakey anticipated Jane's research to be long-term (about ten years), yet critics believed she would not last more than three weeks.

In 1960 Jane set up her camp on Lake Tanganyika in the Gombe Stream Game Reserve. Armed with binoculars, she began looking for chimpanzees. The first groups she sighted fled before she could get closer than five hundred yards. Patiently she established a routine, rising at five-thirty each morning and stationing herself on a peak above a feeding area in the Kakombe Stream Valley. Gradually the chimpanzees became accustomed to her presence and lost their fear of her. By the end of a year they allowed her to observe them from thirty feet, and within two years they were voluntarily coming to her camp for bananas.

Soon she organized what she called the "banana club," a regular daily feeding system that enabled her to keep the chimps under constant, close scientific scrutiny. She came to know and be known by almost half of the one hundred chimps living on the reserve. Finding the chimps highly individualistic, she gave each a name appropriate to its personality, such as "Baby Flint," "Mr. McGregor," and "David Greybeard."

To understand them as completely as possible, she imitated some of their habits, spending much time in trees and sampling every kind of food they ate, including insects. With a minuteness of detail never before possible, she recorded every aspect of chimpanzee behavior, from tree swinging to bed making to their complex social life.

In 1962 the National Geographic Society sent Baron Hugo van Lawick, a Dutch wild-animal photographer, to film Jane's work. Their shared love of the wild and animals suited a union, and they were married in 1964. Shortly thereafter Jane received her Ph.D. from Cambridge University in ethology after submitting her thesis, "Behavior of the Free-Ranging Chimpanzee." She was only the eighth person in the history of the university to be allowed to work for a doctorate without first taking a B.A. degree. Jane's only child, Hugo Eric Louis, was born in 1967. Seven years later the van Lawicks were divorced.

Jane was remarried two years later to an Englishman named Derek Bryceson, the director of Tanzania National Park, who was almost completely paralyzed from the waist down after being shot down as a fighter pilot in the Middle East during World War II. They lived together happily in Gombe until Derek's death from cancer in 1980.

Today, over thirty-five years after Jane entered the forest in Gombe, she and her staff continue to contribute significant findings on chimpanzee behavior.

Her profound scientific discoveries laid the foundation for all future primate studies. One of the many observations that amazed the world was the documented study of chimpanzees making and using tools. This behavior was previously believed to separate humans from other animals.

In 1977 Jane founded the Jane Goodall Institute for Wildlife Research, Education and Conservation, in order to provide ongoing support for field research on wild chimpanzees. Her efforts include protecting wild chimpanzees and improving the lives of those in captivity. It is estimated that for every infant abducted from the wild, ten chimpanzees perish as a result of their captivity. In four African countries, the institute has established chimpanzee sanctuaries, which are responsible for the care and rehabilitation of orphaned chimps. In addition, Jane has founded an international environmental education and humanitarian program for youth called Roots and Shoots. This program teaches care and respect for the environment, nonhuman animals, and the human community.

Since the early 1960s Jane Goodall has been an icon of a woman living an independent, unconventional, yet committed and purposeful life. The remarkable success of recent books about women honoring the "wild" spirit that dwells inside them and in nature gives credence to the respect and awe that several generations of women have reserved for Jane Goodall. She has lived the life that millions of women have dreamed of living.

What is this heroine like in person? After five and a half months' worth of phone calls, letters, and faxes, I was scheduled to meet Jane at her institute in Ridgefield, Connecticut, on a brisk and refreshing New England autumn morning. She was so quiet and unassuming in her jeans and wool Pendleton shirt that she appeared to be completely in the hands of her assistant, Mary Lewis, who whisked her from room to room in which new interviewers awaited her. She bears a surprisingly ethereal quality, considering she has lived the better part of thirty-five years in the forested heart of Africa.

Although I recognized several canned responses to my questions from the sources of my research, I could see that Jane has the quality that many people spend thousands of dollars trying to acquire through therapy, religion, or both:

she knows how to be present in the moment. Her green eyes rarely wandered from mine and were direct, open, and, above all, observant.

"How can you bear to be away from the forest?" I asked.

"I carry the forest inside me," she said.

And, indeed, she does. Her calm is palpable and soothing.

Jane's concern for the environment and for nonhuman animals and her commitment to community enrichment through constructive service projects continue to be the focus of her tireless efforts. At sixty-three she shows no signs of slowing down. If anything, Jane feels increasing pressure to do more, to educate children, who, she believes, are the planet's primary source of hope.

When Jane was just over one year old, her mother gave her a large hairy toy chimpanzee to celebrate the birth of the first chimpanzee infant ever born in the London Zoo. Most of her mother's friends were horrified and predicted that the "ghastly" creature would give a small child nightmares; but Jubilee (as the celebrated infant itself was named) became her most beloved possession and accompanied her on all her childhood travels. She still keeps the worn old stuffed animal at her mother's home in Bournemouth. Who could have foreseen that this gift would be an initiation of sorts into a world rich and exotic beyond imagination and that it was a harbinger of one of the great achievements of twentieth-century scholarship?

She still carries a small stuffed monkey with her when she meets the young people in her Roots and Shoots program. In fact, I'd been curious about the mention of a Mr. H. in the program's recent newsletter. "Who is Mr. H.?" I asked, wondering who this mystery man might be.

"Mary," Jane called out, giggling, "bring Mr. H. in here."

Mary brought in someone's version of a cuddly chimpanzee with a tail. We all had a good laugh. "My mystery romance!" Jane said, shaking her head. "The *real* Mr. H. is totally tattered," she explained. "He's got no fluff left except on his tail. He's been handled by more than forty thousand kids. Mr. H. has been my constant companion for two and a half years because of the inspirational nature of the man who gave him to me."

As inspiring as Jane is to others, she continually finds sources of inspiration of her own. One such inspiration is Gary Haun, a forty-eight-year-old magician who works with kids. He lost his eyesight in the U.S. Marines while commandeering a helicopter unit. He told her once, "Jane, when you first become blind, it's the most frustrating thing—you have to depend on other people for everything." He had been very depressed until he realized he could still hear and smell and touch and walk and learn to write with Braille.

"He's learned to hear your voice and so appears to look directly into your eyes while you're talking to him," Jane told me. "There's no rolling of his eyes or gazing up." At one point he decided to learn magic, although he was told it was impossible. "He's a very good magician, very good," she added.

When he got bored, he learned scuba diving; then it was cross-country skiing, judo, karate, and skydiving. "'How can you be scared when you can't see the ground?' That's what he says; of course it's not true, because you're jumping into a void. Now he's trying to master Japanese swordsmanship." Jane said that he is one of the most giving people she knows. "He's always up—you can call him, as I did accidentally the other day, at four in the morning. We all do. We call Gary to get a Gary fix; he's always positive.

"He gave me the original Mr. H., and he said, 'Jane, take him wherever you go. You know I'm with you in spirit.' I tell everybody Mr. H. is magic because of the man who gave him to me, and if they touch him, they'll never be the same again."

A Woman of the Wild

❖

From the time I was very small I had this love of animals, including insects and all natural life. My mother always supported and encouraged this interest. For example, when my mother found a whole handful of earthworms in bed with me, she didn't say, "Yuck," and throw them out. She just said that if I left them there, they'd be dead in the morning. They needed the earth. So I ran with them into the garden. Another time when I was staying with my father's family on the farm,

I hid in a henhouse to see how a hen laid an egg. None of the family knew where I was—they'd actually called the police—but even so, when she finally found me four hours later running toward the house all excited, she didn't reprimand me and scold me, which would have killed all the excitement. She sat down to listen to my story of how the hen laid the egg.

She obviously nurtured my interest by getting books for me about animals, because that's all I remember reading. When I was nine and in love with Tarzan, I dreamed of going to Africa to live with animals and write books with them. This was at the end of the Second World War and Africa was another world, still considered the Dark Continent. We didn't have any money, and young people didn't go tramping off into the woods and jungles as they do today. So all my mother's friends were apparently saying that she should stop me from dreaming about this nonsense and I should dream about something I could achieve. But she used to say if I really wanted something, worked hard, took advantage of opportunity, and never gave up, I would find a way. She didn't put it to me in exactly those terms, but this was the message, implicit in her response to my dreams. What I got from my own family was the ability to stand up for what I wanted. It gives you a certain inner confidence when you know that your family, although they may not necessarily approve of what you've done, will be understanding and forgiving, and that your family is a place where you can talk it through. So I had that inner sense. I suppose . . . well, it *is* having the courage of your conviction.

Finally, after I'd saved up enough money and gone to Africa and met Louis Leakey, he offered me this amazing opportunity to work in the jungle with the chimps. The two obstacles he had to overcome were, first, that his plan was considered amoral—as I said, no young people went off to live with animals, and certainly not young *women*—and of course I didn't have any training, so it was hard for him to get the money; that was one obstacle. Then the second obstacle was that the British authorities just said, "No." They couldn't take responsibility for this kind of crazy notion. But finally they agreed that I could go if I took a companion, so who volunteered to come but my mother. She was there three months and set up a clinic, and by caring about people, although she wasn't medically qualified, she managed to accomplish some wonderful cures with the old saline drip. There was nothing that you could damage people with. She just used the old-fashioned remedies that my uncle who's a doctor had suggested for her. They considered her a white witch doctor, so this made for terrific relations with the local people, which has stood me in good stead ever since. After three months the government decided it was okay for me to be there after all, so she left. But she really helped set up the perfect situation.

My mother is still alive. She's now ninety-three and just broke her hip—the dog threw her down the stairs. Her doctor said to me, "You know, most people of her age with such a badly smashed hip would not even have tried to walk, and she's going around with just a stick." She has a wonderful attitude about life. She's still deeply involved in everything I do. When people call her, she knows exactly who they are.

When I encourage other people to follow their passions, I tell them what my mother taught me: "If you really want to do something and work hard and take advantage of opportunity and never give up, you will find a way." If someone has a passion for going out and living in the forest, then the fears that most people are concerned about wouldn't bother them because that's the path they've chosen to take. It's actually not nearly as frightening walking in a forest as it is in Chicago or Los Angeles or any inner city; the dangers are absolutely much less. You can be unlucky, but in reality it's not that dangerous. Since I had dreamed about being in the forest all my life, read books about it, and felt that I would have a great rapport with animals, I didn't go around terrified. That doesn't mean I didn't have moments of fear; of course I did—you're very unimaginative if you don't. If you hear something you think is a buffalo snorting and stamping quite near you, you'd be extremely foolish not to get out of the way. So you have a fear response that's appropriate and right, but it's much easier to avoid danger in a forest than in the city jungle.

Observing a chimp mother's relationship to her child only confirmed my experience of my own mother and of myself as a mother to my son. The chimps have taught us that the early experience is just tremendously important in shaping later adult behavior. It's quite clear that young chimps with mothers who are less supportive, less tolerant, less playful, less affectionate, tend, particularly if they're daughters, to grow up into adults who have difficulty making close relationships with other adults—male or female, it doesn't matter. If you have a kind of timid, nervous mother, you're likely to be timid and nervous yourself. If you have a protective, assertive, supportive mother, you are likely to be that sort of female yourself. If you have a bad mother, if her mothering skills are poor, then you're likely to be a mother in your turn who has poor skills. I think it's fairly well proven now in human society that mothers who were abused as infants tend to be abusive mothers, again and again and again.

What I learned from the chimps about the importance of early experience, I had already experienced with my own mother, who made a wonderful home for me. I also grew up in an extended family. With her two sisters and her mother and my own sister, we had this terrific extended family. So if Mum was in a bad mood, probably her sister wasn't; that's what is so nice about the extended family. Everybody is bad tempered or upset one day, but there's always somebody else in the family you trust who's always there for you. That's what's gone wrong with our children today, that family structure is crumbling.

My son now has two children and so I'm a grandmother. I love them, of course, but I don't see them very much. They're in Dar es Salaam, which is one of the two places where I occasionally spend a rare three weeks. The second is at home with Mum where I grew up in Bournemouth, England. She's still there with her sister, who's ninety-five. Now that my mother has broken her hip, *my* sister's coming back more into the fold. We are slightly re-creating our extended family again.

Tanzania is where I would most like to be, but I would feel guilty because this traveling and fund-raising is what I'm meant to be doing now. Fund-raising is something you have to think about all the time—it's desperate. I think one has phases in life. My first one was the preparation phase, which consisted of all the years up until I went to Africa. Then it was the excitement of learning and observing and being out in the forest and living my dream and learning about these amazing beings that are so like us yet they're themselves—trying to feel what it's like to be a chimpanzee.

Then there was a gradual moving toward the "Well, I've got to do something with all this information" phase. That went on all the time, but there was a phase of very intensive analyzing for the big book I did, *The Chimpanzees of Gombe*. That was a phase when I was completely enjoying teasing out all the little observations and compiling them and making sense out of them whilst continuing, but less often, the observation. Also at that time was the beginning of teaching Stanford undergraduates. We had a very dynamic multidisciplinary research center.

Those phases were all going on at the same time, but the really intensive learning came from being with the chimps, which was a phase in and of itself. Then there was the moving into and continuing the analyzing and teaching. Then came what I call my experience like St. Paul on the road to Damascus: of being at a conference where, for the first time, all the chimp researchers came together and we had a session on conservation. It was shocking to see what was going on across Africa. I think we tended a little bit to be ostriches in our little places. We all knew there were problems in the vicinity around us, but seeing it multiplied across Africa was totally shocking: deforestation, hunting, snares, live animal trade. At the same conference, we were shown a piece of secretly filmed video footage from one of the labs that experiment on chimps—it was like looking into the Holocaust, about which I've read all my life. From that moment on, I haven't spent more than three weeks anywhere—that was in October 1986.

It was a complete transformation. The conference happened when I was about to celebrate the publication of *The Chimpanzees of Gombe*. In order to write that book, I had had to go back and teach myself some of the things I would have learned had I been an undergraduate, which I never was. In England, when you do a Ph.D., you simply write up your research; you don't have to go to courses. So I had missed out on all the underpinnings of writing in a meaningful way about animal behavior, such as understanding the endocrine system and the brain and all those things. I had to learn them on my own.

So this lightning strike came at exactly the point when, having published that book, I felt confident enough to go into a medical research lab and talk to the directors; before I'd written the book, I wouldn't have been comfortable. Because there was always the image of the *National Geographic* cover girl—which didn't bother me—I just retreated into my own little world, where I knew that for me I was doing the right thing: learning about the chimps, writing about them, and sharing what I knew.

No, being in my sixties hasn't affected my work schedule at all. I simply have disregarded it. There's not a single day when I think, Oh, I wish I wasn't sixty. Except sometimes I think, Well, I'm on such a roll now with Roots and Shoots and all that I would like is to be ten years younger in order just to have that extra ten years more to work, but it's not something I spend any time worrying about. All the women in my family lived into their nineties—no one ever seems to die in my family! I expect to have a good many more years ahead of me. I suppose the time will come when they won't be able to be quite so brutal to me on a lecture tour and expect me to do quite as much as I'm expected to do and I expect myself to do—Dr. Jane has the image of being totally tough and nothing can throw her, which happens to be true, but it must take a toll, I think.

I don't consider myself vulnerable. I think I've learned enough in my sixty years to know that I can be betrayed. It's a risk I take; it's when you're totally naive that you're really vulnerable. I've been through that phase; that's why I'm bringing it up now. I've been betrayed and it hurts at first, because you're so naive. But if you *know* that even though you think a relationship is wonderful, that things happen, people change, circumstances change, then there's always a feeling of "Let me make the most of it because it could change," and it won't necessarily mean that the person who's letting you down is any worse; it's just that things have changed, so you become much less vulnerable once you've learned that lesson.

I don't have any great romance in my life, but since I never had a brother I have always been very jealous of the brother-sister relationship because I thought that must be so wonderful to have such a good male friend. I like that male-female relationship—it has nothing to do with sex; there's nothing wrong with sex, but I wanted this real platonic relationship. So I decided to choose myself some brothers, and I have about eight or nine, who are at least ten years younger than I am. They're strong and going to be strong when I'm older. They are people whose doorstep I could turn up on, I could ask to borrow money from, I could get them to come and rescue me. It's marvelous, exactly what's needed at this stage in life. They're a wonderful family, just amazing. That's another way of extending my family. They've just about all spoken to each other on the phone; quite a few have met, but not all of them.

One of the brothers is very anxious to arrange a gathering—and it would be powerful, my goodness. They're quite exceptional. I have a Japanese brother, a Tanzanian brother, an American who was originally Russian brother, a Dutch brother. There are also the real close inner ones I've mentioned and then the sort of peripheral brothers. Then I've got nephews, four of them now, absolutely amazing young men. They can't be my sons, because I've got a son; I've got nieces and I've got a sister, so I don't need that—that's real and already exists. Now I've got four nephews. I told them they're not allowed to call me Auntie, though.

Yes, I'm anxious about what's going on in Burundi and Rwanda—it's a nightmare. Zaire is just over the lake from us. We're keeping in touch through the state department. We regularly fax, particularly from the U.K. office—it's much easier. We had chimp orphans in Burundi, but we moved them to Kenya before all this happened. If you allow yourself to despair because people get sick and die, you might as well give up at the beginning. People get sick and they die. Chimps are the same. It's painful, and I suppose if you know the chimps really well, you go through the same stages of grief and mourning that you do with people. But there's something of them that's always with you.

It's the same with the forest. I think I've worked out unconsciously that living the sort of chaotic life I live now—the constant travel, being surrounded by people, everyone wanting a piece of Dr. Jane—if I were to go around in a state of constant agitation because I can't quite do everything, I wouldn't really accomplish anything. So keeping the forest inside is a sort of protection of myself. When wild animals are very stressed, they go to sleep, but I've learned to be quiet, to be quiet in a storm, to let it happen and just concentrate on what I'm supposed to be doing right now. Obviously sometimes it breaks down and I get kind of cross about the way things should work differently. I know the feeling of panic; it's like fear. Of course there are times when I have that, but I send it away quickly, consciously. I don't know what I say, but I make it go away.

I have my three reasons for hope. One is the problem-solving ability of the human species. I truly believe we are close to the point of no return with the damage we've done to the planet. A hundred years ago, who would have thought we could get to the moon. A hundred years ago, if you'd described what I've just been looking at on the CD-ROM, with all its information, it would seem like science fiction. Or a 747 flying off the ground! I fly in them all the time, and every time I have the same sense of absolute awe and amazement and magic. I look at the ground rushing by, and I think we can't possibly rise up from the ground, but we do. It's a very good symbolism, actually; we do fly up with this great weight and all the rest of it. The hope lies in the fact that we've begun to understand there really are very, very serious problems. The hope is we can get together around the world, and people are doing so. There are signs of change, both in the way people are living, in the technology, and in the behavior of industry.

My second area of hope is that young people around the world are getting more and more determined that they *are* going to make a difference, which is why I started Roots and Shoots. It's the main thrust of all my energy now: developing this Roots and Shoots program. You're told to think globally, act locally, but if you spend time thinking globally, you haven't got any energy left and you're totally depressed. There's no way you're going to roll up your sleeves and go out and do something in your backyard, because why should you, what difference can it make? But if you start with the other idea first and get a group of people locally, you see with your own eyes, "Gosh, this has made a difference," and then you know there's people like you all over the world making a difference, and that all these kids are going to grow up and take leadership positions. The young people are my second reason for hope.

My third is this indomitable nature of the human spirit that Mr. H. is exemplifying for me every day.

What I would say to other women in their sixties is: "Don't think about your birthdays; it's not a bit important. It's how you feel that matters. Don't spend time looking back over mistakes you might have made; just think ahead in a positive way and believe, implicitly, that every day you live makes a difference, because you impact the world around you and you have a choice as to what sort of impact you want to make. Do you want to use that day to try to make the world a better place, or don't you care?" It's the Roots and Shoots philosophy, but it applies to people five years old and ninety-five equally. The whole Roots and Shoots ethic is that the individual matters, makes a difference, and that we try to make the world a better place in three ways: for the environment, for animals, and for the human community. That's just as important as you go through your sixties, your seventies, your eighties, and your nineties.

I always had a fantasy of myself in old age. I don't spend any time thinking about it now. But I always used to love old people when I was a child, and I always used to talk to them. If I do have a fantasy, it's in the role of young people coming to me and my being able to share with them some of the wisdom I've gained from the forest and the chimps and the struggle through life and all the rest of it.

When I first entered this field of science there was a great deal of sexism against women. Now it's almost changed the other way. Pendulums always swing, so you've gone from the kind of male-dominated society where males are all-important to a situation where males don't actually count for anything, you can forget them. Of course, the truth is somewhere in the middle. This is why I love the Native Americans. They have the symbolism of the big eagle who can't fly unless its wings are the same size and the same strength. The eagle has both a male wing and a female wing. I was on a platform at the State of the World Forum with women talking about "Beyond Beijing," and one of them, in talking about the next millennium, said, "The next millennium will be the millennium of the woman," and I'm thinking to myself, Do we have to go through another thousand years before we have the eagle flying? Can't the next millennium be a shared millennium, for heaven's sake? We belong together. Men have strengths we don't have; we have strengths they don't have. The world will get right when we link the strengths and make it one, become a whole eagle. I love that symbolism.

For further information please contact:

The Jane Goodall Institute
P. O. Box 599
Ridgefield, CT 06877
Telephone: (800) 592-JANE
Fax: (203) 431-4387

Challenges keep life going. If you don't have a challenge, I think you die. I need challenges, I love challenges. Any time somebody says something is difficult or impossible, that's what I like. People tried to tell me the [hip replacement] surgery would be easy. I didn't want to hear that; I wanted something to fight. . . . If you don't have challenges, you never learn to develop your inner strength.

— ELAYNE JONES

Elayne Jones

Elayne Jones is the legendary tympanist for the San Francisco Opera. On the day we met, the unusually energetic and spirited sixty-eight-year-old woman was home in bed, recovering from a week-old hip replacement surgery. Still, Elayne, svelte and ageless, locked me in a hearty embrace with the most sinewy, iron-hard, yet graceful arms I've ever felt. She then directed me to pull up a chair and continued her dramatic telling with hair-raising details of her successful operation to two women visitors who also perform in the opera orchestra. The only indication I had that Elayne, a mother of three, *might* not be up to her usual self was that she was recumbent—and that, just barely. She did not behave like an aging, frail patient; rather, her Dennis Rodman–like hairstyle and dazzling smile revealed a woman feisty as hell and still ready to take on any challenge—no matter how serious or threatening.

A zealous tennis player, Elayne explained to me when I asked about her hair, "I cut it shorter and colored the center part blond before I went in for surgery. When I used to play tennis, I never wore a hat and the sun would bleach the top part of my hair. So I decided that even though I'm not playing tennis these days, I'm going to make it look as though I am!"

While some women in their sixties are lamenting the loss of their memories, I couldn't help but marvel at Elayne's mental dexterity. Not once in the course of two hours did she stumble to recall a name, place, or date—whether they were from yesterday or fifty years ago. She explained that "as a musician, I have to remember everything. We may have three days of rehearsal. The first day is usually a read-through; the second day, the conductor begins to make changes; and the third day is like a dress rehearsal. But sometimes on the third day, the conductor may say he wants something played a little bit differently—maybe the tempo's to be a little bit faster, a little bit slower, or even the order of the program is going to be changed. When you come in that night, you have to remember. There's no room to forget. If I really had the memory I want, I'd be a politician," she gibed, making reference to the decades of racism she has experienced during her nearly fifty years working in the classical music world.

Elayne was born in Harlem in 1928 of West Indian parents who were both from Barbados. Her parents met in New York and married. Her mother was a pianist and a piano teacher; her father was a Linotype artist. She specified that "neither of them, of course, being black, was ever able to realize their artistic goals (as every story you read about black people makes clear)." As a result, her mother was employed as a domestic worker and her father as a porter. However, Elayne's mother was determined that her daughter would be the extension of her and her husband's artistic legacy. "I was the only child," Elayne continued, "so Mother used to tell me, 'I put all my eggs in one basket!' My parents also realized that black men, generally speaking, didn't make a good living, that black women had to work real hard, so I might as well have a profession that was worthwhile and had dignity. (That's why they insisted on my playing music.)"

And play music she did! Elayne became the first African American to ever have a principal position in a major symphony, anywhere in the world. Everywhere she went, people recognized her. Unfortunately, this public notice did not enhance her position in a racist American society or among jealous members of the orchestras in which she performed. Early in her career (much like her paragon, Billie Holiday), Elayne was seen as a black woman who, in many states, was not allowed to eat in restaurants with her white co-workers or stay in the same hotels with them when they traveled. Through it all she remained focused on playing her tympani. "I just played my music; I love to play," she said, without acrimony.

No matter how tired she gets, "at the end of every symphony or opera, there's usually a long and loud roll of drums—especially in Wagner," so she has to sustain her energy to play until the end. Elayne told me, "Some people say, 'The opera is not over until the fat lady sings,' but I say, 'No, the opera is not over until the black lady rolls.'"

Roll on, lady.

The Rhythm Lover

⁘

I'm writing my autobiography, and I listen to stories of how other black women felt they were deprived of doing certain things in their lives because they had no role models. Well, there was never a question in my life about a role model. There wasn't any! As a matter of fact, the past couple of days I've been lying here thinking, What is there in me that says, "If that's where I wanna go, that's where I'm goin'"? I never think about whether I'm a woman or I'm black; I just do it. You know the Nike ad: Just do it? That's me. I'm the "just do it" person.

Music was important to me when I was growing up because I was very black. Did you ever read the book that says, "When you're white, you're right; when you're yellow, you're a good fellow; when you're brown, stick around; if you're black, get back"? As West Indians, we weren't too well liked by most of the American blacks, either, so I had another thing going against me that I had to overcome. That's something I grew up with; at the same time, I wanted to be liked. All those things made me feel that I had to be the best. I made up my mind I was going to be the best at anything I did—that was the only way I'd bring attention to myself.

As a little girl, I was a tomboy; I knew if I wanted attention from the boys, I had to run down the street as fast as they did. If they were climbing the fence, I would climb the fence, too. If they were playing punch ball, I'd play punch ball. I did whatever I could to be accepted because I felt I didn't have any of the attributes that make you acceptable. Socially I became the pride of the neighborhood because I could throw a ball farther and run faster than anybody else.

I also had my music. Mother taught me the piano. I had an extraordinarily good ear, so I played the piano and entertained everybody. I'd listen to Billie Holiday and Count Basie and play their music by ear. My parents made sure that I always practiced and did my homework.

When it came time for high school, my parents insisted I try out for the High School of Music and Art in Manhattan. "I'm not good enough," I said. "Well, you're gonna try," was their response. You know what? I got into the school! I was the only black in the instrumental classes in 1942. It was my first exposure to the white world. I had never been in a white person's home other than the women my mother worked for as a domestic. But I was determined that when I went into those houses, they would say I was really exemplary. When I started in music at school, I tried to be the best at my music. All the piano students at Music and Art had to take an orchestral instrument. I always liked the violin, so I decided to play the violin. When it came time to select the instruments, I told them my preference and they said, "No, you can't play the violin; you're too skinny."

Why should they give me, a little black kid, violin lessons? It was another form of racism. Of course I didn't analyze it that way then. People don't really understand what racism is all about. It wasn't about being "too skinny"—they weren't going to waste money teaching a black kid to play the violin; there were no other black people in classical music. One teacher said, "Let's give her the drums because all blacks have rhythm." So that's how I got the drums. I liked the drums anyhow, so it wasn't too far out. When I had gone to the Caribbean as a child, I used to hear wonderful music. We went often. I was the only girl in the class, but I practiced and practiced and practiced.

I started out in the third-term orchestra and ended up in the eighth-term orchestra a year or two before I should have. I did very well. I played tympani and percussions, anywhere I could. Percussion has four sections: tympani are tuned instruments; snare and bass drums are the battery instruments; melody instruments are the xylophone, the bells, the glockenspiel; and sound-effect instruments are the triangle and tambourine. I started out learning all these instruments but ended up being a tympanist. I also played in the all-city high school band and the all-city high school orchestra.

When I was a senior, Duke Ellington offered a scholarship to three music graduates that year. Again my parents said, "You're gonna try for that." "No. I can't compete with all these white kids who play the violin," I said. Well, I went, I played, and I won. I was the only black and the only woman among the six winners. That entitled me to a full scholarship to Juilliard for three years. Still I didn't think it was going to be my career, but I really loved playing.

By the time I got to Juilliard I was playing in orchestras with people like the black conductors Dean Dixon and Everett Lee—these people are gone now. Then I got involved in political life. It was a good thing I got involved in all those left-wing organizations because it helped me become aware of the racism and discrimination that existed in the music profession. I began to realize that if I wanted to pursue a career in music as a tympanist, it wasn't going to be easy. I would have to excel in my music but also excel at opening the doors, so that's what I did. I met interesting people and played set drums, not just classical music. I played at summer resorts in New York, in the Catskills—that's where I met my husband.

The year I graduated from Juilliard, in 1949, I auditioned for a tympanist position with the New York City Opera. I passed the audition, but they didn't want to hire me. I wasn't Italian, I wasn't male, and I wasn't white. They said, "How could a black girl [I was twenty-one at the time] play opera?" My teacher was the tympanist for the New York Philharmonic, so he interceded for me and said, "If you want the best person, you have to take her." They reluctantly hired me in September 1949.

Hiring me was one thing; staying was another. They wanted to make sure I would not make the job, that I would collapse. The first opera I played, *Der Rosenkavalier,* was without rehearsal, one of the most difficult operas in the repertoire. They figured I'd fall flat on my face.

Girl, I'll tell you, I felt everybody could see my heart pounding, I was so nervous. I thought my heart was coming through my head. Was I scared! I played and got through it; they all came by and patted me on the shoulder: "What a wonderful job you did, Jonesie."

Then I had another hurdle to climb. Every year we went on tour and they took only the principal players, of which I as tympanist was one. (Now I think, How the hell did I ever get through that?) If you tell me it's difficult, ooh, the stronger I get. That's essentially what happened. I learned those operas like you can't believe, right then and there. At that time, there was another woman, a harpist, but I was the only black. So I had to deal with going into hotels where I couldn't stay with the rest of the orchestra or restaurants where I couldn't be seated with them.

In St. Louis we were playing *Madame Butterfly,* in an auditorium where the pit would rise to the level of the stage. That night they announced that the pit would not be rising. "What do you mean, the pit won't be rising?" The pit would remain below stage level. They had erected some boxes for the conductor to stand on so he could still see the stage and conduct the orchestra at the same time. What was the reason for this? During rehearsal, the opera house management discovered that they had a black girl playing the tympani and they said, "Well, she can't play here in St. Louis." The opera management said, "She has to play; you just can't walk in and pick up a tympani player anywhere." "Well, we can't allow her to be seen." So they kept the pit below so I wouldn't be an embarrassment to the city.

I played with the New York City Opera for eleven years. During that time I married and had three children. I almost gave birth to my son while I was playing in the pit. I was the only woman at that time to be in labor while I was performing. I was playing *Carousel* at the New York City Opera! The same thing almost happened with my daughter. I was playing *Salome* with her. My third child was induced on Mother's Day 1959, because my obstetrician was afraid I'd give birth on the Carnegie Hall stage. ("The way you go, you're going to be playing and the baby's just gonna drop right out.")

It was difficult working full-time and being a wife and mother. My husband was getting antsy, I had rehearsals every day and performances every night. Monday was my day off; my husband was a physician, and Sunday was his day off. We were always running against each other. We had other problems, too. I had to have help with the kids, help with the house. Nobody wanted to work for me as a black woman; there was no status in working for a black woman. This wasn't anything I made up, because people would speak to me over the phone and couldn't detect whether I was black or white. Plus the fact that I was married to a Jewish man. So over the phone I was Mrs. Kaufman. Then they would come to the house, meet me, and say, "I'm looking for the lady of the house." "I am the lady of the house." I actually had one woman run out of the house screaming, "I don't want to work here, I don't want to work here." It didn't matter if these women were black or white; they'd rather take shit from a white person. Since my mother was a domestic worker, I was very, very considerate—overly so—to people I did eventually hire.

My husband wanted me to give up my career. He also didn't like being called Dr. Jones, because I had so much publicity every place I went. Today it would be different, but at that time, I think men resented their wives receiving that kind of attention. He should have been happy to say, "Yes, I am the husband of Miss Jones," but his ego got in the way, so that caused a split.

I had to make a decision whether to give up my career and be Mrs. Kaufman or hold my career and be Miss Jones, so I became Miss Jones. I was thirty-five at the time and thought I'd meet somebody else. I'm sixty-eight now; I haven't even had a date all these years.

Then Leopold Stokowski, who really liked my work, formed his own American Symphony and asked me to be his tympanist. I became the American Symphony tympanist, based in New York at Carnegie Hall, for eleven years. During those twenty-two years at the New York Opera and the American Symphony, I played with just about every renowned conductor and got praise from all of them. I have to remind myself how they all respected me because sometimes I get down and feel that nobody cares.

After my divorce, my kids and I moved to the United Nations Village, where delegates with children lived. My kids went to the United Nations school because it was interracial and I wanted them to live in that kind of environment. I still wanted to play in a major symphony. I thought I'd play in the New York Philharmonic. I had worked with Leonard Bernstein. I also played on Broadway and recorded records. I was very, very busy in New York; I was running all the time. Leonard Bernstein sang my praises. In 1971 my teacher, Saul Goodman, retired from the New York Philharmonic. I had been the first black musician to play with the New York Philharmonic. So when Goodman was going to retire, I auditioned and thought this would be the job for me as tympanist of the New York Philharmonic. I auditioned and wasn't offered the position; that broke my heart. But the guy who did get the job was leaving the San Francisco Symphony. So I said to myself, The only other city I think I'd be happy in would be San Francisco. You wouldn't get me to live in Chicago or Dallas or Houston or any of those places, but I thought San Francisco was a racially unbiased city. I took a trip to San Francisco and auditioned against forty men. I got the job. I was in eighth heaven! Leopold Stokowski was very upset. I have a framed letter from him saying: "For you, I'm happy you're going, but for me, I'm very sorry that you're leaving."

The kids and I packed up everything and moved to San Francisco in June 1972.

Seiji Ozawa was then conductor of the San Francisco Symphony. What I didn't know—and I wish I had—was that the orchestra did not like Seiji. There was so much racism; I walked into a nest of worms. An audience looks into an orchestra and sees musicians playing instruments, but there's a lot going on behind the scenes. I had publicity in every paper in the world—I was the first black person, male or female, to have a principal position in a major symphony in the world. Everywhere I went, people recognized me. Then we went on tour to England, France, Germany, Italy, and the Soviet Union. Everywhere I played, people came up and some would touch me to see if I was really black. My hair was short; they thought maybe I was a guy. That's another story—that six-week European tour. We played in Moscow, where they wanted to interview me, but the orchestra voted against it because they were afraid I would say the wrong thing. For them the wrong thing would be to admit there was racism in the United States. "You have a job; how dare you say there's racism in America?" was their attitude.

After our return to America, reviews came in from the various European countries and they sang my praises. We then went on tour to Japan with Ozawa and had an incredible three weeks there. Every place we went, again I got singled out. I just played my music; I love to play. A lot of European musicians resent that. They would accuse me of using my body too much when I was playing and bringing too much attention to myself. When guest conductors would come to San Francisco, they'd say, "Oh, Miss Jones . . . " and these guys resented me because I was a black woman getting more attention than they were. It was the straw that broke the camel's back. There would be times in rehearsal when the conductor would say, "Follow the tympani" or "Let's balance with the tympani," and they resented that because, after all, they were all white musicians who surely knew more than me. Yet I had more experience than any of these musicians.

After two years, they denied me tenure and voted me out of the orchestra. I thought I would die; it wasn't something I expected after getting so many great reviews: suddenly to be told I could no longer be part of the orchestra. So I sued the orchestra for racism. But I lost my suit. I was a little bit too early. There's no question I would win the same suit today, but this was in 1974.

I should have left San Francisco then, but I was stubborn and tried to prove I didn't deserve to be denied tenure. In the meantime, the opera and symphony had been one organization. Then, when Davies Hall was built, they had separate orchestras for the symphony and the opera. Ironically, there was a committee of seven people who voted me out of the symphony, and six of those people eventually ended up with me in the opera orchestra. So ironic. I just loved it.

It still angers me. It ruined not only my life, but the lives of my kids, because my children were very much affected by that. They gave up their music because they figured if their mother, who was supposedly such a fine musician, couldn't make it, they wouldn't be able to make it. My daughter gave up the cello. My other daughter gave up the oboe. My son, who started the violin in New York and studied from the time he was nine years old, said he would never play in a symphony orchestra where people are so small-minded. He claims they don't really love music—they just play it. So he plays on the streets to his heart's content. In the meantime, I've played with the San Francisco Opera for nearly twenty-five years.

At sixty-eight, I'm now the oldest in the orchestra. When I started with the New York City Opera, I was the youngest at twenty-one. The only reason I would want to retire is because I've done it so long—close to fifty years—and it's time to see if I have the ability to do anything else. I would love to play jazz. What I'd love to do more than anything else is stand up in front of a thousand or more people and talk about my music. I love to bring my drums and play for kids and adults alike. I've done so many things, seen so much. I think because of my age, some of the young conductors are not really interesting for me. I've worked with the greatest, from Leonard Bernstein to Leopold Stokowski.

Even though I'm sixty-eight, I still have tremendous stamina. I think because of my music, I don't get tired. My arms are very strong and muscular, from playing the tympani all these years. A four-hour rehearsal would devastate most people because it's so intense, but I just keep going. My other passion is tennis. The last time I played tennis was August 8, 1995, almost a year and a half ago. I remember exactly. I had gone to Club Med. (Here again is the kind of person I am: I go to Club Med on my own. Everybody—black, white, young, or old— can't get over the fact that I go to Club Med at my age by myself. I go and play tennis, dance, and meet people from all over the world.)

When I was sixty I went alone to Club Med Sonora in Mexico, where they have a big tennis camp. I signed myself up for the most difficult class, and I was one of two women among all these guys. Well, again, a two-hour tennis drill is nothing to me. So the guys would say, "Let's take a break. What about you, Elayne?" "I'm not tired, let's keep on going," I'd say. These guys didn't know how old I was. Then they would see me dancing all night—at some point I heard a man with an Italian accent say, "These guys are older and they work harder; you're just a young woman." I didn't tell them right away, but toward the middle of the week when I told them how old I was and what I did, these guys could not believe that I wasn't really forty or fifty—they really flipped out.

Unfortunately, during that trip I really began to notice how painful my hip was. I don't sleep a lot—four hours, maybe, at home. I would play tennis all morning before rehearsals, then go to rehearse all day and play a performance at night—and, of course, I was standing all the time. I never had any problem with my body. I danced in Barbados, a couple of years ago, at the Carnivale from ten in the morning until six o'clock at night—just one dance after another. And I love to run—you never see me walk. On the way back from Sonora, I had to change planes and I found myself thinking, How far is it to the next gate? That was the first indication something was wrong. How far is it? It was hurting that much. I came home, went right to Kaiser. The doctor said I had arthritis. I said, "Not really, that's for old ladies." I couldn't believe it and spent a fortune going to holistic doctors, chiropractors, osteopaths, acupuncturists, and masseuses, but the condition kept getting worse and worse. I even went to Cuba; I wasn't going to hang around here and be crippled!

I came back, enrolled in a cultural anthropology class at City College; I was the oldest in the class—even older than the teacher. She said I brought an entirely different dimension to the class. I had a wonderful time with all the young people. But going back and forth was getting harder and harder. I started swimming three days a week because I was determined to still get my exercise, so I swam until the day before my surgery. I hobbled in there and managed to get my swim. The pain got worse when the opera season began with *Prince Igor;* I just love that opera. We performed at the Civic Auditorium, where there are so many stairs. So the stagehands let me use the freight elevator. Everybody in the orchestra kept saying, "This can't happen to Elayne." The way they were responding, it must have been very painful for them to see how I had deteriorated. I was determined to play through the season, but, girl, it got worse and worse and worse, and I called my doctor and said, "I want the surgery *now.*" The doctor had one day open, the day before Thanksgiving, and I said, "I want it." It was arthritis all right. When I saw the last X-ray before the surgery, how the hip socket was rubbed flat, that's when I realized how bad I was. I played the opening performance of *Tales of Hoffman* but couldn't do any more.

It's hard for me to accept the fact that I have to just lie here and let my hip heal. I feel good, but my body is still that of a sixty-eight-year-old woman. I have to keep telling myself I had *major* surgery, because I don't feel sick or any less strong. The social services person who comes to give me my bath says, "A lot of young people would be happy to have legs like yours."

Sure, I think of myself as going on forever. I see myself in Barbados, starting a music school—that's what I would love to do. I'm going to leave San Francisco—it's not interesting enough for me anymore—move back to New

York, and travel between there and Barbados. I like to cook, love to entertain, have been a member of the International Diplomacy Council, where you have foreign visitors come to the house. I will cook at the drop of a hat. I can come home after a performance at night and cook a whole meal. I'm never tired when I come home, anyhow.

Challenges keep life going. If you don't have a challenge, I think you die. I need challenges, I love challenges. Any time somebody says something is difficult or impossible, that's what I like. People tried to tell me the surgery would be easy. I didn't want to hear that; I wanted something to fight. While we were waiting for the results of my lawsuit against the symphony, a friend came over and whispered to me, "Elayne, if you win this suit, how are you going to survive? You'll have nothing to fight." Well, I didn't win, so I kept on fighting. The thing that makes me happy is to make people feel good. I'm a humanist. Don't bother me with religion. You use your inner strength. If you don't have challenges, you never learn to develop that inner strength. You realize if that person can do something great, maybe you can, too.

I can't give anybody advice. I don't solely address women, because I see *people* with problems, young black men, young women. I'm not the kind who says that women have problems; we *all* have problems. I feel that, first of all, you have to absorb all that there is. Everybody says my room is cluttered. I'm into everything —you've got to be into everything, challenge everything, read everything. I'm very political; everything that happens is political. You can't let down on the challenges.

There is so much to learn in the world, and don't say, "I can't." Try it, you might like it. I guess that's the way I've been all along. Otherwise how could I have come from Harlem and become a tympanist in a profession where there were no women, no blacks, nothing?—unless from early on I had this belief: I can do it. But not in a Pollyanna-ish way; I would never say, "I did it, you can do it." If I see a challenge, I'm gonna go after it. Do it. Follow your dreams. I think everybody has the ability to do most things if they just get out there and do it. Again, not from a snobbish sense. It takes a great deal of work, but work never hurt anybody. Work is good for you.

It is true that as they age people get more fixed in their ways of being. It's hard not to. Again, I think it takes a lot of energy to keep your mind open on any *subject. . . . I can feel my mind creaking sometimes where it used to swing free. And to hold the door open can be a real tough job. . . . Having watched my father and mother continue to use their minds right up to the end, I feel very strongly that I want to be that way—to stay open and keep learning.*

— URSULA K. LE GUIN

Ursula K. Le Guin

LOSS OF FERTILITY DOES NOT MEAN LOSS OF DESIRE AND
FULFILLMENT. BUT IT DOES ENTAIL A CHANGE, A CHANGE
INVOLVING MATTERS EVEN MORE IMPORTANT—IF I MAY VENTURE
A HERESY—THAN SEX.
THE WOMAN WHO IS WILLING TO MAKE
THAT CHANGE MUST BECOME PREGNANT WITH HERSELF, AT LAST.
—URSULA K. LE GUIN
"The Space Crone,"
from *Dancing at the Edge of the World*

In Ursula Le Guin's popular collection of essays, *Dancing at the Edge of the World,* three chapters in particular held my interest with their feminist slant: "The Space Crone," in which she says, "It requires fanatical determination now to become a Crone"; "Theodora," which is an introduction for her mother Theodora Kroeber's book, *The Inland Whale;* and "The Fisherwoman's Daughter," which is essentially about the writing life of women. For literary and socially concerned readers, this prolific writer's works have been essential reading for nearly four decades. She is the author of more than thirty books of fantasy and science fiction, such as *The Left Hand of Darkness, The Lathe of Heaven,* and *A Wizard of Earthsea*; short stories; children's books; poetry; criticism; and essays. In Ursula's fascination with perceiving and describing "reality" through realism, surrealism, magic realism, and fantasy, she often uses a multiple voice or a mythic voice, because, as she explains, "reality is a slippery fish that often can be caught only in a net of spells or with the hook of metaphor." What would her reality be? I wondered.

Ursula Kroeber Le Guin, besides being a well-known writer, is the daughter of legendary parents. Alfred Kroeber started the Department of Anthropology at the University of California at Berkeley in the 1890s and became well-known as the anthropologist who in 1914 "found" Ishi, the last Native American in California to survive in the wild. Theodora Kroeber was a writer and the author of *Ishi*, the story of Ishi's life among his people and, later, in "civilization." I had heard many intriguing stories about Theodora: she started writing in her mid-fifties, after her four children were grown; she had been married three times, the last marriage when she was seventy-two to a man twenty-seven!

As I drove up the street looking for Ursula's house in Portland, Oregon, where she has lived for thirty years with her husband, Charles Le Guin, and their three children, I noticed how similar the appealing, multileveled brown-shingled architecture is to so many homes found in the Berkeley Hills, where Ursula spent her first eighteen years. I parked in front of the Chinese-red door that Ursula had alerted me to, and she welcomed me with a warm smile and a cup of hot herbal tea. Although our *sympatico* seemed immediate, I sensed a strong reserve, a privateness or shyness, which she eventually addressed, admitting to being "painfully introverted."

"Interviews are difficult for me; I'm not a self-examiner," Ursula forewarned me as we sat in the window seat in the dark wood–paneled living room. "I don't like to reminisce at all; neither did my father. I find it painful and upsetting. It brings up memories that are not very useful to me as a writer—often issues that I've already worked through.

"As an artist, I'm always inventing, and looking back doesn't matter. Artists live in the present; they are more concerned with what they're making now. What they made before is past. It's funny, but I realize this has always been true of me: I've never wanted to look back nor been able to look back very well, which is a loss in that I'd love to remember as well as my husband can. He can tell me the names of the children in his third grade."

"I thought we could begin with Theodora," I ventured forth, hoping to put Ursula at ease. "The fact that she didn't start to write until her mid-fifties is quite wonderful, very inspiring for women." Ursula once asked her mother why she'd waited so long because she enjoyed it so much. Theodora said, "Well, I wasn't ready yet. It didn't feel right."

"My mother was of the generation that was convinced women ought to stay home and bring up the kids. You know—that a career was a sort of competition with being a wife and mother. When she was quite old, eighty, she did tell me, 'I wish I'd started sooner.' One does get behind as one gets older," Ursula said, speaking, I thought, more about herself at sixty-seven than her mother at eighty.

Ursula speaks with equal gratitude about both her parents. "My father was in his study part of every day, writing. He was also a wonderful role model, Pa going off to the study again, all geared up to write, looking forward to it, and enjoying it. I realized at a very young age: this is something grownups do. It's like reading. If the grownups don't read, the kids won't read."

We spoke for several hours. I would ease up on my questions when I saw Ursula's shoulders shrink, almost imperceptibly, or heard a slight tightness in her throat. We confided our mutual love of Berkeley (where I also had lived for twenty years), our enjoyment of literature, cinema, and nature; and she surprised me with her updated view on "cronehood."

Ursula began by telling me how attending college on the east coast at Radcliffe had affected her both positively and adversely.

The Space Crone

‧

My going back east to college was almost accidental. My father taught at Harvard for a year after he retired from Berkeley, and he offered, "If you come with me, you can go to Radcliffe for free." I said, "What's Radcliffe?" I really didn't know. I'd been expecting to go to Cal. There were eight hundred undergraduates when I went to Radcliffe, a quarter the size of my high school. Oh, wow, I can be a person here, I thought. I got a very good education, but also I feel I was taught some things that I had to unlearn, painfully and consciously. In Berkeley we didn't think we were better than anybody else just because my dad taught college. His father had been a clock maker, and my mother's father had been a grocer. The attitude was not simply that of being better; it was work hard and enjoy your work. But the ethic at Harvard is that you're there because you are better than other people. Boy, you buy that so fast at seventeen or eighteen, and you believe it. I had to unlearn that later in life. Who's better? How better? I had a better education, yeah, so what do I do with it? It's hard for me to verbalize this, but I am half very grateful to Radcliffe and half, in a way, a little bitter that they misled this silly little girl from California who just didn't realize what kind of company she was mixing with. I had good teachers and made lovely friends, but I had trouble with the class system.

The ethic of my family was middle class, that work is a good thing. If you are talented in any way, you should learn to develop your talent. The best of the middle class in that sense. A fairly puritanical attitude toward life: you take life pretty seriously and expect to work. It's very egalitarian, actually.

Perhaps the most important gift I received from my mother was feeling welcome. Welcome as a girl. She told me many more times than once how glad she was that I was a girl. I'm the youngest of four and the only girl. She adored her three boys, but she truly wanted a woman in the house, as it were. That's such a great thing to tell a girl. Some girls feel that they should have been boys or feel like second-raters. I never, ever got that from either of my parents. They felt, "Oh, great, we got a girl." Looking back, I think how that assurance at home took me through a lot of misogyny and prejudice that girls went through in my generation. The 1950s was not the greatest time to be a girl. My parents brought me up to believe that one's sex had nothing to do with accomplishment. That I could do anything I set my mind to do, given any luck. My mother put me on to Virginia Woolf quite young. I was fifteen or so the first time I read *A Room of One's Own*. It was real radical feminism, still is.

That doesn't mean, however, that my mother considered herself a feminist. When the second women's movement came along in the 1960s and 1970s, she was a little cross with me for going along with it. She was quite old then, and there were some excesses in the movement. Some women were talking silly, anti-men rhetoric. My mother leaped to the assumption that to be a feminist was to be anti-male, which she wasn't about to be. I couldn't get through to her that it had nothing to do with that, that it had to do with freedom. I've written about men all my life, I've lived with them, I've loved them, I've borne them and raised them. "Ahh, those women's libbers," she would say. People do tend to get more conservative, more rigid, as they get older. It was a pity; it grieved me that she couldn't feel this floodtide of being able to think about things we hadn't been able to think about and finding books that we hadn't known existed and reading them, finding foremothers we didn't know about. It was so exciting.

I am very un—age conscious; I can't tell how old people are. I'm terrible at guessing any age between twenty and fifty. I think it was because I grew up with a grandfather-generation father; a mother-generation mother; and a great-aunt who was like a second mother to me. My father was in his mid-fifties when I was born. I only remember him with gray hair. He was very lively and a lot of fun. He never became an old man to me.

Age was unimportant to me. I never thought of somebody being out of it or different because they were old. I didn't get this youth fixation. So many Americans grow up without knowing any old people. Everybody's under forty. I feel very lucky; mine certainly wasn't a very large family, but it did span generations. That experience helped me to be more at home with older people and, perhaps in some respects, with getting older myself. I've seen it done well, so it doesn't *totally* terrify me.

I think this kind of fixation with aging has increased during my lifetime. I'm getting tired of people in their forties carrying on about turning fifty. "Ooooh, I'm old." I say, Try being sixty-seven, baby! There's a kind of unreality now that I don't remember seeing when I was young. We have a family story about my great-grandmother bursting into tears at her daughter's fortieth birthday party and my grandmother Phoebe saying, "Don't cry, Mother, it's all right," and her mother responding, "I'm not crying about you. If you're forty, how old am I?" She was about sixty-five at the time and apparently hadn't thought about it all that much. She needed a daughter's birthday to make her feel old.

I've got a daughter turning forty next summer. We are celebrating with a big party in the Napa Valley. My husband turns seventy the same summer. I find it amazing. I loved my forties, so I hope she does, too. It was a good decade: I hit my stride as a writer, my kids were good kids and growing up fast. I knew at the time that it was a really nice period.

With any luck, you're perfectly healthy in your forties; you don't get tired as fast as you begin to later on. In my late fifties I realized that I had less energy, less time to do things, and that everything took longer. It's just something you have to cope with; you can't count on things the way you used to. The only thing I've done about it is that, for the first time in my life, I have a lovely girl come in every two weeks to clean the house. I like housework, actually, but I realized that was the only thing I could cut out of my routine. I'm not very good at cutting things, so I'm not coping very well at all. I'm just sort of floundering around, trying to do too much and not leaving enough time for my writing, which goes slower than it used to, so I'm a bit frustrated. I used to be able, as most women are, to do four or five things at once. Do the juggling act. Now, if I can keep one plate in the air, that's good.

Something akin to this is built into the Hindu view of human life as I understand it: when you are young, you are a householder—you take care of your family and home; when you get old, you drop most of your plates and concentrate on learning to be alone and, in a manner of speaking, learn about soul making. You try to concentrate your spiritual powers. "Going into the forest"—that's the technical name for it, which refers mostly to men, but not entirely. Women too can go to the family and say, "Good-bye, look after yourselves, I'm taking my begging bowl and my stick and I'm going to the forest."

That seems very wise and useful to me. But I am not a Hindu, and I live in our modern culture, which is increasingly overwhelming. I'm not sure how we are supposed to handle it. This is one reason I don't have a modem on my computer. I think I will have to eventually because of some jobs I'm undertaking, but I really dread it. It'll take more time, make more complication in life instead of less. Some of the technology available now, though, is wonderful and exciting to a writer. People want to make a CD-ROM of one of my books, and if I work with them, I've got to have the technology. I want to do that, but sometimes I think,

Am I a fool to start this at my age? Here's a whole new technology I've got to learn. But I seem to be drifting into it.

It is true that as they age people get more fixed in their ways of being. It's hard not to. Again, I think it takes a lot of energy to keep your mind open on *any* subject. Sometimes it's easier to fall back into a familiar position, which may be a prejudice. I can feel my mind creaking sometimes where it used to swing free. And to hold the door open can be a real tough job. Sometimes old people fall back onto what they were used to saying, just as an energy saver. Just as you learn to be economical with your movements, you have to practice mental economies, too. Having watched my father and my mother continue to use their minds right up to the end, I feel very strongly that I want to be that way—to stay open and keep learning.

There was a period in my life when I read the psychologist Carl Jung with great interest; he was a help to my thinking. People told me I had to read him because my *Wizard of Earthsea* was so much like what he was saying. My dad was a Freudian; he didn't like Jung. In my forties (even though I was saying they were good) there *were* dark passages, hard places to get through. I needed some help, and Jung was very helpful to me in organizing my thinking. He understands what artists do. But increasingly I find I resist all the talk about archetypes. I think I OD'd, not on Jung, but on Jungians. They tend to talk in categories. For example, the Maiden-Mother-Crone trio, which is Greek in origin—the three faces of Diana. I'm not very comfortable with those archetypal images anymore. These images are useful, like Superman, as an instant reference to something everybody recognizes. But asking myself if I've become a crone yet—do I want to be a crone? No. I want to be me. It always comes down to: I don't want to be any *thing*.

These are powerful images, but to box our perception of women into those categories strikes me as *very* dangerous. It simply says that everything woman is depends on her status as a sexual being and her childbearing capacities. Either she's a virgin or she's a mother or she's past that. Well, give me a break. She is a person, a person changing throughout her life. She doesn't just go from one state to another; she goes through two. Either you're a virgin or you're not. Either you've gone through menopause or you haven't. Men are either virgins or not, but they don't make any fuss about it, and they don't experience menopause.

All the same, in a way we women are lucky; we have this bodily change that says "Who are you now? You're not quite who you used to be and how do you be who you are now? You are now either deprived of or free from your menses and the chance of bearing a child." Most women think about that in one way or another.

They may not make such a fuss about it in other cultures as we do. I hate the way we handle menopause as if it were all a loss and consisted of nothing but hot flashes. I *liked* my hot flashes. If I got a hot flash, I wouldn't get a headache. There's something about circulation readjusting itself. I'd think, I'm getting a headache; I wish I could get a hot flash. And I learned how to work one up. They're very dependent on your psychology. It was like self-hypnosis: "Ooo-ooo-ooo, I'm getting a hot flash; I'm feeling so hot." And sometimes it worked. I've talked with a few other women who had the same response, who really felt something positive was happening. I just read in *Science News* that the term "hot flash" has to be explained to almost all Japanese women; they haven't the faintest idea what we're talking about. Menopause varies enormously from culture to culture. Country Welsh talk about "doing a *good* change"; it's something you *do*, not something that happens to you. Which puts a different spin on it.

This has something in common with the Hindu idea of soul making that I mentioned earlier. I've never been much of a planner, I sort of go along with what happens. But this year I made a conscious effort to try to learn how to meditate, just to sit still. Sit and breathe. Just paying attention. My nice little Vipassana guide says you really can't do it by yourself; you really need to be in a group, sometimes, at least. I always try to do things by myself. I found it *extremely* interesting. I'm not doing it now, but I think I will go back to it when I feel the need to just sit and breathe. In just the six or seven months I did it regularly, I made some advance; I don't even know on what ground, but physically I'm a little bit different. The wheels have stopped moving so fast. Oh, man, do I have "monkey mind"—it's a whole zoo! Hey, all you have to do is breathe. My husband and I learned tai chi with a lovely teacher. That's an increasingly important centering when I'm running too fast. It's so nice when your whole body is involved in a meditative process. As a writer, I live in my head so much, it's important to get out of there—just climb down.

I try to write regularly in the mornings, but I can't write all the time. There are vast periods of time when I don't have a story to write, so I have to make work for myself. I keep writing, but I may just do correspondence. On the other hand, if I don't have a story to write, what am I doing sitting in my office? Chewing my fingernails, probably. When I think I should get out and walk, it's probably raining. When your bones and muscles get older you need to get some exercise.

Old people speak about the difficulty of sitting for a long time in any position, because the circulation isn't as lively. I watch the poor old cat, cat can't jump anymore, cat comes downstairs real differently now—his old bones aren't working. He's probably got arthritis, which, thank God, I don't, but I watch the old guy and yeah, I know what that feels like.

As I mentioned, I'm not self-reflective; in fact, you'll notice in my work, there's very little autobiographical writing. I'm *extremely* introverted. I went off the scale on the extroversion/introversion test. Literally translated, introversion means "turning inward," but I'm not quite sure that's what's involved. It's like *starting* from within rather than turning in from without. We tend to use extrovert as a compliment and introvert as an insult, and I've always resented that ever since I was a kid. "Oh, you're too introverted." All teenagers brood about themselves endlessly; they have to in order to figure out who they are. Writers and artists tend to look at themselves and at their work with a kind of analytical eye. You have to know who you are before you can do what you want to do.

Being an artist is doing something, making something, or trying to be ready to make something. On this subject there are several metaphors valuable to me. One is Gary Snyder's idea of composting; that's what the introverted artist does with experience: take it in and grow something different from it. The idea of the reproduction of reality doesn't make any sense to me. I'm not a mirror; I'm not a camera. Stendahl, the French writer, said he was a mirror. Christopher Isherwood, the British-born writer, said he was a camera. No, you're not. You're a writer, you *invent*.

Readiness is everything. That sitting there in the morning, chewing your nails sort of thing—I call it listening. I'm listening for the story, for the voice. If I allow myself to be bombarded by obligations or duties or distractions, then I'm not listening, not doing my job. Then I'm bad!

A properly made object of any kind has its own shape, own ideal form, including a story or a poem. The artist's job is to find that form, listen for that story, tell it as clearly as possible. *Then* you can worry about what it means or says or why it happened or what it's about or where it came from.

Ever since I was a teenager, I've had very clear in my own mind the distinction between "being a writer" and writing. I've known lots and lots of people who wanted to be writers, but they didn't particularly want to write. They wanted the status and the glory. They think being a writer is glamorous, perhaps will make them rich. I never wanted to be a writer, but I *always* wanted to and did write. That's part of what I'm talking about, which is that I feel lucky that I was somehow wordlessly taught to feel that way, because my parents wrote and read, thought and spoke. I remember asking when I was twenty or so—it was a beautiful California morning, and I think my father had been working before breakfast—"You work all the time, don't you?" He said, "I love it." That stuck with me really deeply; he said it from his heart.

Writing is the most important thing in my life and the activity that I most want to do. I'd rather write than anything else. But it has to fit in with the other important things. When my writing was at its most intense, I was in my thirties and the kids were little. They were right here, running around, screaming. So I wrote at night. There was no way I could shut my door. You can't shut out a little kid for whom you are responsible—you can't shut the door in their face, you can't listen to them cry or fight or whatever on the other side. Kids take your entire attention, and so does writing. There are people like Harriet Beecher Stowe, who literally wrote *Uncle Tom's Cabin* at the kitchen table. She had eight children at the time. One or two hired helpers. I don't know how she did it. Talk about energy. She was probably about forty years old; a tough lady.

How has my writing affected my marriage? Charles has always been totally supportive. We have managed to stay married for more than forty years. How? I think we're lazy! We love each other very much, so all the ups and downs, all the disagreements and quarrels that any long-term relationship that isn't dead is going to have, all the strains and the stresses, never seem to outweigh the simple enjoyment of each other's presence. That's the only way I can put it. It's a long friendship. I think any old marriage becomes a long friendship. It's a great thing. I could wring his neck quite often, and I know he could wring mine, but we have done fine. Charles is a remarkable man for his generation and for having grown up in a small town in Georgia. He never let himself be threatened by my commitment to my art or by my success. I think the success at times has been a little hard for him to stand. It would be for anybody with a partner who's getting a lot of praise and attention. "Why aren't *I* getting any?" But he does his own thing. He's a French historian and loves it. He's now writing a major book with some colleagues, although he's retired from teaching, which he loved. So I didn't have a competitor in the household; I didn't have a man who felt unmanned by what I did. I also had a man who was probably better at handling babies than I was. Totally supportive. I cannot say enough what difference that has made in my life.

A long marriage is kind of against the cultural norm now. Marriage is not being looked upon as a lifetime commitment. My parents were married for over thirty years. Pa was eighty-four when he died, my mother was eighty-three when she died. My father literally worked up to the day he died of a heart attack. He was no longer teaching but still writing and corresponding with other scholars. He loved working. My mother was working on a novel the last year of her life until she got leukemia. She wrote every day as long as she could.

She lived six months after the diagnosis of leukemia. Some people say it was good to think about death and prepare for it, but I wish she hadn't had to go through that. She was scared. How can you not be scared? They did more than made sense to me to keep her alive. This whole thing about cancer is so troubling. When your health just goes down, down, down, and there's no way out of it at all.

I often think about our eighteen-year-old cat, and this eventuality looms. He has been a close friend for eighteen years, but I think I will have the courage to let him go when the time comes if he doesn't find his own way, as cats often do. It's so easy to sound sentimental when you start talking about animals, but several of my cats have been guides on how to die. I have to put it that way—I just watch what they do. How they handle it. The relationship with our animals is a friendship we mustn't let be diminished or trivialized; it's so important in so many lives. We just don't know how to talk about it.

After sixty I think women can look forward to an increase of freedom when they stop being mama. My mother loved her grandchildren but made it absolutely clear that she would never have them dumped on her for full-time care, unless there was a tragedy. There was a certain formality that was very nice for the kids. It made going to visit her a big treat. That kind of decision, I think, older women make more easily, whereas younger ones wouldn't dare say, "I want to do it this way." I see older women saying, "I always wanted to do it this way," and they do. The downside of that is they are often impelled to that kind of decisiveness by realizing they haven't got much time, so if you're going to do it at all, you'd better do it now. Whatever "it" is. You don't want to be driven by that feeling, but it is inescapable.

Carolyn Kizer, a poet, was here recently; she said to me, "Poets think about death and commas all the time." I agreed. And I got funny and said, "Well, fiction writers think about life and commas." Artists *do* think about death in this constant way: what is life, and how does it fit into that? As you realize the number count is getting short, it can lead to a lot of anxiety, and it can also raise you above the anxiety, to take a longer view, and try to get things in proportion. It's difficult. I was hoping the proportion would establish itself as I got older, but I'm not sure it has. It has to some extent by deciding what's *really* important, what *really* matters. That just happens through experience.

I have no picture of myself as an old woman. I have hope: I hope I can continue to work, to be mentally alive and learning Spanish or whatever. I wish my hair would begin to darken again, as my father's did. I hate being gray haired. I'm a dark-haired person, and I still look in the mirror and think, What's all that white stuff? I would dye it, but Charles just won't have it. I really regret my hair. Here's vanity. I help my eyebrows a little bit. It startled me; it never occurred to me that your eyebrows would go gray. Thank God for eyebrow pencil. I don't want to look young, but I want to look recognizable to myself. I want to be able to take my face for granted to some extent. I told my daughter, "I don't understand why I have to spend twenty minutes in the bathroom when I used to spend two," and my daughter said, "It's maintenance work, Ma." There is more maintenance in your sixties.

I do hope that I never have to live in a retirement estate where everybody else is old. In the teaching life, there's always wide-eyed young people coming up; you need that. Human beings are not meant to live in isolated age groups. The tribe ought to include all ages.

Ingmar Bergman's *Wild Strawberries* is a film I saw in college. There were faceless people, clocks without hands. I was so scared; it was existential horror. I'd never been so frightened since I'd seen *King Kong* at the age of six. I was so frightened by the Bergman film, I could hardly watch the rest of it because I was sure something awful was going to happen, something even worse. Of course it doesn't. All the awful things had already happened. He'd made all of his mistakes. He's kind of crippled his own life, yet he comes through to that sweet ending in the sunlight and the memories. I think artistically that is wonderful and truthful. The movie is about a man living with the knowledge that he is going to die. That is still a very difficult thing to do.

Filling up and spilling over . . . That's what I feel is happening for me in my sixties. For the first time I feel my age, I feel appropriate. I don't think that has to do with being sixty or with aging so much as accepting where I am, and that feels full. Full and present, and what could feel better?

— TERRY SENDGRAFF

Terry Sendgraff

FLYING RATHER FAMOUSLY REQUIRED THE EXTRA ENERGY OF
BELIEF, AND THIS, TOO, I HAD IN SUPER-ABUNDANCE . . .
I RAN THE SIDEWALK FULL TILT. I WAVED MY ARMS EVER
HIGHER AND FASTER. I KNEW I WAS FOOLISH. I KNEW I WAS
TOO OLD TO BELIEVE IN THIS AS A CHILD WOULD, OUT OF
IGNORANCE; INSTEAD I WAS EXPERIMENTING AS A SCIENTIST
WOULD, TESTING BOTH THE THING ITSELF AND THE LIMITS
OF MY OWN COURAGE IN TRYING IT MISERABLY SELF-
CONSCIOUS IN FULL VIEW OF THE WHOLE WORLD. YOU CAN'T
TEST COURAGE CAUTIOUSLY, SO I RAN HARD AND WAVED MY
ARMS HARD, HAPPY . . . I WAS FLYING.

—ANNIE DILLARD
An American Childhood

As a child she chose heroines who could fly: Wonder Woman and Mary
Marvel ("They were my early feminists!" she says, beaming). Terry Sendgraff
has never had a fear of flying and was trained as a dancer and gymnast. Rather,
in her performance work called Motivity—a vehicle for "teaching women to
fly," utilizing a combination of the low-flying trapeze and gymnastics—Terry
fulfilled her childhood fantasies of flying. She calls this experience "the fun of
flying" and considers it a system of sensory awareness that allows the participant
to have a kinesthetically sensuous encounter of her own body in relationship to
gravity and to the surrounding environment.

Terry considers the intelligence of her body a close ally. Her body continues
to surprise her with its courage and ability—such as learning to walk on stilts at
the age of fifty-seven. "I certainly hadn't planned on that one," she admits,
clearly relishing her rebellion against the conventional.

As a little girl, Terry endured a troubled childhood in Florida. The tropical paradise of her daytime atmosphere, which included exotic fruit trees and flowers and comic strip superheroines, became a battleground at night for the forces of good and evil in the guise of an alcoholic mother and disintegrating family. An effect of this level of dysfunction has been a lifelong struggle with depression. At the age of fifty-one, Terry was diagnosed with breast cancer and underwent a mastectomy. Eight years later she had a recurrence of cancer. At the age of sixty-three, Terry feels "healthier than I've ever been" and nourished by life.

At her home in a multiracial neighborhood in Oakland, California, Terry awaited my somewhat tardy arrival with a large pot of herbal tea and a plate of meltingly sweet cantaloupe slices on the coffee table in the living room of the home she has shared for thirteen years in a lesbian relationship with her lover and closest friend, Aileen. Intermittently throughout our conversation, a wave of emotion in Terry would express itself in a cascade of tears. "I just feel so moved, so grateful for my life," she explained to me, half apologizing for her tender release. Terry feels gratitude for her hard-earned self-knowledge; for her strong body and vibrant health; for the acceptance and appreciation she receives from her lover and so many dear friends; for the work that means so much to her and, indeed, that has kept her soaring.

The Soaring Woman

❖

In terms of aging, I even surprised myself: I learned to walk on stilts when I was fifty-seven—I certainly hadn't planned on that one. I had been commissioned by the Michigan Women's Music Festival to create a happening with my low-flying trapeze work I call Motivity. Because their stage wasn't particularly adaptable for that, I didn't think I could do it, but I said, "Let me create an outdoor piece and I'll put some trapezes in the trees and do something there."

About eight thousand women go to this event in Michigan, so I had to be high enough to be seen above the crowd. I was going to put ladders and trapezes in the trees. At the time, I had a student, Amy, who was studying the trapeze with me. She was also a stilt walker and a dancer, and I thought, Stilts! So Amy taught me how to walk on stilts, and I gathered four other women to perform at the music festival and we did an incredible piece called "Treelings." It was an inspiration that just evolved and developed. It was tremendously rewarding and satisfying to all of us.

Then, when I came back home, I got even more inspired. I had learned to walk on stilts at Lake Merritt Park here in Oakland, where there is a grove of trees. I thought, I can just see one hundred women coming through the trees on stilts. With the help of a grant from the California Arts Council, I had an opportunity to offer free classes to women and girls in the community. I said, "I want as many women as I can get to walk on stilts to create this piece." My board of directors for the Motivity Center and I talked about seeing these women walking tall through the trees, and that became the name of the project: Women Walking Tall.

It became my mission to empower women by teaching them to walk on stilts. Everybody thinks it is so difficult. It's really easy. I'm five feet two, but suddenly I'm about eight feet tall on stilts. So I started teaching stilt walking in the park. Being in nature and the act of becoming tall transformed us all. We just felt so powerful. We were women of all ages, all backgrounds, all sizes.

Now I go back to Michigan each year and teach more women to walk on stilts. The oldest has been seventy-five. I would say there are probably about five of us over sixty years old who walk on stilts.

During the Women Walking Tall project, I left Motivity for a while and thought I would never do trapeze again, but I've come back now. You must hear many stories of women coming full circle, but I've come back to it with another level of such richness and understanding of what it's really about. What I'm discovering now is that the low-flying trapeze is really a vehicle for teaching people about movement, awareness, and an experience of oneself. It's about learning to be balanced in one's life. I'm fascinated with the proprioceptive system, which is another word for inner balance or the kinesthetic sense.

The low-flying trapeze is a trapeze that is about six feet off the ground.

Everybody has a different height, so the trapezes are at different heights. You can push off the ground and swing and spin and float: that's where the flying part comes in. The starting point is working on the ground below the trapeze. People really get down and explore the body's movements on the ground before going into the air. It can be very primal.

The fact that it has this element of rocking and spinning and the trapeze's suspension from a single point above, giving it an A-shape, is what distinguishes it from other trapezes. It's really beautiful and reminiscent of the trinity, which adds a spiritual quality to it. That one-point suspension gives it an organic quality of moving that developed into the form I call Motivity.

Motivity is a blend of all the ways I really like to move. It is something that I created. When I was young I read history books on dance about the pioneer dancers like Martha Graham and Isadora Duncan, and they all created their own dance. In my thirties I was teaching dance at Arizona State University, and the head of the department choreographed a dance for me and another woman working there. I was doing the dance on stage, and I remember so clearly thinking: This is not my dance. This is *not* my dance; I want to create my own dance. I was also teaching and coaching gymnastics, so those were two forms that I had always been very passionate about.

When I realized that I wanted to create my own dance, I think that was the turning point. I left the university teaching situation, I left my marriage, I left my home in Arizona, and I came to California. That's a lot of women's stories: "I came to California . . ." I was thirty-eight when I came here in 1971. I chose California because I was very inspired by Anna Halprin, another dance pioneer who lives here. That's the thing about being sixty, fifty even, you look back over your life and see these connections. "Oh, yes, this is why I did this. This is why I did that. Oh, look at how this happened. This person was there at that point to influence me."

Now I can see where I made the choices, but at that time I didn't have the awareness that I have now. The choices were impulsive. I just knew I had to leave, I had to make a change, I had to find my own dance. I literally put myself so far on the edge, I now wonder what it was in me that was so sure this is what I had to do. Some people don't make those changes. What was it that stirred in me?

Now I'm sure that I have angels and guides; there's just no doubt. I can even look back further and see, Oh, yes, even when I was asleep, I was being guided to a certain degree. I just feel so moved, so grateful, that I have, with guidance, made these choices in my life. If you're asleep or unaware in your life, you have to have guidance when you make these huge choices. Now I'm more awake and more aware of the choices when I make them. I know when something doesn't feel right. I trust that now. It's so much easier.

When I decided to find my own dance, I didn't know how I was going to do that, but on some level, I knew that these other women had done it and I would do it, too. It *did* unfold, and I see, too, as I look back, the teachers who inspired me and guided me at that time. Al Wunder and Anita Feder Chernilla, two of those teachers, are still a very important part of my life. Al is my dear friend, and Anita is still my teacher. I feel that I've traveled with her for twenty years. When you know someone for that long, and they still have grace in your eyes—she hasn't fallen, but she's never tried to be on any pedestal—they become even more special.

Anita has always been very human. She's been my friend. She's been my mother. She's been my sister. She's my spiritual teacher. I'm just amazed and so grateful, and my tears are of joy and being so touched by the people who have helped me recover from my childhood and grow and nurtured this part of me that I've grown to love. That's what their teachings were about: love.

When I say "recover," I am referring to my upbringing. The first nine years of my life were like night and day. I lived in Florida and it was a paradise. We lived in a beautiful home. My father was a golf pro, and part of the job allowed him to live in this gorgeous home right in the center of a huge, circular yard. There were flowers, animals, a fish pond, and a little swimming pool. There were lime trees, guava trees, mango trees, banana trees, orange trees, and coconut trees.

I was in paradise in that sense. But my family was beginning to disintegrate; my mother was an alcoholic. Alcoholism can be so treacherous. Nobody ever talked about it. So my mother was getting worse and worse; my father didn't know how to deal with it. There were terrible arguments every night at the dinner table.

During the day I was alone a lot, but I had a very rich fantasy life—many dreams and fantasies of flying. I read the *Wonder Woman* and *Captain Marvel* comics. I would practice getting up on anything that was off the ground, and I would jump off. I just knew I could fly. So this was where my power was: in my imagination and in my body, in dancing and flying. I'd wear capes. I even had boots like Mary Marvel, the cohort and sidekick of Captain Marvel Jr. I see her as one of the early feminists! They were out there fighting evil. Pow. Shazam. And all that. That was a very rich experience for me, and I think it was my way of dealing with the other situation of having simply a skeleton of a family that looked all right from the outside. Nobody knew. So nighttimes were awful and daytimes were beautiful. I remember being, I would say, depressed. I've gone in and out of depression throughout my life. It's an awful feeling, you know. That's another thing we don't talk about. When I got to California I could talk about it.

I was late coming to the idea that I'm a dancer because I thought of myself as a teacher. I wasn't an artist, I was a teacher. There were a couple of things that happened at that time. A man named John Waddell, who's actually a very well-known sculptor, asked me to model for him for a dance sculpture figure in Phoenix, which is now in front of the symphony building—so here I am immortalized in bronze. "You're a dancer," he said. "Why aren't you dancing? You are an artist. It's fine to teach, but you should be dancing." That was another push, and I think that fed into the idea that I must go create my own dance and explore what it's like to be an artist. When I was eleven years old, somebody asked me what I wanted to be when I grew up, and I said, "I want to be a famous artist."

In all of my classes as a graduate student majoring in dance, I never felt encouraged. There was always a "way" to dance. You had to look like so-and-so or you had to dance like so-and-so. I never did and I had trouble with it, especially in the classes where you had to know your right from your left and you had to count. I didn't find out until many years later that I was dyslexic. It was really frustrating to try to follow these patterns that were very structured. I just thought,

I'm not a very good dancer, but I knew that I loved to dance. The spirit to dance was inside me. I was more successful in the gymnastics arena, somehow. But it had its rigidities in its competition. Still, I was a pioneer in fostering gymnastics for younger women, as I taught, judged, and formed competitions.

When I came to California from Arizona I did study with Anna Halprin, but only briefly. She is phenomenal. I saw her dance last year, and I was in the dance celebrating her seventy-fifth birthday. When I saw her dancing again, I thought, She's seventy-five and she's dancing as if she were thirty. She's so alive and so aware.

I had culture shock when I came to California. I had just gotten divorced and didn't know who I was. I was in a life crisis where you just let go of who you thought you were because it doesn't work anymore. I literally dropped things, lost things, and discarded things. I got down to the barest essentials. I had hardly any money and didn't care. I just had to get to the basics, the essense of who I was.

When I left Anna Halprin's workshop, I moved to Berkeley because I couldn't stand living in a big city. I had to be closer to nature. I came here to create my own dance. I thought, Okay, I'll just set aside time and do it by myself. I didn't know where to start, and I *didn't* start until I met Al Wunder. He had come to California to find *his* own way of teaching and dancing. Together, along with Ruth Zaporah, we started a school in Berkeley, the Berkeley Dance Theater and Gymnasium.

Ruth was working with theater, and Al was basically doing movement improvisation. I was teaching creative gymnastics. We all shared a love for improvisation. "Action Theater" is what Ruth now calls her work. Al's work is called "Theater of the Ordinary." I created "Motivity."

I define Motivity as the low-flying trapeze dance form, but basically, I think, my work is more than trapeze. I realize that I *really* like having the opportunity to teach, along with the movement awareness, improvisation, dreamwork, and what I call authentic self-presentation. I am currently teaching at Holy Names College in the Sophia Center, which is the women's spirituality program. So there are many tools for my work, but what I'm really teaching is a more holistic thing: I'm teaching people about themselves, the different aspects of themselves. I give the nurturing and the support that brings forth the blossoming of other human beings. I have permission to be fully who I am: physically, emotionally, spiritually, politically.

I created Motivity because it allowed me to have this very full-bodied form that could fly. I always say, "Well, maybe before I die, I'll have learned to fly without my trapeze," but I do it in my dreams. I have many flying dreams.

There's a PBS documentary of me—a wonderful film by Fawn Yacker, *Can You See Me Flying*—in which I talk about my dream of flying. I start out in the documentary by saying, "This is a little embarrassing for me to tell you, but I'll tell you anyway. I would dream of flying up in the sky, flying around doing wonderful things, turning flips and doing amazing tricks and having a wonderful time. But I'd look down and nobody was paying attention to me. I couldn't understand it. Why couldn't they see what I could do? I was *beginning* to realize what I could do, but there was another part of me that couldn't really believe I was okay." Of course, it wasn't only *those* people not seeing me; *I* wasn't seeing me.

Then my dreams started to change; they got more and more powerful, and I did more incredible things: zooming down in spins close to the earth, hovering there, and people were beginning to see me! This also manifested in real life when people were beginning to see me. Then, I think I must have been in my late fifties, not only did people see me in my dreams, they were beginning to fly *with* me. So I began to collaborate more with other people.

Being part of a women's community in Berkeley, coming out as a lesbian in a very supportive environment, was . . . I mean, Berkeley in the 1970s, what more could I ask for? Parts of it were hard, but there was such support. So I really had an opportunity to grow and develop and go through all the stages of development that I hadn't been able to do when I was "asleep."

I had previously been married twice, and both husbands were very nice men, but I was incapable of being in a relationship, incapable of taking care of myself. It is really a blessing I never had children because I would not have been able to be a good mother. I was learning to be a mother to *myself*. That's another thing I've learned in California: the concept of mothering myself. While others are kind of stepping in to be each other's mothers and sisters, you learn to internalize that, to become your own mother—and father.

So, that early time when I first left Florida was critical, and then all those years of struggling in so much pain and denial and alcoholism and those very painful experiences with men, trying to find love in someone else. Finally getting to such a bottom, so far down that—although I wasn't an alcoholic, I certainly abused alcohol and I could have been—I had to seek help. I felt suicidal, so I got to a therapist and my healing began. This was in my thirties at Arizona State University when I was teaching. I cannot imagine how I managed in the state I was in to do all I did—and be successful. I was coaching gymnastics, teaching school, getting my master's degree in dance. And I was in such pain. My husband, poor man, was very patient actually, but he had no clue as to what I was trying to do. He was shut off and in pain himself. I reached that bottom where I knew I needed to get help, so I asked for help and got it.

In my present relationship, my partner's name is Aileen, and we've been together for thirteen years. We met about twenty years ago when I was first teaching Motivity, and she came to study with me. She was and is a public school teacher, and we connected right away about teaching. I was out as a lesbian; I came out when I was forty-six, so I had been out a few years. She's been a lesbian all her life. We continued with our friendship over all those years before we were lovers. She was my business manager as well.

Aileen is one of the few people with whom I've had a chance to experience what it's like when a person comes from a fairly functional family; it's very unusual. She has a core of confidence in who she is, a belief in herself. Her parents gave her roots and wings, very good ones. I love and admire her greatly. I think, in a way, I mothered creativity in her. I taught her a lot about creativity and bravery in emotional existence, but she taught me about fundamental practicality, wise, functional ways of being in the world. So we have a very complementary, wonderful balance in terms of being interdependent.

We became lovers after my breast cancer and mastectomy. I went to stay with her because I knew of her nurturing spirit, and I needed that at the time. She's very unconditionally loving, more than anybody I've ever met.

We've both grown over the years. The way that we've helped our relationship to grow is to continue to grow as individuals. I had an innate determination to do that out of survival, whereas she had that tendency naturally because she grew up with it. Together we were independent, and the ways we were interdependent were very nice and healthful and growthful. I think perhaps I was a little less mature even though I was older. Aileen taught me how to take care of money, how to take care of business, and how to be responsible on an everyday level.

Once she was no longer my manager, there was a hard moment where we wondered if this was a relationship based on her helping me with the practical and me supplying the creativity and excitement for her. But no, we were able to go through that period, and she really went into the development of *her* work; and I had become strong enough, too, so we were both very strong in our work lives.

We've always felt that commitment to a relationship and a partnership comes with the knowledge that you never know what is going to happen, so dependence doesn't work, and I think we both know that. Yet here we are, still here, communicating. I don't think there's anything I've not told her. When you can trust someone that much to love you . . . she has really loved me through everything; but I think I had to learn to love.

That *is* our spirituality, that is our politics. That's the wonderful part about doing women's work: when it works, it's got a spiritual part, too. It must be like that for men, too, but I don't know. I just know that women seem more concerned with the whole, with the relationship among all things. My work is about awareness. So it is my work, it is my play, and it is my relationship.

I feel that the process of coming into my fullness started in my forties—just as the title of your first book describes. I've been filling myself up, filling in the holes, the spaces, and spilling over. Filling up and spilling over—that's a song Chris Williamson wrote. That's what I feel is happening for me in my sixties. For the first time I feel my age, I feel appropriate. I don't think that has to do with being sixty or with aging so much as accepting where I am, and that feels full. Full and present, and what could feel better?

I was thinking, just now, about opposites: full and empty. How sad it would be to be sixty or seventy and feel empty; and I know some people do. I felt empty at thirty. In fact, I got rid of all my things in order to be empty so that I could fill up with what was really mine, not what I had swallowed from my family, culture, education, but fill up with what I chose.

I feel that I'm much healthier now than I've ever been in my life—I mean, I have survived cancer, twice. When I was fifty-one and I got breast cancer the first time, I was pretty depleted, my immune system was very low, and I was depressed —I didn't know how deeply. I was too busy, just too busy. But a lot of wisdom can come from those tragedies, and I certainly did gain a lot from mine. So now, being in such good health, I can't imagine being any different. My skin is different, but I've had wrinkles a long time, so I'm kind of used to those. My body has been a good friend; even when I was asleep during those years, there was still a way that, through my body, I was able to hang in there. Interesting: "hang in there"—it's such a metaphor for so many things. Hanging on, letting go, flying, falling. "Falling from grace."

I was named after my father—Terry was his name, too—and he was named after an Irish fighter who whenever he was knocked down would get back up again. I feel I'm like that. I am very resilient. So when I think about aging, I may fall from grace again only to dig down deeper and come back up higher. It's just a continual series of taking off, flying, coming in for a landing, and resting and refueling. I just can't imagine that I would be much different in spirit, but my body is definitely changing. Even though I can still hang upside-down by my ankles and still walk on stilts, I can feel myself slowing down and my body just telling me, *You don't need to do that.* I don't need to do it the way I did.

Recently I tried to dance on stilts like one of the younger women in my group. I fell. I was trying to keep up with her, you know. We were dancing, performing, and it was in a place where there were tons of people, music, and I could see they were admiring this younger woman. I thought to myself, Well, I can do this, too. And then I fell. I didn't hurt myself, but I learned. Here's the lesson: Terry, do it your way. I dance beautifully on stilts; I don't need to dance like someone else.

Maybe that's part of the wisdom of aging, that we can see what's really happening, what's really going on—if we're paying attention. That idea of who we should be and how we should look is very, very sad to me. There are a lot of things that are sad, but, again, I feel grateful to be so blessed. I don't own a lot, nothing except my little old car, a bunch of trapezes, and a lot of stilts and costumes and journals, personal things; yet I feel so rich. I don't care about money. I want enough that I don't have to be homeless or without food. I don't have health insurance, but I really take care of myself. I need time now to garden and read, to relax and feel okay about it. Being healthy physically certainly is related to mental, emotional, and spiritual well-being. I have a very rich, full-textured life. It certainly has been full.

I find it very interesting getting older, growing older. That is how I see it: growing older, not getting old. Finally, I think, that's the problem. When you stop growing, then comes the difficulty. If you are thirty, forty, fifty, sixty, or eighty, you must keep on developing and growing. I think that it's fine to be older.

—LULY SANTANGELO

Luly Santangelo

DANCE IS A SYMBOL OF THE
PERFORMANCE OF LIVING.
—*Martha Graham*
Blood Memory,
An Autobiography

Her hip-length hair shrouded her head and shoulders and cascaded down her back like a black lace mantilla. The summer evening my son and I went to Theatre 80 on St. Mark's Place in the East Village of Manhattan, I couldn't take my eyes off the striking dark-haired woman who sat outside the theater smoking a cigarette and enjoying preperformance laughs with other members of the noted flamenco dance troupe Noche Flamenca. Her face was one that clearly had *lived,* loved, and suffered. I was certain she must be one of the performers. Her appearance fulfilled every fantasy I have held about flamenco dancers being fashionably thin, but strong and energetic; intense and passionate; colorfully dressed and self-possessed. Could it be possible she was sixty years old, even though her forties seemed more likely?

Asking a woman her age requires subtlety and diplomacy. I asked after her at the ticket booth. As it turned out, the charismatic woman sitting outside had just turned sixty the previous week! When I approached Luly Santangelo with my invitation for her to participate in this book, she seemed delighted at the suggestion. Her deep, gravelly voice seemed to originate from somewhere in the middle of her belly rather than in her throat, like most people's. This added to her sense of mystery. She graciously agreed to meet with me the following week, even though her schedule was extremely hectic.

As it turned out, Luly *is* a dancer, but not a flamenco dancer, as I had thought. Luly is the manager and producer for a group that includes her son Martin and her daughter-in-law Soledad Barrio. Born and raised in Argentina, she immigrated to the United States in order to study with Martha Graham. She has also been a stage director and a dance therapist. Luly spoke slowly and thoughtfully, occasionally repeating a word or phrase for emphasis; her Spanish accent remains thick even after nearly forty years in this country.

The third time we met, Luly invited me to her home—an apartment on the Upper West Side. As I stepped off the elevator, I knew by the large poster of Frida Kahlo and the dangling Mexican tin figures which door was Luly's. Once inside, I felt that I had stepped into the home of Frida and Diego in Coyoacán, a suburb of Mexico City. The walls of the expansive, sunlit rooms were creatively painted in yellow, blue, lavender, and orange. In the sunny kitchen, where we sat, the walls were covered with blue, white, and yellow tiles that friends had brought back from Spain for her and spelled out "Luly" above the sink.

Luly's responses to my questions were often surprising, especially in regard to women's attitude about aging in Argentina and why she prefers to call artists "workers." Like most Argentineans of her generation who lived in Buenos Aires, Luly has her own resource of "Evita" stories from her childhood. "Yes," she recalled when I asked if she had ever seen Eva Perón, wife of dictator "President" Juan Perón. "When she died, I was twelve or thirteen. Our entire school went to the *Secretaría*, where her body was lying in an open casket. The wake must have lasted at least two weeks. Millions of people visited her body. People loved her very much.

"I also saw her when she was still alive. As a child, I performed as a dancer with the opera at the Teatro Colón, which is like the Metropolitan Opera House here in New York. Evita would come and see the performances, and I remember seeing her there."

What does she think about Madonna playing the part of Eva Perón? I wondered. "Coincidentally, I arrived in Argentina only a few days after Madonna arrived with the film crew to make the movie. I was shocked, because from the airport to the city, all the streets were filled with signs telling Madonna to go home. People reacted *very* badly. She had to be constantly protected. And, as a matter of fact, Argentinean actors who had auditioned to be in the film also felt threatened and needed some security." She assured me that the Argentineans themselves are doing a "serious" film about the Peróns. We also discussed the present state of Argentinean cinema and agreed that the director Eliseo Subiela is one of our favorites.

The last time I saw Luly, she had just returned from her son Philippe's wedding in Sweden to a young Swedish woman named Viveka. She described the ceremony to me and said that her son and new daughter-in-law had chosen the exact spot on a beach where Ingmar Bergman had filmed the scene in *The Seventh Seal* where Death appears to the characters in the film. They'd also created a beautiful mandala in the sand on which they stood during the ceremony and which later was washed away by the tide. She called the ceremony "beautiful, just beautiful."

Luly was quite moved by this observance of the "the whole idea of impermanence" in the ritual at her son's wedding, and she spoke at length to me about the notion that by living with this awareness of impermanence in our own lives, especially as aging women, we are better able to accept and live in the present moment.

The Dance of Life

❖

I was born in Buenos Aires in 1936 and began to dance very early, at the age of nine. I don't know what got me into dance, but it has been a powerful influence in my life since I was a child. Contrary to what you might think by looking at me, I never danced flamenco. I was a ballet dancer and did my studies at the Music Conservatory in Buenos Aires. It was at the conservatory that I discovered modern dance. In Argentina there was a strong movement in modern dance because of the influence of the German population that had emigrated from Germany.

Performing came very early to me. As a child I was already performing at the Teatro Colón, a magnificent opera house; dancers and singers, troupes and entertainers, came from all over the world to perform there. I was very lucky to have been able to perform so early in such a grand and important venue. By the time I was eighteen, I was already a professional dancer in my country, and I never even thought about coming to the United States.

But then I discovered Martha Graham. I saw the film *The Dancer's World* three days in a row, and I was astounded by her! After that, I decided I *had* to come to New York to meet this great dancer. It took me a great amount of time, of course, to make it possible, especially economically; and also because I did not speak English *at all*. But I did it. And I've always been glad I did.

When I was twenty-three, I arrived in New York. That feeling of being an outsider, a foreigner, has always remained with me and helped me to have great sympathy for other foreigners. Martha Graham welcomed me with open arms. Immediately, the very next day after I met her, they gave me a full scholarship to study with the Martha Graham Dancers. I also danced with Alvin Nikolai, a marvelously creative person, and many other dancers in the New York modern dance scene at that time in the late 1950s and 1960s.

A few years later I married an American, and within three years I had two baby sons, Martin and Philippe. After that it was very difficult for me to continue with my work as a dancer, especially as a foreigner, because my entire family was still back in Argentina and I had no help whatsoever with raising my children. I did perform for a while, but then my husband and I divorced, and there I was with two small babies. I had to stop dancing professionally in order to raise my sons. It was a very clear decision.

That decision was very painful to me, but still there was no doubt in my mind that dance was my destiny. I have always been with dance. So I created and developed a new profession for myself using dance. I became a dance therapist. At that time, some thirty years ago, there was no dance therapy. As I had done my studies in psychology back in Argentina, I was able to put psychology together with my knowledge of dance.

I then began a very, very important part of my life and my work, which lasted for seventeen years. I made the decision to work only with grownups in my dance therapy, never with children. Because I had two young children at home, for whom I was the only parent, I felt that all my attention to children should go to my own. I worked a lot in the United States and at different universities. Then I was invited to work in Switzerland.

For sixteen years I traveled twice a year to Bern, Switzerland, to teach intensives in dance therapy. I worked directly in a hospital, training the staff. I have done a rich variety of work in dance therapy. In the United States, I have worked with inmates in prisons, with patients in mental institutions. Also I have worked with many individuals. I liked very, very much my work.

But five years ago, when I was fifty-five, I decided that that was it for me. I decided it was time to stop and take time for myself. I traveled in India for four months, and that was a profound experience. All along I had kept dancing in my life. And then the biggest surprise for me was that my son Martin became a dancer. I did not expect that at all. You know, it's funny: I began to dance quite early in life, but Martin came to dance rather late. He arrived at being a dancer in a roundabout way, because he started out as an actor and was doing very well. He was performing with El Teatro Campasino in San Juan Bautista in California. One of the actors who also danced in that particular production was in an accident and Martin was called on to take his place. The part called for him to dance a bit of flamenco, and quickly he became very, very passionate about this form of Spanish dance.

I encouraged him to travel to Spain to study flamenco, and soon thereafter he was invited to perform with the Maria Benitez Teatro Flamenco, which is a very big and important flamenco dance company in the United States. In Spain, Martin met his wife, Soledad Barrio, who is a wonderful and very experienced flamenco dancer. Sole has danced throughout Europe, Japan, and the Americas.

Slowly we created Noche Flamenca, and now I am completely dedicated to this small troupe of dancers and musicians. I am the manager, the producer, and the mother of the whole company, and this work has very much become my life now. It is a beautiful company.

My other son, Philippe, a very interesting young man, spent six years in India studying Buddhism and the Tibetan language. He became a translator for the monastery where he was studying. His area of interest is the study of the mind.

Now he is studying psychology at Rutgers University in order to learn about the workings of the mind from the Western point of view. Philippe is working to connect Eastern philosophy and Western psychology. He is a very capable young man, very bright. I have been blessed with my two sons, who are both passionate about what they do. We have a very special relationship among us. Besides, of course, the love between mother and sons, we have a lot of respect for each other and much admiration.

The other day, I passed sixty years old. You know, to tell you the truth, it didn't make any difference at all, because I always have a lot of energy, a lot of vitality. I sleep only six hours a night and move constantly all day long. I do everything from discussing problems about the production of Noche Flamenca to discussing the artistic part with my son; from washing shirts to cleaning and baby-sitting for my granddaughter; from talking to the press to making arrangements for television and radio. On and on and on.

This position is a great prize because, being a performer myself, I was always on the other side of the stage and I never had any idea about what goes on backstage. But, like everything else, if you have the desire and the will to do something, you work very hard at it. To tell you the truth, I've become a very good manager and producer. It is very surprising to me, but it is happening. It is so rewarding to see this continuity of my son on the stage because I have tremendous affection for the stage. Tremendous affection.

It is very moving to see the company of Noche Flamenca growing and developing, especially because the members are working with the right motivation. It's not a commercial reason, to make money. We live in a time in which everything is equated with money, and my life and work are quite a bit the opposite. Our values are different from most people's.

I don't especially like to talk about what we do as dancers as art, because there is such a confusion about what art is. I always feel that when I watch the dancers and musicians in Noche Flamenca, I see workers more than artists. When I look at my son and his wife, Sole, sometimes I think they could be *panaderos*. *Panaderos* are bakers. The group has the same totality as workers. Their lives are a twenty-four-hour involvement in work before the show, during the show, even *after* the show. It starts when they wake up, and it's still there before they go to sleep. I prefer to translate that intensity into the form of workers rather than artists. That's probably why I like the work of Samuel Beckett so much.

In the last few years I've begun to direct theater—Beckett only, since I feel great admiration for his work. I'm in the process of directing two of his pieces right now: *Not I,* in which the only thing visible is a mouth, and *Quad,* which has never been staged in New York before. Beckett himself directed it for German television. This play has no text, only four figures. It is very beautiful. He is probably one of the purist writers I know of. When you go to the essence of something, the nonsense vanishes.

Probably this feeling of wanting to experience the essence of something also has to do with turning sixty. Aging is a distillation process—you begin to be more economic with your energy. And although I have a lot of energy—and I'm really grateful for that—I don't have the energy I had when I was twenty. You realize that many things are a waste of your time, and you think, Why should I put my energy into those activities anymore? Some things I'm not interested in anymore, but the projects I am interested in, I get *very* enthusiastic about and I put *all* my energy into them.

The attitude that people have about older women in the United States is *very* different from the attitude in Argentina. In Argentina a woman my age, in her sixties, would probably be slowing down and maybe just sitting around all day. That's the great thing about the United States: if you have the vitality and the desire, there are no limits because of age, no barriers, except the normal process.

But, yes, I do think there is more respect for aging women in other cultures. I spend a lot of time in India, and I am quite impressed by their deep respect for the image of the mother. The people in India always approach a woman as a mother. She doesn't need to be an actual mother; just being female is equated with being a mother in India. I found India quite fascinating, really enchanting. It is one of the countries I love very much, and I hope to go back soon. I've been there five times already. And it is clear to me that my life is very much divided into before India and after India.

There was a total shift in my values. That's the best way to put it. I made my first trip when I was fifty, when my son Philippe was already there. Since that experience, there are certain things I don't participate in at all. Notions about achievement, reputation, goals, results, all have disappeared from my life, and I tell you, it is a *wonderful* feeling.

I find it very interesting getting older, growing older. That is how I see it: *growing* older, not getting old. Finally, I think, that's the problem. When you stop growing, then comes the difficulty. If you are thirty, forty, fifty, sixty, or *eighty*, you must keep on developing and growing. I think that it's fine to be older. It's fine.

Aging is the progression of time, it is inevitable. I'm not too affected by being sixty, but I am aware that it is a different time in life. I don't feel a rush, an urgency, to utilize my life, because I have been using my life since I was a child! I am healthy, but I am very aware that death is there and we live surrounded by that knowledge. I think it is important to realize that the nature of life is impermanence. Signs of it are everywhere. Just a few days ago, I found out that a friend of mine has cancer and must be operated on immediately. She is in her forties, and up until last week she seemed fine.

Perhaps part of the difficulty with old age is that we don't want to realize that we are just passing through in this world. That knowledge of impermanence makes it so important to understand and appreciate the moment. I don't have much concern with death. I know I'm not going to be here forever. We have to have the courage to keep going and to follow our own course. Finally, I think, it is a matter of courage—life. We have to have the faith and courage to be ourselves. It is important for anybody at any age to know that.

There is one problem with my age that bothers me, though: my memory. I have spoken with other friends my age about how the memory goes—it's quite upsetting. But the only thing we can do is accept it. What else can we do? That's one change that is very annoying about age. It seemed to start in my fifties.

Also at this age, I need a great deal of solitude, and my apartment provides that for me. It is like a refuge, a protection from the city. I always say that I need to keep myself sane. And I need time alone for my sanity! I value that time very much. So I have both: the solitude that I need and, when I want it, the stimulation of the city—it's right there. I *love* New York. Not only the culture, but the nature that is in Central Park. I *love* to walk, and I love to walk in New York City.

I haven't been able to take advantage of the summer here because I've been so busy with my work. I finally decided to take a few days away on St. John Island in the Caribbean, but when I had my ticket and was ready to go, a hurricane was coming! That was the end of my summer vacation.

Then I thought, Well, I have two possibilities: to be upset about it or to take a vacation in New York City. So I decided to take a vacation in New York City, and I had a great time. First, I went to Jackson Heights for an entire day. I told you I've spent a lot of time in India; it was like going back to India. There in Jackson Heights I was surrounded by Indian ladies speaking Hindi, colorful saris, the smell of many spices, Indian foods. It was wonderful. Then the following day I went to Chinatown and I did exactly the same thing. I spent that entire day in Chinatown. It was wonderful! Then two days later I went to Battery Park with all the tourists. It was a beautiful day, a Sunday. I tell you, I really felt like a tourist in my own city. That was my vacation in New York City.

Over the years that I have been a single woman, I have been learning to live by myself. I come from a background that would have you believe if there is not a body next to you in bed, you are not complete. Once I believed it, but not any longer. Not any longer. That was a big process for me to accept that I can exist without certain things, like a relationship with a man. I don't know too many relationships between men and women that work well. When they work, it's wonderful, but when they don't, it's hell. That realization probably relates to the distillation process I was talking about. I really feel that everything begins and ends within oneself. I've had such profound experiences in my life, but the most important thing to me has been my maternity. That doesn't mean that I need to have my sons next to me all the time, but my relationships with them are very important.

The other side to that question, of course, is that it is probably dangerous when you begin to live alone for too long because you get set in your ways and it becomes hard to change. Change is difficult, either way. It was hard to accept being alone in the first place, and at this point it would probably be hard to integrate my life with somebody else's.

The important thing is to find out what makes you feel good and what has meaning in your life. There are not too many things that have meaning, at least for me. But I'm *all* for whatever does have meaning for me. That's where I put my passion.

In my sixties I have had the gift of my granddaughter, Gabriela, who has brought me peace, joy, and hope for the continuation of life.

At sixty I fell in love again. I've been falling in love all my life, so what were the odds? Rather high! . . . Because I'm past sixty does not *mean that I am past the period of wanting romance in my life. There is no contradiction between being mature and romantic.*

— FAY WELDON

Fay Weldon

"Never trust a fiction writer," Nick Fox told me in an ironic caveat as he motioned his head toward his wife of two years, the English novelist and playwright Fay Weldon. Her third husband (who bears a strong resemblance in looks and style to rock-and-roller Mick Fleetwood) introduced himself to me and brought Fay's glasses to her. I was appeased by this explanation of Fay's discrepancies. Did Fay mean it when she said, "You can't expect to be happy if you're in love, no"? Was she serious when she told me, "Of course it's no fun being a feminist! Being a feminist is the opposite of fun. I recommend it to nobody"? Her sideways glances seemed to be testing my limits of gullibility, while her perpetually smiling eyes and good-natured laugh helped make her words less formidable.

We were engaged in conversation at a local bookstore, Capitola Book Cafe, in Northern California, prior to Fay's talk and book signing for her twenty-first novel, *Worst Fears.* The protagonist is an actress, Alexandra, who returns from a run on the London stage as Ibsen's sweet and timid wife, Nora, to find her real husband mysteriously dead of a heart attack and her female friends ominously invested in smoothing out all the complications of the tragedy. She begins to be suspicious and searches furiously for evidence to confirm her husband's rampant adultery—and her own worst fears.

In a review of an earlier novel, Anne Roiphe wrote of Fay, "[She] writes as if she were Virginia Woolf and Roseanne Arnold joined at the hip." The reference to Roseanne is more than apt, as Roseanne played the fat, dowdy, once dutiful, then revenging wife of another philandering husband in the American film

She-Devil, which was based on Fay's acidic novel and diabolical best-seller, *The Life and Loves of a She-Devil*, a distinctly unforgiving piece of feminist fiction. As a writer, Fay's gifts lie not only in her wickedly funny wit, but in her insightful and persuasive social commentary. During our interview I learned that she is as fun and funny in person as she is on the page.

Although born in England, Fay was raised in New Zealand. In 1940 she was casting horoscopes for neighbors, because her "mother and grandfather could do it" and they considered it quite an accomplishment for young Fay. She assured me it never occurred to her that it was *true*. She used astrology to entertain friends and as a guide to character, but *never* as "fortune-telling."

At the age of fourteen, after the war, Fay returned to live in "austerity Britain" with her mother and sister. On a scholarship, she attended St. Andrew's University in Scotland, where she received her M.A. in economics and psychology. After a series of jobs from waitress to chambermaid, Fay entered the world of advertising. An advertising problem that might take other people a fortnight to resolve took her only an hour. She quickly discovered her ability to express herself in writing. She considers "having babies quite helpful to the creative process," because, as she reasoned, "it reminds one that there is always more where that came from and there is never any shortage of ideas or of the ability to create." Because she has borne four (and is now stepparenting three) children, and has written two nonfiction books, twenty-one novels, and even more television and theater plays, one dare not argue with her assessment.

Even though, professionally speaking, she may be "the quintessential anti-romance novelist," as the *New York Times* defined her, she continues to work out the man-woman debate both in her work and in her personal life. In her novels Fay tackles Western culture's most cherished state of self-delusion—romantic love—while wholeheartedly embracing the practice of romantic love in her own life. After two divorces and with four grown sons, she began a long-term friendship with Nick, who is eighteen years her junior (and who has three sons himself by a previous marriage), four years ago when Fay was sixty years old. The friendship transformed itself into love.

At first, it seemed that whatever I asked or said to her, she persisted in taking the opposite view. In all earnestness I questioned, "Are you contrary by nature?" True to form, Fay insisted she is "not the *least* bit contrary"—indeed, she said, "I am extremely obliging, do what I can to help others, put other people's interests first, was well brought up as an English girl to put other people's needs before my own." (This I could not refute as we sat opposite each other: she was clearly putting *my* need—and her *publicist's* urging—to interview her before her need for some quiet time and space.) Still, I felt that all I had to say was "tomato" and out of her mouth would pop "tahmahto." When I remarked on her many contradictions, Fay said with a shrug, "I see no virtue in consistency."

For nearly two hours I queried, probed, challenged, and discussed with Fay Weldon her views on feminism, the characters in her novels, "insanity" in California, paradoxes, men, the current state of the world, and, of course, love—past and present. She offered a refreshing perspective on aging and mortality. At times disarmingly frank and darkly humorous, but always original, Fay maintained a gracious and even generous disposition, even though she feared that her husband, who had traveled to the United States with her on her book tour, might be "lost" in Santa Cruz and unable to find his way back to her. ("He has no bits of paper or documents with him that will be any help at all," the concerned wife in her worried.) Occasionally, it seemed clear that, being six thousand miles away from her home in London, she would much rather have been doing *anything* else besides giving *another* interview. (I wouldn't be surprised if Fay felt that—to paraphrase Sartre—hell is not other *people*, it is interviewers!) Be that as it may, I decided I was willing to trust this fiction writer.

New Love at Sixty

LOVE CAME AND WENT;
IT WAS THERE OR IT WASN'T.
THE BLESSINGS OF THE GODS,
AND THEIR CURSE.
—*FAY WELDON*
Worst Fears

⁘

When people ask me if I love writing, I say, "No." It's like asking, "Do you love breathing?" It is simply a natural thing that I do, and I consider myself extremely fortunate not to have to go out to work or have to do in my daily life what other people order me to do. Although as a writer I end up spending a great deal of time doing what other people tell me to do! As a child I had a peculiar need to write. This is very different from wanting to *be* a writer. Wanting to write has to do with a general and understandable desire for self-expression. But I come from a family of writers, so perhaps it's genetic!

The characters in my novels are not necessarily affected by my getting older, I don't think. Although I may have become slightly more moderate or more understanding in my views than, let's say, I was in my thirties, when I preferred to blame men for everything. I no longer prefer to blame men for everything because, it seems to me, *people* are to blame for everything, regardless of their gender. And gender makes remarkably little difference. Men may be villains for any number of reasons, but I don't hold their gender against them. Now, this may be a function of age or experience or the effect of the world changing around me. All these things move together, but I'm not sure that it has anything to do with my being older.

I suppose my only view of aging is that one would rather not. So why bother, why do it? I think at the slightest sign of age, mental or physical infirmity, I would make my will and remove myself from this world rather sharply. There's no reason to cling to something if it's not affording you much pleasure.

This age mania is an American obsession. Americans think there is some value in youth. I think the young tend to be obsessed by age. In my twenties I can remember thinking, *God, at thirty I will have to kill myself.* Then every decade, you simply put it off for another ten years. Once you stop counting, it doesn't really, honestly, seem to make much difference. My birthdays no longer mean anything to me; otherwise, I mean, you would find yourself incredibly defined, wouldn't you—now I am forty or now I am fifty. You would feel that society was laying some peculiar fate upon you. If American women feel that way, they have only themselves to blame for taking notice. They don't have to play along with it. Of *course* it's better to be younger than older, but it's simply a fact of one's existence. If you are born, you get old and you die. This is just it. Why bother about it?

I'm not against face lifts. I had my eyelids done ten years ago so that my eyes would focus better and I would take a better photograph. I was in Hollywood at the time, and everybody did it anyway. Again, why not? You want to put on some lipstick or wear clothes that you look nice in. I see no reason at all why you shouldn't look your best. It's just not good if it gets obsessive or takes up all of your time and attention. Or if you look in mirrors all the time and worry about looking older and you never have time to *do*, to *live*.

When someone says, "I feel so young," what does feeling young mean? Why should you feel differently when you are young from when you are old? It's like role-playing. This is a form of ageism. People should learn better than to say, "I feel so young," because this is attributing to youth qualities that youth does not have. If anything, youth is self-obsessed and age is interested in the outside world. If, when they say, "I feel so young," they mean "I still feel so self-obsessed and desperately want somebody to love and fancy me, and I want to have power over them and sexual control over them," then they should say so. Let them define their terms.

As one gets older, I think, you get better at predicting what is going to happen next. Because you have seen it before, you know what will follow somebody's particular behavior. When you find yourself behaving in a certain way, you know what's going to happen next. That comes with experience. You know you won't change, but at least you know what to expect.

In California everybody's into personal growth. It's *insane.* Who wants to grow? What do you want to grow *for?* What do you want to grow *into?* Perfection?! Perfection is just the ironing out of emotion. It's the turning of an incredible mass of individual response and individuality into one sort of homogenized boring person. And to see a whole culture bent on self-improvement by virtue of such self-negation is terrifying.

Wanting to eliminate negative feelings, or aiming for peace and tranquillity, seems to us [the English] insane. It just means you're not alive. It's a journey to absolutely nowhere. If you want to wake up happy every morning, you would be nonexistent. Worry is reasonable. Depression is the proper response to a terrible world. You are all in denial. It's a way of feeling justified in ignoring the horrors of the world. People feel anxious because they are getting old and they feel they shouldn't be. It's misplaced anxiety.

I don't *try* to accept myself. I'm not in the business of looking for peace, happiness, fulfillment, or any of these things. I don't know what the word "fulfillment" means. It's a completely artificial word used by people who see a lot of discontent in their lives, who feel that to be discontent is somehow unnatural, unhealthy. In a way, I think we live in the kind of world in which we are not entitled to be happy. Why *should* you be happy? How *can* you be happy? It just seems to me that people ought to be a lot kinder to themselves. Stop trying to grow when it's quite obvious there is no potential for growth there. I think you ought to have a little less Calvinism in America. A little less passion for self-improvement or perfection.

It seems to be people's profound belief that nature made everybody perfect; but nature has no interest in personality or happiness or behavior. Nature simply designed you as an organism that would reproduce itself by the age of twenty and then, for all it cared, you could die. It doesn't need you to be happy. Nature is simply a sort of reproductive energy. That doesn't mean that if you are born restless or full of resentment, you don't work to train yourself in ways that would make your life more enjoyable, but it has nothing to do with returning to some tranquil, happy state that never existed in the first place.

Somehow this extraordinary belief pattern that we are born happy and good overwhelms any real attempt to live well with another person. It leads to us breaking off our relationships with one another because we expect perfection. If you feel discontent, you feel that someone else is to blame. It becomes impossible to have lasting relationships because no one is prepared to believe that the discontent is in themselves. You just can't put up with the people around you because they aren't providing a solution that you have been led to believe is available. It *isn't* available, so you might as well put up with what you've got.

At sixty I fell in love again. I've been falling in love all my life, so what were the odds? Rather high! What you have to do is not want it to happen. That seems to be the art! I had known Nick socially for about ten years. When my marriage collapsed and then his marriage collapsed, we got together and it's been lovely. I don't think a disparity in our ages makes any difference. Occasionally, very occasionally, you realize you have concepts in your head that are rather different from the other person's because you were brought up in different generations. I was brought up with a generation that worried about the inevitability of war. That particular discussion, as it were, is more *relevant* to my generation than to his. So I will know all the arguments on either side, but he will have to work them out.

Nick is completely different from men of my generation. For one thing he isn't a dinosaur! But that has nothing to do with his chronological age. The difference is cultural; he was brought up in a different culture—in a society that believes women are human. This is a vast improvement over the society in which men now over sixty-five were raised. However hard they try intellectually to take on board the fact that women are equal, they have been reared to play emotional games with women. This is a big difference. It has nothing to do with youth or age, simply that society changes; the expectations of what men and women are has changed. And I am fortunate enough to have the benefit of that change.

The differences between my husband and me are not as great as they would be if one of us had been brought up in the tropics and the other had been brought up in the land of ice and snow. If you come from different backgrounds, those differences can be geographical or they can be cultural. In our case, the difference is cultural rather than geographical. The fact that two people come from a similar geographical locality directly develops their taste and forms what they feel to be aesthetically desirable and influences the kinds of foods they eat. Understanding that is probably more important—I'm *sure* is more important—than age. So you don't necessarily look for similarities with another person. I'm not talking about the coincidence of taste, but you don't need to like the same things in order to have an enjoyable relationship.

Because I'm past sixty does *not* mean that I am past the period of wanting romance in my life. There is no contradiction between being mature and romantic. The whole pleasure in relationships is what you invest in them. I don't see why that should be any less because you are older. In fact, it's probably *more* reasonable to be romantic in older age because you have less time in which you have to maintain it. The difficulty for the young is you can be ever so romantic at twenty, but by, say, seven or seventeen years later you've probably worn it out. If you feel romantic when you are older, you don't have so long to wear it out. You don't think, Oh God, I'm going to have to keep this romanticism up for the next sixty years; thank you very much.

But you can't expect to be happy if you're in love, no. Who ever thought love would make you happy? Of course it doesn't. It's very difficult. These are difficult emotions. You can't have love *and* happiness. On the whole women limit their choices enormously because they have in their heads the idea that the man ought to have the same political opinions or vote the same or like the same music. You just simply limit your choices. If I was to do a sort of checklist of the men I thought I would have the relationship I now have with my present husband, it wouldn't tally.

Why did we get married? I think, essentially, you get married because you don't want anyone else to get your partner. Mutually. I think this is a lot of the reason for marriage. You take it seriously and you feel that you need all the help you can get from society to honor that union. But if I had looked for the "right" person, this wouldn't be it. I would have found somebody in my own age group who felt the same politically—all kinds of things. Love has to do with a combination of the sexual and the intellectual. It comes down to the fact that you only feel comfortable in a certain person's company. If they are away, you think there's only half of you there. I suppose that's being in love.

About the question of feminism: I was never a staunch feminist. Feminism is something that other people attribute to you: if you have a certain set of views, you are seen as a feminist. Most certainly, what the feminists thought and what I thought very often coincided, but what brought about feminism is what brought about me. The same sorts of pressures in society were the same sorts of pressures on me as a woman and as a writer. So of course what I write is going to be feminist.

Before feminism there was a situation in which women had to work and earn money and look after the children while society pretended they didn't. Now, women, poor things, just assume that they will have to do the whole lot. This is probably a very natural state of affairs because it happens all over the world. We were lucky for a time in Western Europe when the women of the middle class were allowed to stay at home and look after the children, which at the time seemed a boring thing to do. Now a lot of women would do anything to be supported by a man. But, at the same time, being supported by a man is a terrible thing, because if you want a new pair of shoes, you have to ask, "May I have a new pair of shoes, please?" and he will say, "What's the matter with the ones you have on?" and you will be obliged to look at him and say, "Well, nothing, really—I mean, they keep the water out, but it's just not much fun."

Of course it's no fun being a feminist! Being a feminist is the opposite of fun. That means, if you are going to be a proper feminist, you need to live by your principles, and this is impossible. You have to see the emotional as the political, and that's a very hard thing to do because it means you can't enjoy your emotions, which are inevitably going to be politically and emotionally incorrect. So it's no fun. I recommend it to nobody.

What do I do for fun? Nothing. I just enjoy whatever happens next. So nothing is separated out from anything else, really; it's all mixed together. It's not fun. It's just life—difficult and complex. One is ambivalent about most things, really. One would usually rather be doing something else than what one is doing. I just wouldn't separate it out or think, I will go and do this for fun now. Relaxing? I *hate* relaxing. *Hate it.*

Perhaps when one gets older, a sense of proportion seems to settle in. When

I read the newspapers and listen to the news I think, How lucky I am. And I take pleasure in thinking, How lucky I am. Not at the expense of the tragedies I read and hear about, because you also know that even though terrible things happen in people's lives or they die terribly, they had a whole life before they died that was probably all right. You learn to see your own life in a kind of proportion. You know that if things are terrible now, they were good for a long time. Or that while they may be good now, they were terrible for a long time.

If you've had enough people die on you, you learn to value life. One of the things one learns about getting older is that if you are born, you'll die. You know that you are going to die and that everyone dies, and you don't try to evade that knowledge. Americans are terrified of age and mortality, terrified of disease, and the more they search for nirvana, the more terrified they become. This is a strange, rather cowardly way to behave, instead of just being extremely glad to be alive and not caring how long you live.

I never played sports. I never found any enjoyment or encouraged any enjoyment in myself or my children in any physical activity at all. But what is exhilarating is *thought*, and what remains exhilarating is the mind and jokes and wit. That doesn't go unless you get Alzheimer's or something, but then you would think you'd have enough sense before it got too bad to organize your own demise.

It seems to me, wit and humor get better with age because you have more to base it on, more experience. This is why old people used to be respected and listened to, rather as astrology is now. You wouldn't cast your horoscope to try to find out what would happen next or what you were likely to do next; you would go and ask your grandmother, and she would tell you. Because she had lived long enough, she knew what to expect from people and life.

I suffer from free-floating anxiety. That means my anxiety wanders. It attaches itself to so many different things. But you really don't have to take any notice of it. It's sort of like a flu or cold; it just goes away. It may be attached to money or to "God, I've got cancer" or "I'm getting old and there's nothing I can do about it." It's just anxiety. If you say, "Oh, anxiety attack," and explain to yourself that "it has nothing to do with this; my life is really no different than it was yesterday," you can just wait for it to go away. Anxiety is not a nice feeling. It creates a sort of paralysis, because you think there is something you ought to do, but there's nothing you *can* do about it. It usually is about issues in the face of which you are powerless anyway. So you might as well wait for it to go away, and it *does* go away. Usually, that state of anxiety was seared into the mind at some stage of your life when you were very reasonably anxious about something, and the anxiety was the trigger to action and you acted. But in later life it becomes the shadow of an earlier anxiety. If you know that, then you ignore it. I was eight years in Freudian analysis and it was interesting, but it cured nothing. Talk never cured anybody.

*O*ne *of the wonderful results of my own aging has been that my life has become a lot simpler. What is superfluous has been stripped away. It is such a relief to see it go. . . . My yearning now is to be free of all physical encumbrances. That's where my empowerment is.*

— M A R I O N W O O D M A N

Marion Woodman

. . . FOR HERE THERE IS NO PLACE
THAT DOES NOT SEE YOU. YOU MUST CHANGE YOUR LIFE.
—RAINER MARIA RILKE
"Archaic Torso of Apollo"

Nearly every woman in Western culture is haunted by an "addiction to perfection." She is deluged with images of seemingly flawless bodies and sculpted faces from movies, magazines, and television. Yet when she looks into the mirror, she sees only her own unadulterated reflection, not the artificial ideal the culture expects her to reach. At some deep level, she is forced to wrestle with the repression of the feminine principle and with the effects this repression is having on her attitude to her body and to nature.

Marion Woodman is a Jungian analyst from Toronto, Canada, whose particular interest is addictions—specifically the eating disorders: anorexia (a pathological fear of weight gain, which often leads to malnutrition and excessive weight loss), bulimia (a compulsive drive to overeat, often followed by forced vomiting), and bingeing (the tendency to go into an extreme of overeating).

Marion's interest in food addictions originated from painful firsthand experience. After years of struggling with an eating disorder herself as a young woman, she came close to having a physical breakdown in midlife, an experience that forced her to retire from her beloved career as a high school English teacher. She went to Europe to study at the C. G. Jung Institute in Zurich, Switzerland, where her dreams became her guide. Through her body she received a message from her soul: "You must change your life."

Over more than two decades of exploring, through private practice and hundreds of lectures and workshops, her own addiction and those of numerous other men and women, Marion has written seven books, the most recent of which is *Dancing in the Flames: The Dark Goddess in the Transformation of*

Consciousness, coauthored with Elinor Dickson. Her earlier books, *The Owl Was a Baker's Daughter* (1980), *Addiction to Perfection* (1982), and *The Pregnant Virgin* (1985), dealt in part with eating disorders. Through her work, Marion has discovered that the addict's real search is not for some physical object—food, alcohol, drugs, money, another person—but for meaning in life, for sustenance for the hungry soul. That sustenance comes from a deep connection with what Carl Jung called the archetypal world.* "That's where the *true* nourishment is," Marion says.

In 1968, still in early midlife, Marion thought she had almost everything her middle-class status could offer: a beautiful home, a fine husband, an excellent teaching career. Then, one snowy winter's evening, she found herself unable to hail a cab. She thought, Here I am, an adult woman, and I am helpless when I'm alone. She knew right there that she had to find out who she was. In a dramatic move, she decided to travel solo to India, where she hoped she would find spiritual guidance. Six months later, in New Delhi, Marion found her belief in a male deity challenged. "*He* turned out to be *She.*" In a "modern initiation" of sorts, she encountered a hitherto unknown feminine principle, which she later came to call "Sophia."

Though raised a minister's daughter, she walks her own path and calls herself "a gypsy outside the collective." "In a way," she says, "that's where I am now: not quite in and not quite out of the collective." Her childless marriage to an English professor remains strong after nearly forty years, and, she says, it is "central to my life."

Now sixty-eight years old, Marion believes that a blessed wisdom inhabits the body, a wisdom that can lead us to self-acceptance and love if we let it, a wisdom that can relieve us from our terror of and preoccupation with death. She says that illness has been her greatest teacher. In her battle with cancer, diagnosed three years ago, she sees an opportunity for continued learning.

As we spoke together for several hours in a rented beach house, just before her week-long workshop entitled "BodySoul Rhythms," Marion's long,

*Archetypes are universal patterns or symbols that come from the collective unconscious and are present in individual psyches. They are the basic content of religions, mythologies, legends, and fairy tales.

thoughtful pauses were punctuated by the pulse of Northern California's winter surf.

The Body's Wisdom

⁘

For four and a half years, I was in Zurich. My husband, Ross, continued teaching at the university in London (Canada), and I went back and forth between Europe and Canada. We would meet at Christmastime and during the summers. Ross allowed me the freedom to explore without guilt what I needed to explore. At first it was chaos, because I would come home from Zurich quite a different person from the one who had left. It was extremely difficult for Ross to relate to the new me. Each time I returned home I was a little different: I had found my own voice, I had developed my own empowerment. They weren't easy, those four and a half years. The marriage we had committed to in 1958 was not the marriage that evolved from 1979 onward; it had become a very different relationship.

It's curious that I became a Jungian analyst and writer as a sort of by-product of going to Zurich to work on my own health. I had never intended to be either. I never imagined that *The Owl Was a Baker's Daughter* would ever be read by anyone. And, in a way, it is the purist book of all, because I wrote it as a thesis, alone in my room in Zurich. I talked to myself and wrote it down. But so many people were interested in eating disorders and asked me for photocopies of my thesis that I thought, I can't go on making all these copies! At about that time, Daryl Sharp had begun his Toronto-based publishing company, Inner City Books, and suggested that we print a hundred copies of *The Owl*. Well, they sold out, and so the writing began.

When I wrote *Addiction to Perfection*, I still had no sense of constriction, no awareness of the expectations of my readers, because I never imagined that anyone would read the book. But it, too, was published and sold well. When it came to writing *The Pregnant Virgin*, however, it was a different story. By this time I knew that my books *were* being read. In fact, I remember the first time I went to lecture in California, in 1981. I couldn't understand why everyone was kissing and hugging me. I thought, How forward these people are! Why are they doing this? Later that evening, I realized that it was because they had read my first book and they felt closer to my soul than most of the people who knew me personally. They felt a real sense of intimacy with me.

It's interesting how things work out. I hated teaching grammar, but now I realize that it served my ultimate destiny. As a writer, I need to know how to handle a sentence. Looking back over my life, I see how all the threads have miraculously come together: the teacher, the writer, the actress, the dancer that I wanted to be—and of course, the analyst—all are woven together into the single tapestry that is my life and work.

How I came to realize the importance of the feminine in my life is another way in which the threads have come together. As an anorexic, I was the personification of addiction to perfection. I was in control of my life as far as I could be: one hundred percent. That's how anorexia works. I was extremely efficient as a schoolteacher. But I became sick trying to live that way. I knew nothing about the feminine, thinking that being thin and stylish *was* being feminine. That was my understanding of what it meant to be popular with men and valued as a woman. That was my horrible misconception, but that is what the culture told me—and still tells us.

The watershed in my life was the trip to India in 1968. I went alone, thinking I would live in an ashram. That didn't work out, however, because I became extremely ill. In my aloneness in India, I began to understand a great deal. Vulnerable though I was, I had wonderful things happen to me as I opened up to the new culture. I was able to overcome my fear of death. In India I became aware that for the first time in my life my feeling function and my intuition were being valued. Gradually I surrendered to life in India.

Back in Canada, stepping off the plane, I remember thinking, I've got nothing to lose. After India, though, I was unable to accept the culture at home. There seemed to be too much food, too much everything. Compulsive materialism disgusted me; that's what sent me into analysis. I could not find my place in this culture because I had started to move into a femininity that was taking me outside my culture as I knew it. I had tried to be part of the culture by being thin. That hadn't worked. Then, when I tried to live the feminine as I had come to understand it in India, I felt even less a part of Western culture. I knew I had to find a different way of being, and that is what has brought me into the psychology of the feminine. Without the anorexia I would never have encountered Sophia and the feminine. I now thank God for the addiction, for had I not been caught in that life-or-death situation, I would never have had to face the challenge: "Change something or die!" Determined to work it through, I entered analysis—with a man. He had a magnificent feeling function and a wonderful intuition, and it was, ironically, through him, a man, that I began my exploration of the feminine.

Mind you, it was also through my dreams that he was able to help me understand my psyche. There is still much to be learned about the relationship between psyche and soma. I have been fascinated with this relationship all my life. Early on, my illnesses had been my guide, and once again, with Dr. B., my analyst, I had to try to find a relationship between psyche and soma, between body and soul. That's my whole point about psyche and soma: it is the experience in the body that gives resonance to the knowledge in the mind. That's where the wisdom is—in the body, in the experiential side. My quest took me to Zurich and into an entirely new level of dreamwork. At that time, no one was doing bodywork there. I had to rely on my own dreams, and they did serve as a guide.

For me, the relation between Sophia and God is like the relation between two complementary energies, the masculine and feminine faces of God. I think of God as mystery, as the unknowable, as magnificent energy manifested through matter. As for evil, I do believe it exists, but it has deep philosophical ramifications. I have had dreams from which I have awakened sweating, knowing that I had been in the presence of something horrific that I could not deal with. In one dream, I was driving a car and came to a border. Sensing an evil presence, I pressed my foot on the accelerator to get out of there, knowing that as an individual I was powerless to combat the evil. On the other hand, what we sometimes construe as demonic may, in fact, be the face we are turning toward the unconscious. When I was anorexic, for example, I often asked God: "How could you be so cruel to give me a body that, to me, is so *un*beautiful?" It was my turning against myself that was creating the evil. As I grew older, I realized that the evil was my own projection. As I began to see the benign side, what had once seemed cruel now became the source of my creativity.

I see the manifestation of God in everything—those trees, those flowers, your eyes, your smile. That manifestation I call Sophia, the feminine, the form that spirit takes. She is matter. She is wisdom. I think of wisdom as surrender to Oneness, the unifying divine. The energy, the pulse that beats in that flower, in that tree, in that cloud, in everything, is one Soul. Wisdom is knowing that we are all part of the whole and part of each other. Knowing and accepting exactly what we are is also wisdom. We have so much trouble accepting ourselves as we are because we try so hard to be what the collective wants us to be.

One of the wonderful results of my own aging has been that my life has become a lot simpler. What is superfluous has been stripped away. It is such a relief to see it go. It takes a lot of work to simplify. It takes what I could call a very good sense of the inner masculine to discern what needs to stay and what needs to go. There is no way you can hold on to everything as you get older. You just do not have the physical and emotional stamina to hold it all together.

I don't want to leave a lot of things for other people to take care of. I'm getting rid of all my files of notes, boxes of pictures, and boxes of clothes. I'm getting life down to the essence. Something similar is going on in my thinking. I am focusing and concentrating more, holding center, so that instead of being diffused, my energy focuses like a bright fire. I find it very releasing. This ties in with discipline. With cancer, I've had to be one hundred percent disciplined. Sophia has laws, and I know I have to obey them. When you are young and you disobey, you can still survive. But when you are my age, if you disobey those laws, you *don't* survive. So you learn to eat the right foods, to exercise, to rest, to meditate, in order to have a balance that brings you freedom. If you don't have balance, you will never have freedom. Being able to achieve that freedom, I think, is the glory of aging.

In regard to the cancer, before being diagnosed, I was working as fully as I could. Then I had three immense losses, one right after the other. I was working at my peak, but the stress of my brother's death and the death of my closest friend of thirty-five years did me in. In retrospect, I knew it was time to change, but I put it off by one year too many.

Cancer was my second initiation. It turned my life inside out. Everything I'd thought about in terms of the feminine, in terms of surrender, in terms of oneness, in terms of the relationship between psyche and soma and the development of the subtle body—all these huge questions—I'm now dealing with all the time, every minute. What does it mean to live in the moment? With a disease like cancer, you have no idea what the future holds, so you live in the now. There is no certainty of a future; you try to experience essence in each moment.

There is another beautiful aspect about living to this age: what once appeared to be contradictions are no longer contradictions. For example, between my husband and me, sometimes it's funny when we don't quite hear each other or don't quite see each other—I mean literally—because of our age. Or we talk about something that happened twenty years ago; I tell him what I thought happened, he tells me what he thought happened, and it's as if we weren't in the same place at all! It's very funny—and, at the same time, tragic. To have lived so close and yet so far apart! We now see the discrepancy between the tears and the laughter as a paradox rather than as a contradiction. Being able to hold that paradox—that's what holds our relationship together. That is the secret: we see and embrace both sides.

There is a perfect illustration for what I mean by "holding the paradox." Ross and I once played the characters Nagg and Nell, the old parents who are thrown into garbage pails by their son, in Samuel Beckett's play *Endgame*. It was a fascinating experience because the people in the audience who were close enough to see our eyes cried, while those who were farther back laughed. It was interesting to play to these opposite reactions from the audience: we could hear gasps coming from the front rows and realized that the people there were participating intimately in the human tragedy being enacted on stage, yet we could hear the laughter from the back rows and realized, too, that the perspective afforded by greater distance—greater detachment—can help one see the humor in a tragic situation.

I find when I travel now that some ticket agents and flight attendants pat me on the head and call me "dear." That condescension irritates me. What they are saying, in effect, is, "You are too old to take care of yourself. Just do as you're told and you'll be all right." Well, I won't do as I'm told! They assume that just because my body is frail, my mind must be, too. Well intentioned though they are, they fail to realize that I am still in charge of my own empowerment. A person who comes from a place of empathy honors age. Unfortunately, our culture as a whole has lost that capacity for empathy.

Interestingly, the values that I had when I was twenty-one are back, but in a different form. When I was twenty-one, I put a rucksack on my back and went to Europe and youth-hosteled. When I started out in the morning, I had no idea whom I was going to meet or where I was going to go. I was a gypsy, outside the collective. In a way, that's where I am now: not quite in and not quite out of the collective. I'm walking my own path. What comes up in my dreams is this twenty-year-old with her full body strength. I can feel that strength in myself. I can feel that person who wasn't afraid to voice her opinions, wasn't afraid to be who she was. Now my body isn't as strong as it once was, but for all that, this fortitude that would not be conquered is still there. It refuses to be defeated.

My philosophy of aging is expressed in W. B. Yeats's "Sailing to Byzantium":

> An aged man is but a paltry thing,
> A tattered cloak upon a stick, unless
> Soul clap its hands and sing, and louder sing
> For every tatter in its mortal dress. . . .

That's my philosophy. I celebrate every wound, every sacrifice, every joy, every passion—"every tatter in [my] mortal dress." If I can keep my soul singing and clapping its hands, that's all that really matters. For me, that's what aging is all about: allowing the soul to expand even as the body fails. There is no real grief in the loss of the body because a new balance is emerging. The soul is becoming empowered in recognizing its own voice and using it.

Another thing I love about getting older is that I now have no desire to control anything or anybody. That is so releasing. I used to go to workshops thinking, Oh, we have to do this, and this, and this. There was an agenda. Now I think, We'll do what we can. As long as we are right in the moment and are dealing with the issues of the moment, it doesn't matter *what* is done. If somebody else takes over, that's fine with me. Shedding the desire to control has been part of the simplifying process.

When I was younger, I was possessed with trying to be what I wasn't. I always wanted to be a sylph, a Balanchine ballerina. That's the kind of body I wanted. Now, knowing I was born of Scottish ancestry, I accept my sacred matter with love.

Simplifying is crucial. If we are still trying to figure out how to care for our too large house and garden, and what to do with all our goods and chattels, we can't let go into a new life. If we *can* let them go, we have the joy of seeing their beauty released into new energy in someone else's life. We see our life as ongoing. My yearning now is to be free of all physical encumbrances. That's where my empowerment is.

In our sixties, we still have a fairly strong body and strong mental capacity—if we are lucky—but the spiritual dimension is becoming paramount. Looking back over my life, I see that transition now taking place. My first initiation came in 1968 in India, as I mentioned earlier. That's when I saw that if I persisted in what *I* wanted to do, I was bound to be defeated. But if I gave up my own aspirations and surrendered to Sophia, the divine feminine, then life would be an adventure—and it certainly *has* been! I *did* have to make that surrender, though—not in defeat, but in consciously yielding to an unknown destiny.

If I were to advise other women about aging, life, and death, I would say: Try to imagine yourself at ninety-seven and ask yourself if at ninety-seven you will be able to say, "I've lived my own life." That's all that matters. I cannot imagine anything worse than facing death knowing that I had not lived my own life. When I was really ill with cancer, I had no fear of death because I really had lived *my* life. The last twenty years, particularly, have been a huge adventure—expanding everything I am and demanding everything I've got.

When I was young, I used to ride my bicycle with my arms flung wide open.

I *loved* life. I feel that even more intensely now—an immense love of people and nature and life. Expansion. I say to women: "Open your arms and embrace paradox." More and more, that is what's going to be needed, as institutions and relationships of all kinds break down. Everything is changing so fast, we cannot keep up. There is no way of surviving the splits without holding paradox. In the world we are moving into, it's going to be "both/and" or war. And there is no room on this tiny little planet for war. That's true at the individual as well as the national and international levels.

When we accept paradox, we automatically expand. Expanding is what being an adult is all about. It takes adulthood to embrace paradox and expand into totality. Jung would call it the transcendent function: we move into a third place, where the two opposites are held, no longer in opposition. You see, that ties into something else. In that move to a third place, there is no more "power over," no more control over anybody or anything. That's the place where love moves through us. The love moves us, and we are expanded.

So often in life we are given the chance to grow, but instead we shrink. Something in our culture discourages us from standing to our full stature. I think that if we fail to stretch to our full capacity when our moment is upon us, then we are going to miss the next opportunity, too, because every time we are called everything in us has to come forth. I believe that that is success: recognizing the moments when we are called, and being able to respond with everything we've got, no matter how frightened we are. In that moment, the soul is empowered. It begins to "clap its hands and sing, and louder sing/For every tatter in its mortal dress."

I would encourage [women] to be more active if they haven't been, not just let someone else do it. We can make change if we work together with like-minded people in organizations. I see some women so engrossed in their own world that they don't realize change is possible. . . . I don't understand how they can live like that. [But they] probably don't understand how I can live like this.

— NELLIE WONG

Nellie Wong

I WANT FREEDOM, THE RIGHT
TO SELF-EXPRESSION, EVERYBODY'S
RIGHT TO RADIANT, BEAUTIFUL THINGS.
—EMMA GOLDMAN

An Emma Goldman poster that hangs on Nellie Wong's office wall bears the above quote. When I questioned Nellie about it, she said that these words from her heroine exactly conveyed her own philosophy and ideals. Nellie is proud of her Marxist-Socialist-feminist values and sees them as an ethical standard by which to live ("It's acting out what I believe in"). For more than fifteen years she has been a member of Radical Women and the Freedom Socialist Party, which works to bring about changes in this country's economic system as well as in attitudes of racism, sexism, and homophobia.

Nellie is also a poet whose poetry is permeated by her personal politics. As a first-generation Chinese American growing up in the San Francisco Bay Area, Nellie has experienced more than her share of racism. She spoke poignantly on the subject and shared with me some poems about being "dark-skinned in a white woman's world." Her poetry has been collected in two books and numerous anthologies and has been called conscious, militant, feminist, realist, and radical. Susan Sherman wrote of Nellie's book *The Death of Long Steam Lady,* "It is political writing at its very best, combining concrete imagery and social reality with compassion, sensitivity, and imagination."

When Nellie began writing, Asian American writers were hardly known. Now we are all familiar with Maxine Hong Kingston and Amy Tan. "They are a lot more mainstream," Nellie said. She doesn't consider herself part of the mainstream because her poetry is so politically oriented. "Writing poetry is really a political act to me." Eventually she would like to write a novel about her family that would intertwine her autobiography. "I think a lot of stories have been told, but mine would be different from what other women write. Mine would be more political and set against the contemporary background of a revolutionary Asian American woman."

At the age of sixteen Nellie started earning her living as a clerical worker. For the past thirteen years she has worked at the University of California at San Francisco. She is now a senior analyst in the office of Affirmative Action and investigates discrimination complaints based on race, gender, sexuality, age, Vietnam era status, and disability. The program also monitors the Affirmative Action plan on campus and offers diversity training. Now, at the age of sixty-two, Nellie looks forward to retirement, when she will have more time to write, to work for her political causes, and to be able to indulge her lifelong passion of going to the movies—at a senior discount.

The afternoon we met at her office, Nellie was working excitedly to wrap up several projects in anticipation of a six-week sabbatical during which she would help organize and host a conference for the Freedom Socialist Party. As we sauntered down the street to dine at a local Thai restaurant in the quiet, slow-paced neighborhood of the San Francisco Sunset district, Nellie's colorful story began to unfold. Her language was rich in imagery and narration, and it became clear to me that her "joy is a battle within a storm."

A Radical Poet

. . . HAVE THE DETERMINATION TO DRIVE AHEAD TO THE END.
WOMEN WHO ARE FULLY AWARE OF THE PRESENT MOMENT HAVE
TO KNOW HOW TO SHED EVERY ROSE-COLORED FANTASY. OUR JOY
IS A BATTLE WITHIN A STORM AND NOT PLAYING THE HARP UNDER
THE MOON OR RECITING POETRY IN THE FRONT OF A FLOWER.

—DING LING

Thoughts on the Eighth of March (1908)

⁘

My father came from China at age sixteen in 1911 and worked in my granduncle's herb store in Oakland. He returned to China, married his first wife, and had a baby (my oldest sister). His first wife died when Li Hong was about a month old. Then he married my mother and returned to Oakland, leaving her in China. He made three subsequent trips back to China. In 1933 he brought my mother and their three China-born children over to the United States. I'm the first of four U.S.-born children. There are seven children altogether. It's almost like two families.

I went to China once in 1983. Since my mother emigrated, I was the first one in our family to go to China. I was very thrilled. I think what impressed me the most was how poor the family is. It was emotional for me to stand on the soil in the village where my father was born. An auntie in her nineties who was sick got off her bed and took pictures with me. I met so many cousins, a whole generation, and I was able to speak the village dialect and communicate with them. It was exciting. I was in the village only part of a day but was in China for three weeks. I went with a group of American women writers, Alice Walker and Tillie Olsen among them. I was the only Asian American woman on the tour. I have good memories of that trip. When I turned sixty I thought, Oh my, I'm an older person now. I'm a feminist and don't have a hangup about aging. In fact, I thought, I can't wait until I can get into the movie theaters at a discount! It's funny. As I've gotten older, I'm much more confident in believing I can do things that I didn't have the confidence to do when I was younger. That's why activism is attractive to me.

My feminism and activism came out of a time when I was looking for change. I discovered writing in my mid-thirties when I was still single. My youngest sister, Flo, suggested I take a writing class because she thought my yearly newsletters to the members of my family were amusing: "You're really kind of funny; you should explore writing." So I did.

I didn't know what I was looking for; I'm gonna learn to write, I told myself. I had no background in writing whatsoever. In my first class, we had to write a short story, so every week I had a new story. I was one of the most prolific writers in class. My future husband was in the class, too, and we started going out. We got married about a year and a half after we met, and we moved to San Francisco, found an apartment, then signed up for writing classes at the Marina Adult School. My teacher said, "You should be going to San Francisco State." I'd never gone to college. Two of my sisters had gone to UC Berkeley. I realized there was something I was missing, and I was resentful. So going to college was a dream of mine. My husband at the time encouraged me and I wanted to go, but I was scared. I passed the SAT and finally started at SF State as an undergraduate.

I began to take evening courses in creative writing, poetry, literature and Asian American and feminist studies while I was working full-time at Bethlehem Steel as a secretary. For several years I took two courses per semester. I was very, very excited about going to college, taking all these courses—I was thirsty for knowledge. I became interested in Asian American history, Chinese history, and Chinese American history. My writing and reading helped me to see who we were, how we fit into the United States of America as a people who have been discriminated against and had laws enacted against us. When I learned that, I was very angry.

I like to share this story, which I think is important. My poetry writing teacher said, "We're going to start alphabetically, and next week those whose names begin with A and B are going to read their poetry." My name was Balch at the time. Read my own poetry? What poems? I didn't have any! I didn't know what poetry was about, but I wanted to find out. I called up my niece's friend who was a creative writing major and asked her to help me. She asked me if I had ever written poetry or written down my dreams or done any automatic writing. I hadn't done any of that ever. So she gave me lots of suggestions. That day I remember I told Jim, my husband, "Leave me alone, I am going to write poems." And I did. I wrote in a stenographer's spiral-bound, Gregg shorthand notebook. There's a line in the middle of the page, so you've got two columns for writing. I wrote several poems in it—long, skinny poems. Amazingly, I just wrote what came out and didn't stop myself. About a week later, I had to read the poems in class. The professor said, "Bitter, bitter, bitter," because it was about being Chinese American and being critical of the Miss Chinatown, U.S.A., contest, which I believe dehumanizes women. I was devastated. I was pretty shy and naive and just going to throw it away. I didn't engage in discussion with him, but a couple of students said, "Nellie, I really like your poetry."

I told some friends in a feminist class I was taking about what had happened. One of them said, "You don't have to listen to him." I said, "I don't?" My mindset was that professors, doctors, and lawyers knew everything. I was just a small woman who didn't know anything. I didn't get discouraged because I had support among my female classmates and they invited me to join their own writing group.

When I first joined the Women's Caucus in Creative Writing and Literature (which later became the Women Writers Union on campus), I was discouraged because the women were too loud for me. There were forty women in a room, making a lot of noise. Feminism was really rising on that campus. The combination of feminism, Asian American studies, and creative writing and literature became formative for me. I went to all my classes—never skipped a day—plus worked all day and cleaned and cooked at home. I never did graduate. I got enough credits to be a junior, but I was getting tired. I was getting published, doing a lot of reading, being active in my organizations, and being married. I couldn't do it all. But the classes I took at SF State were very valuable; they really opened up the world to me.

I had started writing in the early 1970s, and by 1977 I had my first book out. I met a lot of white women and many lesbians—and here I was married, but I felt we had a lot in common because we were concerned about who we were as women. At that time, I didn't care that there weren't any women of color in my classes. I guess I was unusual. My friend Karen Brodin, who died about eight years ago from breast cancer, encouraged me to publish my writing. She was a Socialist-feminist and a member of Radical Women and the Freedom Socialist Party, two organizations I'm now a member of. I began to learn about Socialism and Marxism. I did a lot of organizing with them. I'm still a Marxist. I feel very working class because I rent the house I live in, I don't own anything. I don't need much money to live, but at the same time, I know there's a lot of suffering by people who don't even have that.

I'd like to help people have somewhere to live and not be homeless. Women should have a chance to fulfill their lives as women and as people, but not with prescribed molds. There's a lot of courage among women who work—those who strike for higher wages, those are the women we should emulate. They link with other workers. The exploitation of workers will continue until we organize to overthrow the ruling class, which decides how we eat, sleep, and what we do. Oh, yes, I think that will happen. It's happening now. Open the papers and read what's going on: there are lots of pockets of resistance to the ruling class, but change will take a long time.

The Freedom Socialist Party is a group of men and women of all professions who are anti-capitalist, pro-Socialist. We work to bring about change in the United States in the economic system, which engenders racism, sexism, and homophobia. The structure of the organization appealed to me. I felt that writing was great but was not the only thing I wanted to do. If I had three or four more lives, I could use the time. The Freedom Socialist Party wants to make things better for everyone, particularly women and children, people of color, people with disabilities, and older people. I've been a Marxist for about fifteen years, but before that I was doing a lot of work in the Socialist-feminist community: organizing and picketing. It's acting out what I believe in. As a secretary I'd never belonged to a labor union. There were no unions in the jobs I'd ever had. Now I'm active in my union at work, University Professionals and Technical Employees.

After twelve years of marriage, my husband and I grew apart because of our political differences. As I was getting radicalized and politicized, I began to find marriage stifling. He was supportive of my writing, publishing, and reading, but he didn't like my becoming a Socialist, although he didn't seem to mind the feminism too much. Part of those married years, I was supporting both of us because he wasn't working. He loves books and was very encouraging of my wanting to study and bought me a lot of racist books about the Chinese. I have a whole collection of them. I was changing, and I don't think he was. A lot of men want to be in a relationship with someone and don't want anything to interfere with it, but I was becoming very full with everything I was learning and doing and excited about. I didn't want anyone telling me I couldn't do something. I've been single since 1982. I have no problem with being single. I'm not dating, not chasing after a relationship. I had some relationships a few years ago, but they didn't work out. Some men find it difficult to be with a woman who is strong and independent and also, politically, a Socialist.

When I began writing, Asian American writers were hardly known, and now they are a lot more mainstream. I don't consider myself part of the mainstream because my poetry is very political. Writing poetry is really a political act to me. It doesn't mean that I can't write something that's very tight and small, but at the same time there's a lot of politics going through it. Some editors don't like it. So I do get rejections, which upsets me. It's part of writing.

I hope to retire in a few years. I have to make sure I have enough to live on, and then I will continue my activism and my writing. I wouldn't do part-time work for anything. I've worked forty-three years, and the only break I had was when I went to China. Ten thousand of us were laid off by Bethlehem Steel at the end of 1982, and I thought I was going to retire then, since I had eighteen years there. With my severance pay I went to China. I had never stopped working, so that was really another change for me.

I never had any children. My ex-husband and I tried but couldn't. It was hard at the time. I always wanted a child or two so I could be like everybody else. I wouldn't mind having a teenager running around, being a friend. I'm glad now because I've always been free. I have a lot of nieces and nephews and grand-nieces and -nephews. For a long time we were told we couldn't be fulfilled unless we had children. We could not be real women unless we had children. I don't have a partner, I don't have children—we've all been defined and judged by that. The world tries to tell me I'm no one or I'm not female if I don't do what everybody else does. Not everybody gets married and has children. They choose to stay single. In a poem called "Enter the Mirror," I wrote:

I have no children. The other night I dreamt I gave birth to an insect. What terrified me even more was that the insect was sucking up a glob of pink goo. Was it a strawberry milkshake? And did it ooze from my vagina? This is not a metamorphosis. This is a dream, and I am perplexed now at age 44 why the process of birthing seeps up through the subconscious at night when the moon should be napping.

When I was growing up, I felt insignificant. In my family, we have six girls and one boy, who is the youngest. I don't think I grew up resenting that; it was a fact of life. Another thing I've struggled with since I was young is atopic dermatitis, a skin condition. As I was growing up I had a lot of rashes. I scratched and itched a lot. It really affected my life. Often I was sick because of my respiratory system, and I couldn't breathe easily or eat many different foods because of allergies. I was not a normal child. Because my mother had to raise seven children, she would say things that really hurt me, such as "You cost me a lot of money." I'd always say, "I didn't ask to be born," in my own rebellious way. But times were hard and there were a lot of mouths to feed. My parents worked very hard to feed and house us.

When I was growing up, I was very affected by movies and magazines. I always wanted to be like those beautiful women in the pictures I saw on movie screens and in calendars. I thought, Why are we different? It's very interesting, because I always wanted to be well dressed and beautiful. I knew I looked different, but I didn't like the way I looked because of my skin allergies and because I was darker than a lot of other people. There is something about color in all our lives that made a difference. We were despised or disrespected.

Many things that happened to me personally changed me. I'm not saying I had the worst life in the world, but it was pretty traumatic at times. My skin would be so raw from scratching, my mother used to wrap my hands in nylons so I couldn't scratch. My nails would dig into my skin and I'd just bleed. They didn't know what to do about it except tie my hands back. I worried about my life as I was growing up. I didn't have a lot of friends. Never had a boyfriend in junior high or high school. I did go to my junior prom—in those days you could ask a man to take you. I did ask someone; it was the most uncomfortable experience of my life. I thought I looked fine, but I didn't realize that how you feel about yourself doesn't necessarily have to do with your physical being. It is tied in with the emotional, with the spirit. When you're young, you don't really know that. I didn't know that. I saw a lot, but I think I put on blinders and escaped to the movies, to books, and to fashion magazines. I knew everything that was going on in *Vogue* and everything about the movie stars. I was caught up in their lives when I was young. All the images were white. I grew up wanting to be white. I wrote a poem about that called "When I Was Growing Up." One of the stanzas reads:

> *when I was growing up, people told me*
> *I was dark and I believed my own darkness*
> *in the mirror, in my soul, my own narrow vision.*

Now in my sixties, I accept my skin condition, which I still have to take care of through light treatment, which keeps my skin from erupting. I exercise at a gym to help keep my health problem under control. I want to have energy so I don't tire as easily. I do get tired now, but I think I'm pretty healthy for my age. I seem younger than a lot of people I know. I want to continue being active. I don't think I'll be able to vegetate, live in a mountain cabin, do nothing. If I were ever incarcerated for my political activities, I would say, "Don't take away my books or my notepads, pencils, and pens. I need them in order to live."

There are other up-and-coming writers, representing a mosaic across the Asian American community. We have so many ethnicities, languages, so much diversity. I feel I have a lot to say about how our lives were. I'd like to put it into a novel. Once I had a fantasy about writing a musical; I love musicals, grew up on *Oklahoma!* I knew all the songs. I'd like to write another one against the backdrop of the Great China restaurant my father bought in 1944 when I was ten years old. We all worked there, waited on tables, did everything. I loved that restaurant backdrop. Whether I'll ever get to do it is another story. In "Reminiscing About a Chinese Restaurant" I wrote:

> *This Chinese restaurant demands love,*
> *demands attention.   Its walls expand,*
> *I slither inside.*

I have to fit my writing into everything else I do. I do not write every day, I write when I can, at midnight or early in the morning. Poems come when I'm out, a line crosses my mind, and I just try to remember them when that happens.

If I had any advice for women, I would encourage them to be more active if they haven't been, not just let someone else do it. We can make change if we work together with like-minded people in organizations. I see some women so engrossed in their own world that they don't realize change is possible. They're very private people, and I don't understand how they can live like that. They probably don't understand how I can live like this. There's a lot of richness and rewards from what I do. I feel that I have a lot to give. What I give will always come back. Sometimes I think, Who cares about what you're writing? And in my journal I write, "*I* care, so I'm going to keep on writing."

𝒲omen let themselves be so bamboozled by these completely denigrating views of chronological time and what it means. It's our fault; we should not allow that. We should insist that people respect and enjoy us for the receptacles of knowledge . . . that we are. Just for the sheer amount of time we've spent on the planet.

— RACHEL ROSENTHAL

Rachel Rosenthal

She has been called the Great Mother of Performance and the Mother of Unconvention. Both are accurate. Rachel Rosenthal, an interdisciplinary solo performance artist and animal rights activist, is the only sixty-nine-year-old woman I know (or ever heard of) who sports a shaved head and wears a gold hoop pierced through her eyebrow. In person Rachel is authoritative and compelling—her mouth, sensuous; her eyes, mesmerizing; her soft, calm voice, reminiscent of her French upbringing; her body, burly, as befits any Great Mother, yet displaying the grace of the dancer and actress she is. She does not bear the conventional beauty of a film actress, but resembles an ageless Nefertiti.

Born in Paris to Russian immigrant parents, Rachel began performing at the age of three for her parents and their artistically prominent friends. When the Nazis invaded France in 1939, the Rosenthals fled to New York. Rachel attended the High School of Music and Art in Manhattan and later studied art with Hans Hoffmann, dance with Merce Cunningham, and theater in Paris with Jean-Louis Barrault, the great French stage and mime actor. In 1955 she moved to Los Angeles, where she met and married the actor King Moody. After twenty years of marriage, the feminist movement "rescued" her and she devoted herself full-time to her art.

Her art became more than a personal expression: for the past twenty years Rachel has worked with passionate concern for the environment and animal rights. Her multimedia performance pieces range from storytelling to autobiography to polemical harangue. They utilize sound, image, music, movement, and spoken word to conjure ferocious metaphors about the state of the biosphere and its inhabitants. Talk about building a bridge to the twenty-first century: Rachel Rosenthal is a national living treasure and a force of nature all rolled into one.

Articulate and informed, she spoke with an earnest intensity about issues that most concern her: the fate of the arts, our reckless depletion of the earth's resources, and our utter lack of care and respect for animals. She studies everything: history, biology, physics, myth, ecology, literature, chaos theory, feminism, geography, anthropology, philosophy, and aesthetics. These subjects are reflected in the titles of her pieces: *Gaia; Mon Amour; Taboo Subjects; Grand Canyon; Rachel's Brain; Amazonia; Pangaean Dreams; filename: FUTURFAX; Timepiece.* Since 1975 Rachel has written and performed over thirty-two full-length solo and group pieces.

In addition to performing throughout the United States, Europe, and Australia, she has taught at UCLA, the Art Institute, Parsons School of Design, and NYU, among other institutions. Rachel currently is the director of the Rachel Rosenthal Company in Los Angeles. We met at the converted storefront building that serves as her home, studio, and business office. Her two dogs rested quietly on their own double-size mattress in her office while we talked. At sixty-nine Rachel possesses a dedication and drive that put others half her age to shame. In many of her performance pieces she confronts the taboo subject of aging. On her sixtieth birthday she used a tube of lipstick to write "60" on her bald head, and she flirts with the question of androgyny and how Western culture tries to push older women into sexlessness. But true passion is not necessarily sexual, and the passion of Rachel Rosenthal is inextricably woven into her art.

An Unconventional Woman

I was born in Paris in 1926. I was thinking recently about the fact that I've lived almost seven decades of the twentieth century. I left France when I was thirteen. My sense of place, of belonging to a specific place or a specific group, is so skewed because my parents and I were Russian Jews. Both my parents emigrated from Russia: my father when he was fourteen in 1888 and my mother, who was twenty years younger, in 1918. But both of them were nineteenth-century people. She arrived from Russia as a result of the Russian revolution, and he came simply because he wanted to make his fortune, like the story of the penniless kid who is a multimillionaire by the time he is twenty-five.

My father was adopted by France and was very patriotic, very French. They were both what were called in those days "assimilated Jews." I didn't even know I was a Jew; there was nothing Jewish in my upbringing, nothing Jewish about any of the festivities and celebrations. My first language was French, and then, when I was three, I was upset because they were saying secrets in Russian, so I asked to learn Russian with a Moscovite, a woman with a beautiful accent, so I still have my gorgeous Russian accent. Then my next language was English; I learned when I was six because I had a British governess.

I wasn't really a French person, although I was born there and my schooling was French. We were still Russian Jews. My mother was a wonderful singer who sang Russian songs all the time. My parents had Russian friends, although they also had French friends. Then in 1940 we emigrated—actually fled—from France and went first to Brazil, where I learned to speak Portuguese. Shortly thereafter we moved to New York. I was thoroughly confused as to what my identity was. But having gone through all of that, I have a very strong panoramic view of the century. It's good to transcend nationalism when you're young.

My father was a wholesaler and importer of precious gems and stones and Oriental pearls before the war. Then, when he came to America, he went into cultured pearls. I was always supposed to be an artist, encouraged to be an artist, and I've loved art since I was three. We had a beautiful collection of art objects and paintings. The house itself was decorated by Jean Dunand, a very famous decorator who worked in lacquer. My father adored art. He was a self-made man; he was a self-*educated* man who would surround himself with art historians, art critics, artists, and big-name musicians, like Yehudi Menuhin, Horowitz, and Heifetz, who would come and play for my parents' parties.

I was going to be a painter. But even though I was talented, I didn't have the temperament for being a studio painter: the ability to work alone all day long. Very early on in my childhood it was obvious that I was a performer, but my father had very old-fashioned ideas. Being from the nineteenth century, he thought that women in the theater were whores. He was so important to me that of course I would defer to his opinions. He definitely was my hero in every way. Because of his influence, I didn't develop myself as a performer or as a theater person until after the Second World War, when I went back to Paris.

I couldn't stay in Paris longer than a year at a time because I'd been naturalized and the law was that you couldn't go back to your country of origin for more than a year at a time or you would lose your naturalization. For eight years I spent a year there, two years here, etc., uprooting myself repeatedly. I was a displaced person everywhere because I didn't belong here, I didn't belong there. I moved here to Los Angeles in 1955.

I always saw myself as a citizen of the world, but I didn't develop a sense of *home* until very recently, actually, here in L.A. It's only in the last few years that I have felt this is my home. For a long time I felt that L.A. was just a place where I alighted, a sort of headquarters from which to radiate in the world, even though I owned property.

Probably habit has given me the feeling of home. Forty years is a long time. I have seen the permutations of this town, have experienced them, and been here longer than I was in any other place. In spite of that, it's still kind of light-headed. The atmospheric pressure on my life in Los Angeles is still lighter than the atmospheric pressure of my childhood in Paris, which was very strong and remained so all my life. I am still so European, which always amazes me because I have no true contacts or real attachments in Europe, or any sense of wanting to live there, but the European in me is very strong in spite of all my ideological changes.

In Paris I read the work of Antonin Artaud and was totally zapped by it. At first I thought I would be a director, but it became very clear that I had talent as a performer. So eventually when I came to Los Angeles I formed a theater company where I could be both! All the influences I had picked up over the last few years in Paris and New York melded into this form that I was teaching and developing. I called the group Instant Theatre. It was totally improvised theater that was unique and imaginative in the way we approached things and the philosophy behind it. I did that from 1956 to 1966.

The company had a three-year commercial run in a theater on Melrose Avenue after years of playing in storefronts, dance studios, and in my home. We had performances for adults every weekend and matinees for children. We did something like eighty-eight different fairy tales from all over the world. It was a wonderful success, but my knees were deteriorating because I had degenerative arthritis, so I stopped. At the beginning of the 1970s, I became very involved with the women's art movement and feminism. I was one of the women who was active in creating new feminist galleries, cooperatives, and collectives.

In 1975 my mother died, exactly twenty years after my father, and my knees flared up again—I could hardly walk. The owners of a gallery in the San Fernando Valley, the Orlando Gallery, had seen Instant Theatre and now wanted me to do a performance in their gallery. It wasn't the real *beginning* of performance art—a lot had happened in the 1960s and early 1970s—but galleries were getting more interested in showing performers. That was my first actual performance piece that I had done as a soloist because up until then I'd improvised pieces in collaboration with others.

The piece was called *Replays,* and I decided to do it about my knees because they were in such bad shape. After the play, the swelling in my knees went down, which was really interesting. It was a very ironic and funny piece, very much like the kind of work that was done at the time. We would do pieces one time only, so there was a real quality of magic ceremony to the performances. They were very transformational, both for the performer and for the audience.

I wouldn't try to define performance art today because it's changed so much. In the 1960s and 1970s, it was very personal and often dealt with the body or at least with autobiography. It was a work that was developed in time and space as opposed to just space. Also, the time element was often nontheatrical—a performance could be ten seconds or it could be a year. It was usually documented and almost entirely controlled by the artist. But the one thing that was constant was that it was not marketable because it was a one-time-only, ephemeral event. That came about as a reaction to the commercialization of the art world; it was a political statement. But that changed when it became obvious that this expenditure of money, effort, time, and energy to be done only once and seen by only a few friends just didn't work. So people started to create works that could be repeated. As soon as you do that, you go into theater.

Today, all the political flak in government concerning art has completely changed everything because the venues are the ones getting the money, not the artists. Therefore the artists are completely at the mercy of what the venues want to show. If artists want to show their work, they have to create pieces that may be presented, so they don't have the freedom, spontaneity, and imagination that they had in the past when artists listened to their own creativity. Now if you want to make your mark or get a fee or even be *seen,* you have to do things that the presenters will show, and the venues are very timid. They want to be surefire because putting performances on costs a lot of money. They want the work to be entertaining, and it can't offend *anybody.* So the work has become very thin.

Where do I see performance art going? There is an increased coopting of art by the fashion industry, and there's such a seemingly endless appetite for novelty. Audiences so badly want to be shocked. So it's very hard for artists these days to remain clear as to what they're doing and why and how to present it and how to stay afloat and keep food in the fridge. So I don't know exactly where it's going.

I shaved my head in 1981 as part of a performance. It was like a ritual. Then I found I liked it. I liked the fact that it sent mixed messages and confused people. I liked the fact that it was a statement against the rigidities of gender, the fact that it recalls World War II, the fact that it recalls illness and also concepts of beauty from the ancient Egyptians and some African nations who shave their heads for beauty's sake. The statement was really based on cultural differences. In your culture you may think it's horrendous; in the other culture, it's considered beautiful. I liked the fact there were all these mixed messages and that people would get kind of taken aback and maybe question their mind-sets.

It also helped me in my work because very often the actions that I took during my performances would be facilitated by having no hair, like putting objects on my head, painting my head, pouring things on my head. I did a piece called *Rachel's Brain,* where I talked about the human brain and the mind. It was good having my head exposed. When I turned sixty I did a piece called *L-O-W in Gaia,* in which I took a lipstick and wrote "60" on my head and then, later on, after a very dramatic section, I had a big candle on stage lit for most of the performance, so by the end it had a lot of hot wax and I poured the hot wax on my head as part of an outcry about cruelty to animals. So my shaved head has become a sort of signature look. If I grew hair now, nobody would know who I am!

When I don't wear my finery and my makeup, people call me "sir." Then they notice I have big boobs and they get flustered. One day I was walking my dogs in the park and a man—I could have been his mother—was cleaning the park and he called me "son." I was really flattered.

I've taken it a step further with the body piercing. In 1981, the same year I shaved my hair, I did a piece called *Taboo Subjects.* It had three women doing three monologues. Mine was called "Performance in the Masochist Tradition." The whole piece was about piercing—this was long before piercing came in vogue. In this piece I talked about masochism and its relationship to performance art. As an illustration, I had two hooks that I asked the audience to insert into my wrists. I did the performance many times, but only once did two men out of the audience come forward and actually put the hooks in my wrists.

The whole point was that the audience is in the role of sadist and the performer is in the role of masochist. When people didn't come out of the audience, I had an assistant do it, so I always had the hooks in my hands and they were attached to fish lines. Then I would ask the audience to pull the fish line. They wouldn't do that, either. I said, "The masochists say that sadists always stop first; they always give up before the masochist does." It was interesting.

When you pierce the skin, you feel it, but I'm pretty tough to pain. It looks worse than it feels, believe me. Pain is in the brain. If your brain wants to hurt, you hurt, and when the brain doesn't want to hurt, you don't hurt. I feel that the body-mind connection is the wave of the future. I mean, it's already started. I saw the development from the beginning: when Western medicine considered the body-mind connection totally ludicrous and now is completely involved in studying it.

To come to the real point, I have never "felt" my age. Not because my body is so young, it's not. It's deteriorated and I have problems with my hearing and my sight; I have arthritis and the whole schmear, but that doesn't count. What counts is that I have not felt the passage of years because I have always lived in the present. So my take on time has been constant and very detached from a sense of motion. It's only when I turned sixty that suddenly I realized it was the big six-oh. For some reason it hit me. Up to that point, I had not gone through any of the usual so-called passages when you reach thirty, forty, or fifty and you're supposed to feel, "Oh, my God, I'm turning . . ." whatever. I was constantly involved in projects and art, in doing and performing.

The other thing that also helped, in a weird way, was that my knees were so bad, I've lived in pain since my mid-thirties, so it wasn't as if suddenly I developed old-age pains, because I had been in pain all this time. Also I've been very emotionally immature all my life: sweet sixteen, never beyond that, so I always felt like a kid. To this day, I look at people who I know are younger than I am and I'm thinking, Oh, that old fart, because I feel as though I'm still in my thirties. It just never quite hit me, except that people behave differently toward me when they see that I'm an older person. I've been asked questions from the point of view of aging, and it makes no sense to me, frankly, because inside I don't feel that I'm in any way different from before. The limitations are superficial.

Another aspect of aging is that I feel so much happier now than I ever did, because I spent so many decades in conflict with myself, having feelings of guilt and angst and regret and misery and self-deprecation and dumping on myself all the time. It's only in the last few years—I don't know exactly when it happened—that this has been lifted from me. Suddenly one day I realized, It's gone. When did that happen? It was kind of a strange discovery.

I've always felt funny about the past; I've never liked the past. It's strange that

I use so much autobiography in my work because it was really painful, even things that are not inherently painful or unpleasant. The fact that they were in the past made them difficult for me to contemplate. I love the present. I don't look at the future. I have been forced to in the last few years because of grants that want you to have five-year plans and all this bullshit. It's not in my nature at all to do that. What's in my nature is to do what I want to do *now*. I'm very spontaneous. I have no continuity whatsoever by nature. I've been forced to have continuity.

So I don't even know what it is to feel my age, what that means, or how other people are experiencing this, you see. To me, time stands still. I'm in the middle of this raging river, but I'm in my little boat and I just move along. I just try to stay afloat and do what I need to do day by day because there's so much to do. It seems to get worse with every decade.

It's because technology has taken over and gone way, way ahead of what biology can do. We're organic beings; we're not machines, but we're asked to compete with our machines and we can't. So it's getting harder and harder to stay abreast of what's happening.

I try to live what I teach, and that's a big practice. I'm very, very involved with animal rights, which I consider a basic and all-important issue in our civilization. This is not addressed one-thousandth of what it should be addressed. Very few people are actually aware of the ramifications of our treating animals the way we do. In everything. Why do we eat them? Why do we breed them by the billions and have them live lives that are so abominable, lives of constant suffering, until we take them to be killed in the most horrendous fashion? In this country, it's very bad, but in third world countries, it's just atrocious, an abomination. In this country, we raise and kill eight billion animals a year. In the 1960s it was only two billion. The meat industry has grown to such an extent—meat used to be an occasional treat.

This raising and killing of sentient beings in *total* confinement, and in circumstances that induce disease and madness, goes completely against their biological nature. It's like having torture chambers on a vast scale all over the nation all the time. People just don't realize that the food industry is so insidious. It has become so sophisticated and such a fashionable thing. Going into restaurants: the meals are lovely and beautifully presented, and they have excellent writers who have developed a style of describing food in such a way that your mouth waters. They make you want to run out and go to that restaurant. So the demand has, again, been artificially increased. People are clueless and don't *want* to know what suffering they're causing and what horror this industry brings.

We eat violently, we ingest madness and sickness, and we wonder why we're sick. You are what you eat—let's face it. It's not just because there's *e coli.* or some other virus. It's not just cholesterol. It's because we're eating flesh of animals that have been rendered mad. It's not just mad cows; it's mad *everything*. That's the biggest complaint that I have, because many people are concerned about animals in laboratories, which is, God knows, bad enough, but in terms of numbers, they don't come near the billions that we eat. Those people fret about lab animals, yet they eat other animals. Everybody has pets, a dog or a cat they lavish attention on. What's the difference: you love this dog, why don't you love this calf? Someone has a parrot that cost them $4,000; what about all these chickens? So there's a lot that's so painful and so discouraging because whenever you see a little bit of progress, there's still so much regression and callousness. As I said, the numbers are astronomical and rising. It's awful. At least in this country, there are ways of reaching government officials.

I write letters all the time. I send a lot of money, all that I can spare, to organizations that do my dirty work for me, basically. I try to do rescue-and-placement in the pet industry—that's another story, not a good one, either. I'm a resource for people when they have problems with animals; they usually call me and I direct them where to go, what to do, and so on. I go to demonstrations, and I always talk about this subject in all my lectures. People hire me to talk about art, then they're lectured about animals and ecology! The state of the earth is as bad as the state of other species. It all comes from the fact that we, as humans, are so full of shit; so full of hubris and arrogance and conquest and domination and competition. We enslave everything for our own benefit. Gandhi said, "The greatness of a nation and its moral progress can be judged by the way its animals are treated."

This is the big problem: we don't recognize the importance of others. It's a real problem, but I think there's a little bit of light at the end of the tunnel. Some people are beginning to get a clue. Now with the DNA and genetic research, people are being told we have almost the same genetic makeup as apes and that there's just a difference of one gene between us and chimpanzees. Still, it hasn't helped the fact that chimpanzees are abused in labs. Unfortunately, people can rationalize almost anything if they think it's in their interest.

The media is forcing us into an economy that is killing the earth by making us buy things that we really don't desire or need. At some point, we have to gain enough wisdom to say, "Enough; I'm not interested; this is not affecting me. This is not what I'm about." Then it will die of itself. Unfortunately, it's got its grip on us and has addicted us to so many things: tobacco, fashion, sex, shopping till you drop. This is obscene when you know that we are depleting resources at a rate that the earth can't put back.

When I thought about the end of my life, I used to see myself dying at eighty-six. I did a performance piece in which I am supposedly eighty-six and I die during the piece; it takes place in 2012, and the piece is about life and the world in 2012. During the performance, I get a fax from the future (from the people who live in 2092, because I created the piece in 1992). It's also about the end of our species in 2092. The whole piece is played very funny, but it's horrendous. It talks about a world that you and I wouldn't want to live in.

I'm torn between not wanting to live in the kind of world I see it developing into and also seeing every so often a little glimmer of consciousness that might bring about true change. I'm so curious that I want to know what happens next. I see that people are living longer and longer lives, and if I can keep all my marbles and remain independent and healthy, I wouldn't mind living longer just to see what happens. I know that any time I'll be dying, I will feel, Oh, now it's really interesting. I want to know what happens next. It's like reading this great mystery story and then finding that the pages are missing at the end. That's totally frustrating. That's the one thing that bothers me about dying. Otherwise I think dying is swell; it's a lovely thing to do.

I don't have fears for my personal future. In terms of financial security as I get older, I have money squirreled away—not a great deal, but some—and I know that I can live very, very simply. If I ever reach the point where I need to retire and stop what I'm doing—which doesn't seem likely for a while—I think I would go someplace where the living is inexpensive. I would hope that my eyes hold out so I can read a lot of books, and I would probably go back to painting, to the visual arts. If I don't have my eyes, I've already decided I would work on sound pieces. I would keep doing what I'm doing, only do it differently. I don't worry; I'm not a worry bird at all.

I think androgyny is a state that society pushes us women into as we grow older. Women are not supposed to be sexual after a certain point, and certainly older people are not supposed to be sexual at all—women or men. This is a cultural thing, a societal thing. I haven't stopped having sexual feelings just because I'm older. Not at all. I'm celibate out of choice, but not because I've stopped having sexual feelings. You don't. Your body is still just as interested and just as responsive, possibly more so and probably more savvy as you grow older.

The androgyny comes from the fact that what we associate with beauty and sexuality is youthfulness, smooth skin. As an older woman you're no longer an object of sexual attraction, yet I know and I've heard of women in their eighties and nineties having passionate affairs or getting married. We just get pushed into being put on a shelf: "Oh, you're no longer part of the game." That's too bad, because some women are totally interested. I'm not interested, but a lot of women are. I wish I were a lesbian because I think women are so much more interesting than men at this age. But unfortunately I'm very hetero, and I just decided I'm not talented at relationships and I don't like doing things unless I do them well. So for me it was just better to quit than to kind of bumble through. I'm very happy being on my own—it's such a relief.

My work is very important to me, and success means the ability to continue with my work. That means I have to get bookings, I have to get good reviews, I have to get good interviews in journals, I have to be recognized. I'm always trying to find angels who will underwrite my company or trying to get grants or doing fund-raisers. There's always the business aspect that I loathe, and I'm not so good at it to begin with. But I have to do it; this is part of it.

The *true* success for me is when I feel that I'm communicating my ideology, because I'm really a proselytizer. I need to have everybody believe what I believe, so that's what my work is about. I do it through teaching and through my performances and lectures, so when people come to me and say, "Oh, that piece that you did ten years ago changed my life" or "After that workshop we did five years ago, I went on to a career"—that's success for me.

I live in L.A., the heart of youth obsession, but I've never touched my face—except for piercing, but I consider that "putting on jewelry." I've never had any cosmetic surgery. I'm too fat. I'm bald. I'm certainly not a model. My advice to other women would be for them to strike that word from their vocabulary: aging. The word "aging" has connotations that are so negative, they drag you down, they are meaningless in our experience of ourselves. They simply help other people relate to us, but why should we make it easy for them? It doesn't mean anything; it just means that you're closer to dying, and everybody knows that. We're all going to die at some point or another.

It doesn't change anything about how we see the world, how we behave in the world. Our creativity only gets better. We get more knowledge. We get a bird's-eye view of the world and of the century and of the big movements of civilization. We should be getting wiser. People should be coming to us for that wisdom, and we should insist that they do.

Women let themselves be so bamboozled by these completely denigrating views of chronological time and what it means. It's our fault; we should not allow that. We should insist that people respect and enjoy us for the receptacles of knowledge and experience that we are. Just for the sheer amount of time we've spent on the planet.

Instead we allow ourselves to be put away and just forgotten; that's such a waste, such a shame. The only tragedy for me would be if I felt I was losing my marbles. I think that I would very soon kill myself because I wouldn't want to wait until I could no longer do it. But if you have your marbles and you know what you're doing, if you have your memory and can still function creatively—my goodness, it's terrific. Just sticking around long enough to see the parade—the earth is so extraordinary and so pathetic, you know. All the things that are being discovered every day in all the sciences.

I realize that the hardest thing for us would be to get to the point where we are no longer the slaves of our egos, the slaves of our hubris, the slaves of positioning ourselves on top of the pyramid and looking down on everything else as inferior, not necessary or important. To learn and to keep learning, because it's so easy to forget, the lesson of interconnectedness and of respect. We have lost the sense of respect; we don't respect anything. For instance, we take for granted things like air, which is the psyche, the spirit, the vital medium in which we are on this particular planet, which was created against all odds and is unlike any other planet in this solar system. I don't understand this lack of respect, because it's like spitting on the food you eat or the air you breathe or the water you drink or the person you love or yourself. It's like having a basic contempt for all the things that mean life and happiness and whatever it is that people want.

To me it's incomprehensible because it goes against logic, and I'm a very logical person. To have contempt for these things is like slow suicide, and that's what we're doing to ourselves—maybe not even so slowly. Those are the issues that really concern me the most.

You know, this idea about age is funny. When I was growing up, telling your age was a mortal sin . . . a real no-no. . . . I never could understand why. To me, if you're fifty, you're fifty; if you're sixty, you're sixty. You can't change that. So I always went the other way: "How do you do? My name's Maureen Stapleton and I'm sixty years old."

— MAUREEN STAPLETON

Maureen Stapleton

This Stapleton is Maureen, *not* Jean, "the broad who slept with Archie Bunker" (as Maureen describes her) in the long-running television program *All in the Family*. To this day, according to Maureen, "People come up to me saying, 'Oh, you're Jean's sister.'" She tells them politely, "No, we're not related."

"Finally," she told me, "I saw Jean a few years ago and said, 'Oh, my God, Jean, all I get is, "Are you Jean Stapleton's sister?" I go into detail in order to explain to them that I'm not.' Jean looked at me with a straight face and said, 'Why don't you just shut up and say, "Yes"?'"

From the time she was a child in Troy, New York, Maureen, who is descended from Irish stock and was raised a Roman Catholic, knew she wanted to be an actress. After school and on weekends she spent every day in the many movie palaces in Troy. "There were lots of theaters then; there aren't so many now," she said a little sadly.

After being a member of the renowned Actors' Studio in New York City for several years, where she made friends with such luminaries as Marlon Brando, Montgomery Clift, Julie Harris, and Elia Kazan, Maureen went on to win two Tony Awards as Best Actress for her Broadway performances in Tennessee Williams's *The Rose Tattoo* (1951) and Neil Simon's *The Gingerbread Lady* (1970). Other Broadway productions include *Playboy of the Western World, Plaza Suite, Antony and Cleopatra, Cat on a Hot Tin Roof, The Cherry Orchard, The Glass Menagerie,* and *Orpheus Descending*.

Maureen was nominated four times for an Academy Award for Best Supporting Actress in films. The first three nominations were for *Lonelyhearts* with Montgomery Clift (1958); *Airport* ("Can you beat it—me in a movie about airplanes?" she joked, making reference to her terror at the mere thought of flying) (1970); and Woody Allen's *Interiors* (1978). Finally, on her fourth nomination, she won the award, for *Reds* (1981). When later that night she was asked backstage by the press if she had expected to win, Maureen answered, "Yes, because I'm old and tired and I lost three times before." In addition to these four screen credits, Maureen created memorable roles in the films *Bye, Bye Birdie, Plaza Suite, Cocoon, The Fugitive Kind, Heartburn, Nuts, Passed Away,* and *The Last Good Time.*

People outside the entertainment industry are eager to fantasize about the lives of celebrities they admire, envisioning them as golden and without misfortune. One need only read an autobiography or biography of an illustrious figure to learn just how "ordinary"—in terms of difficulty and hardship—his or her life really is. A friend of mine who was studying acting more than twenty years ago went to visit a retirement home for aging actors and actresses just outside Los Angeles at that time; the experience immediately altered any desire (or fantasy) he may have had about becoming the great American actor.

After recently spending an autumn afternoon with Maureen Stapleton, I found that two qualities about her stood out for me: her indefatigable sense of humor (often at her own expense) and her vigorous observance of independence. A tumultuous life is recorded in her autobiography, *A Hell of a Life,* written with Jane Scovell. In it the reader is witness to the domestic violence Maureen suffered as a child; her ambiguous relationships with both parents; the struggles of an emerging actress tempered by contact with some of the great names in theater and film; the sorrows of two marriages and eventual divorces; the joys of motherhood; the torment of alcoholism; and the ecstasy that seemed accessible only when Maureen was on a stage or in front of a camera. "It's what I know best."

About the loss of her marriages, Maureen says in her autobiography, "I still attribute my failure as a wife to my inability to *be* a wife. It wasn't my table; I didn't know the rules. The searing memories of my parents' unhappy marriage were baked into my soul." Later she admits, "Bottom line, I loused up two marriages. But I'm the greatest ex-wife a man ever had," she says, offered as a consolation to a predominant disappointment in her life. "Lousing up two marriages were the worst times in my life," she says with regret.

In rich and sometimes hilarious detail, Maureen recounted her phobias about travel. No more travel by plane, ocean liner, train, and, "You can also forget bridges and tunnels." Thank you very much! "And throw in elevators while you're at it," she told me resolutely.

At the age of sixty, she moved to the picturesque New England town of Lenox, Massachusetts, in the Berkshires, in order to be closer to her daughter, Katharine, and her two grandchildren. Ten years later she still hopes that someone will call with an offer of a new role for her to play, watches *Jeopardy* and *Wheel of Fortune* on television, does crossword puzzles, reads poetry at benefits for the Lenox Public Library, sees her grandchildren as often as possible, and tries to heal her bad back, her "busted" arthritic knees since replacement surgery, and an abscessed heel.

Her words were often punctuated by a cough so deep in her lungs and so ominously predictive that it could convince *anyone* to quit smoking. Anyone, that is, except Maureen herself, who started when she was "eleven or twelve" and still chain-smokes. In *A Hell of a Life* she discusses in depth her many destructive years of alcoholism, but about the subject to me she said only, "I haven't had hard liquor in years. Now I only drink beer and wine, but *lots* of it."

Maureen's life in Lenox is supported by "a pension from the Screen Actors Guild, a pension from Actors' Equity, and Social Security." Again, she leaves little room for an outsider's fantasy about "wealthy movie stars." "I don't live high off the hog," she told me, indicating an acceptance of her financial status, "so it's fine. I don't have to worry about money." Her typically working class and "proud of it" demeanor, her tendency in earlier years to be overweight, and her notorious "foul mouth" make her a 1950s precursor of television star Roseanne. One would have to look far and wide to find anyone less pretentious than Maureen Stapleton. When she opened the door for me she was barefoot, wore a knee-length gray cotton T-shirt, and had no makeup on. She has a grandmotherly kindness about her and often called me "dear" or "sweetheart."

Her two-bedroom condominium is crammed with a lifetime of movie mementos: movie posters, photographs, and awards—Academy, Emmy, Tony, Golden Globe. Even the bathroom walls are covered with autographed photos: an Eli Wallach here, a Tyrone Power there. These treasures reveal the thrill and excitement that once must have stirred the little girl from Troy, New York, and propelled her to follow her "destiny" into acting.

Acting remains Maureen's passion still. "I'd like to keep working," she admitted to me. "It's what I know how to do best." Indeed, after more than fifty years as an actress, she still hopes the curtain will rise again.

An Actress's Life

.·.

I would like to work more, but I don't travel well these days. I can't go to California or Florida. I received offers to work in Minnesota, Texas, Mexico, Florida. I can make New York and Toronto, but I can't do those long trips anymore. Travel scares the pants off me. My anxieties seem to be getting worse as I get older. My phobias—acrophobia (fear of heights), agoraphobia (fear of open spaces), claustrophobia (fear of closed spaces)—are part of the cause for my fear of travel.

Flying is certainly out! I have never forgiven the Wright Brothers. I've flown one and a half times. I was nineteen or twenty the first time I went up with a guy I was dating who piloted his own plane—a two-seater Piper Cub. It was in Rahway, New Jersey, that he took me and my two girlfriends one at a time for a so-called spin. I didn't even know I had this fear of flying until we left the ground. I went ape! I immediately began to hyperventilate and almost went into convulsions. Fortunately, he got me back down on the ground pronto.

As if that experience weren't enough, when I was in my mid-twenties and married to my first husband, Max Allentuck, and on tour for *The Rose Tattoo*, he convinced me to fly from California to New York. It was even more excruciating because it was *not* a direct flight. We flew from Los Angeles to Dallas, from

Dallas to Washington, D.C., and finally on to New York. I'll tell you, I was a wreck! Flying? You can have it. I can't even stand to watch shots taken from an airplane on television. You can also forget bridges and tunnels, and throw in elevators while you're at it. Years back, I could ride in elevators—can't do that anymore. I want to be *on* the earth, not above or below it.

Troy, New York, was where I was born and grew up. It's about an hour's drive from Lenox, maybe fifteen minutes from Albany. It was during the Depression, and no one was what you would call well off. There were five or six movie theaters. I just went to the movies all the time. I mean, *all* the time. Going to movies was my favorite thing to do. I think I was five years old when the dream of acting first took hold of me. By the time I was twelve, I definitely knew I would be an actress. It was like my destiny to act in movies.

In those days, you could get into a movie for five cents if you were under twelve; it cost a dime after twelve. I discovered that I could get a whole nickel back on a big empty bottle of ginger ale or club soda. I knew almost every back alley in South Troy, 'cause I'd go through the huge garbage cans, looking for those bottles that would pay my way to that day's movie.

Films became my obsession. To me, there was no such thing as a bad movie. I loved everything about them—the actors and actresses, the costumes, the fantasy, everything. I guess movies helped people a lot during the Depression because you could watch someone else's troubles and forget your own. You know, there was nothing "artistic" about it for me; it was just that all the women were beautiful and all the men were handsome. It was like a dreamworld.

Probably my favorite actresses were Greta Garbo (I swear I saw *Camille* twelve times—no! more), Myrna Loy (who was a heavenly woman, the nicest creature; years later I acted in my first film with Myrna Loy), Barbara Stanwyck, Jean Arthur, Jean Harlow, and a whole bunch of other dames. In fact, it was watching Jean Harlow in *Red Dust* in 1932 that clinched my idea to go into movies. She was somethin', that broad. But, let's face it, as much as I loved the women, I absolutely *adored* the men. Robert Taylor and Clark Gable. To this day I dream about Clark Gable. I've probably seen *Gone With the Wind* thirty times. That's either passion or craziness.

At the age of seventeen I headed by bus from Troy to New York City. Everything you read in the books about acting said: If you want to be in movies, you should go to New York, not Hollywood. So, like everybody, I went to school. I started out at the New School for Social Research, where in night classes I studied with Herbert Berghof, who was one of the pioneers in the teaching of acting. Originally from Austria, he staged the first American production of *Waiting for Godot.*

Soon, however, Herbert opened his own drama school, and that's where I met Mira Rostova, who was a wonderful teacher. She was Russian and had acted on the stage in Germany. Mira always reminded me of Edith Piaf: so tiny and almost sorrowful. She became Monty Clift's mentor.

For the first five or six years in Manhattan, I worked at odd jobs and shared an apartment with various girlfriends like Janice Mars (another actress) on West Fifty-second Street. Our place became a pit stop for, it seemed at the time, every struggling young actor in the city. I hung out with my chums: Wally Cox and Johnny Fiedler and a guy nicknamed "Bud," who was Marlon Brando (to drop a name). You knew Marlon was going to be big; you could tell just by looking at him.

Then it was on to the Actors' Studio, which was originally started by Elia Kazan, Bobby Lewis, and Cheryl Crawford, not by Lee Strasberg, as most people think. Although I felt I should have been in the beginners' class with Elia, I was put in the more advanced group. Some of my classmates were Marlon, Monty, Sidney Lumet, Karl Malden, E. G. Marshall, Pat Neal, Eli Wallach, and Annie Jackson. I was in very good company.

Some of my first plays were *Playboy of the Western World, The Barretts of Wimpole Street, Birdcage* with Melvyn Douglas, and *Antony and Cleopatra.* (God, no! I didn't play Cleopatra. Katharine Cornell was Cleopatra. I was Iras, one of the two handmaidens to the Queen of the Nile.)

Playing Serafina in Tennessee Williams's *The Rose Tattoo* in 1951 was my big break. I was still so young, only twenty-five. His earlier plays—*The Glass Menagerie, A Streetcar Named Desire,* and *Summer and Smoke*—had already been staged, and to great acclaim. Although Tenn had written the part of Serafina, the betrayed widow, for the Italian actress Anna Magnani, she declined, because she was afraid her English wasn't good enough for the American stage. I later heard that Tenn wrote about me in a letter to someone in the production: "She's an American Magnani." I still have the photocopy of that letter. We soon became very friendly, and I had great times with him and his companion, Frank Merlo. Tenn was absolutely captivating. *The Rose Tattoo* ran for almost a year on Broadway, and I won a Tony Award for my performance. That role established me as a Broadway actress.

As far as my family life goes, my son, Daniel, was born in 1950 and my daughter, Katharine, in 1954. Max Allentuck was my first husband and the father of my children. We divorced when our kids were about five and ten years old. Max passed away a few months ago, but we had remained very close. In fact, we are a weirdly close-knit extended family in which everybody is friendly with everybody else: ex-wives and current wives, stepchildren and natural children. It worked well for us.

After making so many films, I was asked in 1980 to play Emma Goldman in Warren Beatty's film *Reds*. I remember reading Emma Goldman's autobiography —two volumes long—and thinking to myself, Oh, boy, those people were remarkably humorless. Emma was a fanatic who had no life of her own—just a cause. For example, she asked Jack London to write a preface to a book by one of her beaux—I forget his name. This man had gone to Pittsburgh and stabbed Carnegie and then tried to shoot him. He didn't kill Carnegie, but he went to prison for a number of years for attempted murder.

After he was released he wrote a book on the United States' penal system. Jack London did write a preface, but Emma never spoke to him again because he closed the preface by saying, "Any guy who can't shoot straight can't think straight." Emma did not get a laugh out of it, and she didn't use the preface! The entire two volumes of her life were very heavy-duty; there was no humor about anything. I realized I'd better not do too much research on her, just do what was in the script.

My part for *Reds* was to be shot in London in about six weeks. Now I had to get there. That's another story! I'd already had a scare on the *QE2* in 1976 when

I signed on to play opposite the great Laurence Olivier in a televised version of Tennessee Williams's *Cat on a Hot Tin Roof*, with Natalie Wood and Robert Wagner playing Maggie the Cat and Brick. Even though the production lay across the Atlantic Ocean, nothing could keep me from appearing opposite the greatest actor in the world. The *only* possible mode of transportation acceptable to me, of course, since flying was out of the question, was by boat.

I decided to take my kids, Kathy and Danny, along with me as a special event for them. The trip over seemed to pass without incident. There was a heavenly crew on the production, and it was a great privilege to work with such talented actors. But the return trip was a major nightmare. We were about two days out of Southampton when one morning at around four o'clock we were awakened by fire alarms. I had heard an explosion, and everybody—a thousand passengers—went up to the deck, where we were told there was a "small" fire and we'd have to return to Southampton for repairs. The Cunard line had arranged for air transportation to the States for all the passengers, but at least two hundred of us were D.F.'s (don't flys), so we headed to London to wait out the repair time. I eventually returned home safely.

I had thought my ocean-crossing career was over, but then came Warren's offer to be in *Reds*. Because it was winter and most of the liners weren't making the crossing, they found a Polish freighter that was going to Rotterdam, from where I'd then take the boat train to London. This time I took my son and his new wife, Nina, with me. For the first twenty-four hours everything went fine, but then we stalled in the middle of the ocean for three days and nights! The freighter, called the *Polarski*, took fourteen days to reach Rotterdam. I made a vow that once I got back home, I would never cross those big waves again. I returned on a French freighter on which I was the only passenger; that was nice. Nothing happened. But when I got off, I said, "That's it; no more with the boats. Even if Clark Gable himself invited me." But Diane Keaton is a darling, and Warren is so smart and charming. They made crossing an ocean worth it.

I moved to Lenox when I was sixty to be close to my daughter and two grandchildren. My granddaughter is now twelve. I guess I thought I wouldn't be able to see them much unless I moved to where they lived, so I came here. I always said, "If my kids moved to Calcutta, I'd move to Calcutta." When my grandkids were young, I got them every day, when they were in kindergarten. I could walk a lot then. Now, of course, they go to school and have soccer practice and visit with their friends. But I take 'em when I can get 'em! My son, Danny, still lives in New York City. He and his wife come up to see me regularly. I can't take New York anymore.

Perhaps from fifty to sixty were the best years of my life. That's when I won my Academy Award. I could still get around pretty well. A couple of years ago I needed to have knee replacement surgery due to arthritis, and I've had a lot of trouble with an abscessed heel for the last year. Then my back went out. You know, you get to feel like a busted couch: you reach over to push that in and this pops out! But if the knee ever gets better and the heel gets better, I'm sure seventy to eighty will be nice, too.

You know, this idea about age is funny. When I was growing up, telling your age was a mortal sin, right up there with "Thou shalt not kill." I never knew how old my mother was or my aunts Julie and Jeannette. As far as I know, I could be *eighty-five* because it was a real no-no to even ask my age. I never could understand why. To me, if you're fifty, you're fifty; if you're sixty, you're sixty. You can't change that. So I always went the other way: "How do you do? My name's Maureen Stapleton and I'm sixty years old."

I remember when I was about eleven years old and a friend of my mother's came up to us—my mom hadn't seen her for a long time—and said, "Oh, Maureen, my, what a big girl you are now. How old are you?" I said, "I'm eleven." I still can feel my mother's fingers on my shoulder, digging in *so* deep. Later Mother said, "Don't you *ever* tell anybody how old you are." I thought, Well, I've committed another mortal sin. The funny thing is, now my aunts *do* tell their ages. So how do you figure? And they are both in better shape at eighty-four and eighty-eight than I am. They're incredible. Wow!

The interesting thing about age is that I've *always* played women who were older than me, sometimes *way* older. You see, if you're a character actress, it doesn't matter. I suppose if you're a leading lady, you have to try to preserve your youth. You have to keep being young. But as a character actress, it doesn't matter how old you are.

I've been so fortunate, you know. Wow, when I think of everybody I've worked with and been friends with: Elizabeth Taylor, Eli, Annie, Diane Keaton, Walter and Carol Matthau, Meryl Streep, Colleen Dewhurst, Monty, Tennessee Williams, Barbra Streisand, George C. Scott, Woody Allen, Burt Reynolds, Joanne Woodward. Oh, my Lord. That's the beauty part; that's the best part. And my kids and grandkids. Friends and family—that's the best and most important.

Every day is a present. I don't look forward to death, by any means. I gotta give myself pep talks about trying to stay healthy and keep in good spirits. I'm still eager to work, to act, or do benefit performances for the Lenox Public Library. I think you oughta hang in for as long as you can.

If you don't have a grandmother or a grandfather, then go and adopt one. We cannot understand the cycles of life unless we have old people around us. The wisdom that comes with being an older person is wonderful. We need older people in our lives.

— OH SHINNAH FAST WOLF

Oh Shinnah Fast Wolf

"I drive a red four-by-four Subaru," Oh Shinnah Fast Wolf had told me on the telephone when she offered to pick me up at the airport in Colorado Springs. Within minutes of my arrival, the said red 4×4 Subaru pulled up in front of me and a fair-skinned woman with kind green eyes welcomed me into her life. Beside Oh Shinnah sat her great-granddaughter, Kayonna, a dark-haired three-year-old who entertained herself with doll figures of Esmerelda and Quasimodo.

We drove through the naked plains of Colorado Springs until we entered a suburban sprawl with its endless single-level malls that gave new meaning to the word "barren." Colorado Springs is home to the largest community of right-wing conservatives in America. But why was Oh Shinnah, a model of radicalism, living here?

"This is where my people lived," she answered logically. After nearly an hour, we spiraled up Garden of the Gods Road toward one of the highest points in the Rocky Mountains, Pikes Peak. Tucked into the crease of the terra-cotta-colored earth is an artists' colony named Manitou Springs. It was like coming home; I could breathe again.

"My home is like a museum," Oh Shinnah forewarned me as we entered the cool, dark, two-story house. Indeed, photos of the rock stars Janis Joplin and Jimi Hendrix, and others—mementos of her years as a folksinger—share equal wall space with images of Native Americans, woven rugs, hanging plants, and books.

Oh Shinnah is the matriarch of four generations, many of whom live under one roof—hers. She assured me that the family dynamics are always changing. Currently the household is composed of Oh Shinnah; her daughter, Heather; her granddaughter, Calico; her grandson, Sky Bear; his wife, Sabra; and her great-granddaughter, Kayonna. It's a full house in every sense of the word. Her living arrangement follows her own advice that "people on this planet need older people in their lives."

Her life has been patterned after Cochkolta, a woman warrior who rode with Geronimo. "This was not his real name," Oh Shinnah says with urgency, as if wanting to finally set *that* record straight. "His real name translated to He Who Sits and Waits. This is not information that came from the archives of the Smithsonian or the military accounts; this came through the voices of the people." Her family dedicated her life "before I was born" to becoming a woman warrior. Oh Shinnah's name translates as the heartbeat or song of the Earth. She takes her name seriously and accepts her indigenous responsibility to "sing on behalf of our Mother."

Oh Shinnah refers to herself as "a renegade," because she inherits traditions from her father's people, the Apache, and from her mother's, the Mohawks and the Scots. "I'm an eclectic," she says provocatively to some Indians who challenge her status because she is not a full-blood. But she feels that the white man's blood she carries in her veins keeps her from being prejudiced. She has received a great deal of academic training and holds a bachelor's degree in music theory and an M.A. in voice from the University of Denver, as well as a master's of science and an honorary Ph.D. in experimental psychology from the University of Chicago, where she worked with Dr. Karl Menninger. As a folksinger, Oh Shinnah performed in top folk-music clubs around the country and helped develop improvisational theater techniques at Second City in Chicago and the Committee Theater in San Francisco. She also enjoyed playing a part in the movie *The Trial of Billy Jack*. "I was the one who started the riot," she says conspiratorially.

Among the many contributions Oh Shinnah has made in her life is the co-creation (with her friend and adopted sister, Dolores Krieger, author of *Therapeutic Touch*) of an organization called the Center for Grandfather Coyote.

"Our Native elders are a national treasure," explains Oh Shinnah. "With them end ancient traditions." The center operates two programs to assist elders on reservations: Support an Elder and Adopt an Elder. Through these programs individuals are assured that their food, clothing, shelter, and medical needs are met and that they receive some human companionship from someone who cares about them.

Oh Shinnah's ability to cut through the trivial right to the heart of a matter earned her the nickname "Laser Lips" from Al Gore—before he was the vice-president. After a meeting in Northern California in the 1980s to prevent off-shore oil drilling, at which Oh Sinnah was especially vociferous, Gore walked up to her and said, "You're some kind of lady." She said, "Well, thank you very much. Is that a compliment?" "Yeah," he replied, "you've got laser lips. You cut through everything and get right to the point. You sound like a very religious, spiritual person. What church do you go to?" She looked at him and, proving his point, said, "I beg your pardon. The dome of my cathedral is the everlasting sky. And where my feet are standing is the center of the world."

Her life experience is far removed from the monastic image many might hold of a spiritual teacher. Oh Shinnah feels that it is imperative to "live what I teach." No one could accuse her of retreating from the world. She is a curious blend of spiritual insight, political advocacy, everyday aphorisms, and personal disclosures too dramatic for a soap opera script. She has spent time in a mental hospital due to "compulsive suicide attempts," had near-death experiences, survived six marriages ("If somebody walked into my life and there was a real love between us, I'd do it again," she confided). She has given birth to three daughters and buried one. She calls her life "messy," but it is also utterly human. Oh Shinnah is the first to admit it is our struggles that bring us closer to enlightenment.

Like her "people before her," she is an enchanting storyteller—full of narrative images, anecdotes, and allegories. About her ability to read people's minds she said, "Apaches don't look into a person's eyes very much; we're like wolves. We look in the eyes and then drop our eyes to the mouth in conversation, then come back up. There is a way we know we can go inside a person and read their interior, so we avert our eyes, because that's an invasion of privacy, unless we are invited to do so. The wolves are the same way." Oh Shinnah and I welcomed each other into our interior.

At her invitation, I stayed for the night, and until well past two in the morning, we talked about her formative childhood experiences and the wrenching ordeal of her daughter Fawn's untimely death at the age of thirty-seven from a brain aneurysm and how the entire family and community helped to honor her death in traditional Native ways. Earlier that evening, Oh Shinnah's great-granddaughter, Kayonna, had smudged everyone in the house with a red-tailed hawk feather and sage. As her proud great-grandmother watched over and coached her, it was clear that a new woman warrior was in training.

The Woman Warrior

❖

My comprehension of the world is quite different from most traditional people's because I'm not really a traditionalist—even though I practice a lot of very strong traditions that I learned from my father and my great-grandmother, who was a Mohawk and also a Balinese temple dancer. She spent twelve years in Bali learning to dance the sutras or prayers. The meditation of the day was in the dance, so when the nuns and the priests would come in for a meditation, the dancers would come out and give them what the meditation was to be for the day. I'm also a fourth-generation Theosophist, and that makes a difference.

So I have a crazy family here; there are four generations living together now, right here in my house. We have a very profound bond. I mean, we have our problems, we scream and holler at each other; but although Kayonna, my great-granddaughter, is not with her mother, she's okay because she knows she has family. That's a big part of what the Western world doesn't understand, what family *really* is. Family is not Mom, Dad, and apple pie; it's Mom, Dad, and uncle, cousin, grandmother, great-grandmother.

My people, who are called the Apache, were the most nomadic people in this country. Every tribe had a certain duty to perform, for the earth itself, as caretakers. The Hopi people are Keepers of the Peace. The Shoshone people are Keepers of the Medicine. The Iroquois Six Nations are Keepers of Unity. Apache people are Keepers of the Four Directions. Number four is the most sacred number. We were everywhere. They found a contingent of Apache people in Honduras. To the south they were in Palenque, Chiapas, in Mexico, which the Hopi people called the Ancient Red City, which is where *they* went for initiations into the higher arts. It was a place of alchemy and metaphysics.

I once spoke at a conference at the University of Alabama for the anthropology and archaeology departments; it was titled "If You Want to Know Where We Come from, Just Ask Us." Archaeologists don't know what they're talking about; you will not talk to any Indian people on this Turtle Island of the Americas (which is down to the isthmus of South America and all the way up to the Bering Straits) who say they were created anywhere else but here. We didn't come across from Mongolia. We *went* over there, didn't like it, and came back. Now they've found archaeological digs in the Americas that predate anything they have found in Mongolia, so that's why I say, "If you want to know where we come from, just ask us." Many people think that all people came from Africa, but I don't believe it. I think cultures were developing simultaneously all over the world.

I used to be one of Martin Luther King's organizers for the marches in Chicago. I was the reason we all went to jail in 1962. The issue was the rents in the black ghettos and the fact that paint was peeling off the walls and babies were dying of lead poisoning. So we did a march. He was my kind of pacifist. (I was reading Gandhi when I was eleven.) Martin Luther King was not a man who lay down and let somebody walk over him, either. He wouldn't raise his hands toward anybody, but he wouldn't let them walk over him. He was a warrior, and the warrior will do whatever is necessary for the good of the whole regardless of the emotional response to that event. That's what I am to my people, a woman who is a warrior woman.

The police weren't allowing us access to the courthouse. I was standing on the top of the steps with Jesse Jackson and Medgar Evers. A policeman said to us,

"You can't come in here," and I said, "This is a public building; I pay *your* rent, so don't tell me I can't come in here." And he said, "Well, you're not comin' in here," and I said, "Well, watch my smoke," and he knocked me down. When he knocked me down, a riot ensued.

It's unfortunate that five people were killed. They arrested so many of us, they couldn't put us in jail, so they stuck us in a warehouse. We yelled out to the police, "Hey, we're bored, we want to sing." A policeman went and got us a guitar and, instead of standing guard outside, came inside to sing with us. I don't think people really understand what pacifism is; it's not surrender.

I have studied languages and music and psychology. At the University of Chicago I did my master's thesis, which I entitled "The Invalidity of the Current Psychological Testing System When Applied to Indigenous People, Re: Language," and I used the Beck system of psychological evaluations. (This was a big mistake because he was my senior adviser. If I'd known that before the fact, I would have chosen another subject. God, he was really hard on me.)

I entered the university when I was fourteen. I had been educated by the Ursuline Sisters at the Loretto Academy in Santa Fe. These sisters recognized what Sister Mary Cecilia used to tell me, that I had an advanced intelligence. The nuns recognized this intelligence and a deep hunger for knowledge inside me. She told me I was an old soul and that she would help me to remember. You don't meet many Catholics who talk like that. But I have a T-shirt that says "Recovering Catholic."

Sister Mary Cecilia, my music teacher, recognized that all my mathematics translated into music, so she started teaching me language. Silence is a universal language. That's why so many Indian people pray in silence. The word "surrender" in English means to give up, and that's how we got to the subject of my thesis. In my language the word means to give over, and you can only "give over" to that which is above, because if you give over to anything that walks equal, you become a shadow. I tell my students, "If you follow in the footsteps of the guru, you become their shadow."

My father speaks fourteen foreign and nine Indian languages, so language was easy for me. The nuns taught me Greek and Latin. Spanish was my second language; Apache was my first. English was my third. I think and dream in Apache. The school was mostly for Navajo girls, but there were five Apache girls. The Apache and the Navajo are cousins, but we don't agree on certain aspects, like reincarnation—the Navajos believe once you're gone, you're gone, and that's the end of it. We don't believe that. We think that the reason why certain places feel familiar, why when you look into the faces of certain people, you think you've known them before, why there are periods of history that you feel compelled to understand, is reincarnation. It's connected to Tibetan Buddhism in that way. At night Sister Mary Cecilia took the five of us into her little cubicle and had us teach her Apache so the language would stay alive. They recognized me as a Warrior Woman.

I needed to be a Warrior Woman when my daughter, Fawn, crossed over. I'll tell you the whole story; it's really important because of the way we did it. There's the moccasin telegraph; it's faster than Western Union. I couldn't believe how fast the word of her death spread. The first message I got was that she had had a heart attack and was in the hospital. When I called the hospital, a woman told me, "Yes, we have her here, but unfortunately she didn't make it." The next thing she said was, "Which funeral parlor would you like her to go to?" and I said, "Her father and her uncle are on the way there; don't touch her."

They didn't touch her, even to the point of not removing the tube from her mouth. George (Fawn's father) was about to sign the death certificate and an autopsy report, and Dan (there's not blood between us, but he's my brother, if you know what I mean) took the pen out of George's hand and said, "I know she's your baby girl, but this is not a white woman; this is an Indian girl." So he smudged her and performed the crossing-over ceremony for her. Then he called the coroner. He sat there six hours with her because that's how long we sit with somebody after they die. We think it takes that long for the soul to detach from the body so that the spirit can encapsulate that soul and carry it back to the Well of Souls, back to that reunion with Source.

When Autumn and I went to view Fawn's body the first time, she was still in a body bag. We walked into the room and Autumn looked at her and said, "Ena, Ena, wake up." ("Ena" is the Apache word for mother.) It was the most heartrending cry I ever heard. I took this double Scorpio in my arms (she does not cry, she doesn't reveal her emotions) and I said, "That's not your mother there. That's the shell of the person who used to hug us and sing for and with us."

In this country, it's a law that if a body isn't embalmed, it must be buried within twenty-four hours after death. The state of Colorado protected me against that "law." The coroner called the DA, who called me and said, "Oh Shinnah, if anybody gives you any problem about this, you have them call *me*. The only people you have to worry about is the Health Department." The mortuary people hid her from the Health Department for us. She died on a Tuesday; we didn't get her into the ground until Sunday. It was May and the ground was still frozen. Every night I'm goin' out, I'm talkin' to the Mother, and on Friday I went out, I didn't talk to Mom, I said, "Hey, Fawn, what the hell is going on here? You're the one who's in control. Where do you want to be buried?" Because every piece of land that was offered to us was frozen solid.

During my prayers and while I was talking to Fawn instead of Mom, a voice came in and said, "Gale." My close friend, Ellen, was doing the same thing at the same time. The name "Gale" popped into her head also. She called her friend Gale and left a message to return the call. Later that morning the phone rang and it was Gale. She said she would count it as a *privilege* to have Fawn sleeping on her land in La Veta, Colorado. Two other people picked out a spot that (without our realizing it) was Gale's favorite place when she was a child. It's an old homestead piece of land, one hundred eighty acres that they have never let go of. Gale said she would deed us a big enough place for the whole family. The guys who dug the grave didn't know that Fawn's direction was south. You walk north when you cross. They dug the grave south to north.

We went to the mortuary and did a ceremonial washing. The wife of the man who owned the mortuary was there with us, and afterward she said, "I've never seen anything like this in my life." Fawn's daughter, Autumn, put makeup on Fawn and painted her eyes. She put on red lipstick and said, "Well, Ena, I know that you don't like this color lipstick, but it looks great on you, so this is what you're getting." I braided her hair while I was singing the chant.

I invited the funeral director's wife to the "good-bye" ceremony; she turned up in a Navajo velvet skirt and top with a concha belt. I said, "You're incredible," and she said, "Well, I was at work in my red sweats, but I couldn't say good-bye to Fawn that way." We said good-bye to Fawn at the mortuary, then we came over here to my house and told stories about her.

We didn't transport her to La Veta in a hearse; she was driven to La Veta in the back of my brother's station wagon. We stopped at a convenience store and bought all the junk food that she liked; that's what went into the grave first—her junk food, so that she wouldn't be hungry on her way over there. Then the grave was lined with cedar and pine boughs and hodentin, cattail pollen. Then we put her in her burial clothes—she wasn't in a box, she wasn't embalmed. Nobody messed with her. Everything was exactly the way she would have wanted it. The state of Colorado protected me to make sure that it happened *our* way.

When we drove her to the land, there were two fawns sitting on the side of the road; it was as if they led us. I couldn't believe it. We sang our favorite songs for her. Heather, Fawn's sister, was like a pillar that stood guard over any force that might try to penetrate that circle.

For the last part of the ceremony, I planted crystals in the four directions, counterclockwise, because we do everything sunwise. I put the first one at the north, then the west, the south, and the east. Just as I planted the last one, they all fell straight down. Two red-tailed hawks came in, flew counterclockwise three times around the circle, and then split. One went to the north and one went to the south, and her bird is the same as mine: a red-tailed hawk.

We fed them with corn. Everybody had a flower; they put an offering in and said good-bye. I put water in a tiny blue ceramic bowl (she was like me, she loved cobalt blue). She was covered over with cedar and pine boughs and with a pint of hodentin. It is one of the most sacred things to my people. I put a whole jar on her, and one of the Navajo ladies came up and said, "Boy, I know she was a very honorable woman if you're going to put a whole bottle of hodentin on her." I said, "More than that, she was valuable." Everybody threw a rose in; it was her *favorite* rose, right? Autumn said, "I don't want any stranger to put one piece of dirt on my mother." Dan went over and told the guys, "Thank you very much, but we don't need your help." That little girl stood there like a rock in *her* direction, the west, and watched every shovel of dirt that went in on her mother.

Losing my daughter was probably the most difficult thing that has ever happened to me. Cancer was easy compared to saying good-bye to my precious daughter, who was the most gifted person in the world. She could do anything. She carved and did beautiful beadwork. Amazing. She's become the teacher to me. This Western world doesn't allow us to grieve, but we grieved. We fed her for a year; there were over two hundred people in this country who were feeding her every day, because that's what we do, and then we have a Feast for the Dead one year later.

I think this is an amazing story. Fawn has really become the teacher. I can tell people now, "This is how you can do it. You don't have to buy into this Western society. You don't have to do it a certain way because somebody else tells you, 'This is the way it has to be done.' You make up your own mind that *this* is the act of a warrior. You do what you know is necessary for the good of the whole. This is what my daughter would have wanted, and that's what she got."

I went on because I'm Apache. Fawn is as close as my heart. She talks to me all the time. Heather dreams of her all the time. I don't dream of her very often. I wish she'd leave my car keys alone, though. I find them in the strangest places—everybody in this house puts things in one place and then they're gone; we know who's doin' it. We keep tellin' her, "You don't have to do that. We know you're here!"

The Western world denies that the energy of that person is accessible, until we come back. My mother died when I was eleven years old; she was murdered. I never told my children much about it until they got older because I didn't think they needed to know that their grandmother was murdered by a doctor who was in love with her. She wouldn't have anything to do with him. He was doctoring her for ulcers. At one point (and there are records of this) he gave her an injection that she was allergic to. He knew she was allergic to it; so did the nurse. The day she died, all the records disappeared, but the nurse didn't. Eventually she testified against the doctor. My mother was thirty; I was eleven when she died. Autumn was eighteen; her mother was thirty-seven. It was exactly the same number of years between my age and my mother's, and Autumn's age and her mother's at the time of her death. Really strange.

I used to have repetitive dreams about my mother. There was a frog and a road, and I was walking down the road and she was standing in a certain spot. I could see only the top part of her; her hands were reaching for me, and I'd start to go toward her, and some other energy would put a block between me and her. Since the day I got pregnant with Heather, I have never dreamt of my mother again. You can *see* the resemblance between them. Nobody else in this family has curly hair. She's short waisted like my mother and has these teeny tiny delicate bones just like my mother. My mother took after the Scot side of the family, and so did Heather. Heather knows. That's why she bosses me around, because she still thinks she's my mother. I have to keep telling her, "This time *I* get to be the mommy."

The story of my life . . . I can't even begin to tell! You know, my first recollection was when I was still in a cradleboard and I saw a crystal hanging off the edge of the cradleboard. There was a little hood, so if I fell, I would be protected. That's my first recollection. Then, when I was three and a half, I was told *not* to go out and play with my pet pig because it was very stormy (this was in Durango, where I was born) and they were putting a roof on the barn. Of course I went right out to the little pen that was right next to the barn and played with my pet pig. The wind came up and blew a piece of tin off the roof. My great-uncle Dee, my favorite person in the whole world, was coming around the corner and he saw it comin' down and put his hand out to protect my head. The tin took off two of his fingers. It fractured my skull, but it didn't kill me. For years he was known as Two Fingers Gone. He wrapped them in buckskin, sage, and cedar and put it in the ground. These two fingers were sacrificed for my life.

I was in and out of consciousness, they said. My father finally called my great-grandmother, who was an incredible person and knew how to deal with energy and healing. When the tin hit me, there was a tall Indian man who said, "Do not be afraid; you are not alone," and then there was a ruby rain, which was blood, and then I was gone. I told my great-grandmother, "That man is here," and she said, "What does he do?" and I said, "He puts his hands over my head."

Then my great-grandmother told me she had a conversation with this man and he said, "The doctors need to go back into her skull; there's something wrong." My great-grandmother told my father, and of course he told the doctors, who said, "This is ridiculous; this is stupid." My father said, "I will take her to another hospital if you don't go back in there and find out." They took seven teaspoons of hair out of the inside of my head, and that's what was giving me the brain fever and why I was in and out of a coma. Amazing. My great-grandmother lived until I was nineteen. I was very fortunate to have her that long. She's the one who filled in the edges of that story.

As far as romantic love goes, I've had six husbands: four of 'em I married legally, two of 'em I married the Indian way, and the Indian ones are harder to get out of, I can tell you. People ask, "How come you got married so many times?" I say, "I think it's either that I'm a glutton for punishment or an incurable romantic, one or the other." But I love men. I think men are wonderful. At sixty-two I don't think about getting married again or having a romance. I'm just doing what I'm doing. If it comes into my life . . . if Anthony Quinn walked in the door, I'd leave tomorrow. Other than that, I don't know. I've never asked for any relationship. It's just something that comes into your life.

My last lover was eighteen; I was fifty-nine—and he couldn't keep up with me. Before him I was celibate for five years. I don't believe in sex, I believe in love. I've never in my whole life laid my body down with somebody unless there was a real love between us. I think that's a matter of choice, that's not a judgment, that's just what worked for me. So I was celibate for five years the last time, for four years this time. If somebody walked into my life and there was a real love between us, I'd do it again.

The only bad aspect about aging is seeing pictures of myself when I was younger and then looking in the mirror in the morning. Everybody said I was a pretty little thing, and now they tell me I'm beautiful. Beauty is an inner kind of understanding about yourself. I don't mind getting older, I really don't. I sometimes object to the fact that I looked like I was thirty until I was fifty-five and still had a twenty-inch waist.

At one point, I became compulsively suicidal. I was already a clinical psychologist, and I was doing therapy in the Illinois State Psychiatric Institute, which was a very prestigious place. I would be in a crosswalk and I'd get hit by a car; that happened eight times. I have no recall of any of that ever happening. Finally, I got hit by a truck and a psychologist said, "There's something wrong here, this is compulsive behavior." So, I was doing therapy on the eleventh floor of the Illinois State Psychiatric Institute as a therapist and I committed myself to the fifth floor as a patient because I was dangerous to myself. It was great—all I had to do was push a button and I was at work—I didn't have to drive through Chicago. I made arrangements for the supervisor on each floor not to tell the other floor about my comings and goings. It worked.

When I think of myself as an old woman, I see myself living as long as my grandfather did, about a hundred and thirty-five years old. Maybe he was older. Nobody really knows, because in those days there were no records, but his oldest daughter said he was really a hundred and fifty and *lying* about his age. I can believe that. In my workshops, every time I said anything about him, he wanted me to tell people he was still sexually active.

That's sort of the place I come from. We live until we die. My daughter was thirty-seven, and you never expect to put your children in the ground; it's against nature. They should put me in the ground. It's not how long you live, it's how well you live. And how you die. This is the thing I try to share with the people I work with who have AIDS or cancer.

I had cancer when I was twenty-seven, which is the same age that Jim Morrison and Janis and Jimi all died. I was twenty-seven when they told me I had Hodgkin's disease, cancer of the lymphatic system. This doctor looked at me and said, "You're going to be dead in two years." I was so angry I just threw my hand across his desk and everything went flying. I said, "You are a liar. You didn't tell me that I had a life-threatening situation: you handed me a death certificate, and if I believed you, I'd die. But I don't believe you," and I left. I never had any allopathic medicine. I did do a lot of alternative remedies, I changed my diet, moved out of Chicago—that was probably the most important thing I could have done at that time. I went to California, and I'm still alive thirty-five years later.

So I don't think it's how long you live. Although I want to live a very long time. I want to see my great-great-great-grandchildren. I've got a great-grandchild already at sixty-two years old, so I have the possibility of seeing my great-great-grandchildren. But it doesn't matter because, you see, my continuance is instilled in my children and my grandchildren and my great-grandchildren. It's not about how long I live in my body; it's about how long they contain what I am teaching. It continues through generation to generation.

My children were hippies. I was a beatnik—we were much cleaner than the hippies, and were into poetry and espresso and coffeehouses. My mother was a Bohemian, my grandmother was a flapper—I could tell you some funny stories—and my great-grandmother was a Theosophist and a Balinese temple dancer. She had twelve natural children, eleven daughters and one son. She married my great-grandfather, who was a Scotsman. His people were part of the contingent that came over from Scotland during the Great Wars. I'm only an eighth Scot, but I am *so* proud of that.

I knew my great-grandfather until I was six, so I learned a lot of things from him; he raced Irish trotters in Georgia. He taught me Celtic songs, made comparisons about the Indian peoples and the Celtic people. One of the best stories I could tell you is about how he died. One day I was sitting on a fence at his ranch. He never gelded his male horses—and he won all the time because his stallions still had that strength—but he always broke a stallion in with a mare. One day the stable boy brought in a horse that he didn't know was in heat, and this stallion went crazy and kicked my great-grandfather right on the temple and killed him instantly. My great-grandmother was standing on the porch and she ran over to him. This is when my great-grandmother taught me about living and dying.

The first thing she did was just cradle him in her arms and sing him across. It was hot that day, and she made the workers build an arbor over him. The priest came and said, "You *have* to take him inside." She said, "I've had twelve children with this man, and each one of them has been baptized Catholic. The only reason I had twelve children was because he was Catholic. But this man is not *your* husband; this man is *my* husband, and I will do with what is left of him *my* way because I have never been Catholic. I am a Mohawk woman." She wouldn't let them move him. She taught me how to deal with death in a beautiful way. She held him and cradled him, sang him across. She told me this was a blessing. I said, "Why is it a blessing?" and she said, "Because the very thing that he loved the most is what took him out." He was ninety-eight years old—many years older than her. They had met in New York when she was dancing at a concert with Isadora Duncan.

I think death is all around us. My great-grandmother sat there for six or seven hours, explaining that when rigor mortis sets in, the soul leaves the body. It's like birth, it takes time to be born. The internal element of spirit is infinite nature; we all have that. We all die, but that infinite nature is in all living things. The finite nature is what makes you different, what makes the garden beautiful. This is what my grandmother was trying to tell that priest. This is not your man, this is my husband.

Grandfather David, who was a Hopi and adopted me when I was three, taught me that we are timeless. It's not about when we die, it's about how we die. It's about how we live our lives, the goodness we put out, not the hardness we put out. Sometimes life becomes very difficult and we don't want to be here anymore, but that's a cop-out, you know. I could have died from the cancer, but I didn't.

I'll tell you, I learned more as a patient than I did in school. What they do to these people is astonishing. An eighty-year-old woman walked in and they took off the wedding ring that she had worn for sixty-two years. They took her wedding ring away from her; I couldn't believe it. I was *so* angry. And they gave the patients medication as if it were candy. At the time, I was an insomniac, so they gave me sleeping pills. They didn't check to see if I was swallowing them or not. I was smart; I collected them. I collected eighty of 'em and took 'em all in one day. This is the reason why I believe in guardian angels: I opened my eyes and there was an angel standing in front of me and she said, "You cannot do this to me." I fell off the bed and the girl in the room next door heard me fall and called the doctor and they pumped out my stomach.

They called my husband, George, and he held me in his arms and said, "Don't die, don't die." The doctor said, "She's gone, we lost her." Now I'm outside of my body and looking at them. I went through a gray, murky kind of fog and I found my great-grandmother there. She said, "Naughty, naughty, naughty. No, no, no. You are not complete; you have to go back." Then I woke up six days later and there was a nurse standing beside me and I had tubes going everywhere and she said, "Oh, we're back." I said, "Where have *you* been?" We're back! The doctor said, "You would be really dangerous in the world if you had the brain cells of that five-minute lapse." I said, "So you don't think I am already?"

I finally got a hypnotherapist who regressed me to an experience that happened when I was six years old. My great-grandmother and her sister, my great-aunt Minnie, went out for the day and left me with my uncle Eddie, who was an alcoholic. He was supposed to take me to the zoo, but he got drunk instead and I screamed, "I wish you were dead, I wish you were dead!" He went upstairs and then he called me up. When I opened the door he had a gun in his mouth and he pulled the trigger. My conscious mind could not accept that. My great-grandmother would say his name and I would say, "Who's that?" and she would say, "Well, that was your uncle Eddie."

So, my compulsive suicide attempts were in reaction to the fact that my husband, George, and I were going through a separation. My subconscious mind was trying to push this old trauma into my conscious mind, which was saying, "I can't handle this." The result was my compulsive suicidal tendencies. I listened to the hypnotherapy tape over and over and over again, and then I began to remember things around the edges of it, and then it became more real; and once it clicked into my conscious mind, I was no longer suicidal or alcoholic. It taught me something about the human psyche that I don't think the current psychological system understands. It only deals with what's going on right now; it doesn't deal with the effect a *memory* has on you now.

The point I'm trying to make is that we really are the same people. We all come from the same place, the same creator, That Which Created All, Great Spirit, Great Hooha in the Sky—I don't care what you call it, it's the same energy. Spirit is infinite nature, and that's what makes you and me the same. The soul is where we individuate, and sometimes that individuation becomes a teacher. We don't learn through the easy times; we learn through the hard times. We're born like iron, and iron will break at the first blow. Steel, which is iron in the beginning, is tempered through fire and water; fire is the events in our lives that either make us fall apart or become strong. The emotions that we feel, the tears that we shed, are the water that turns us into steel. If we don't become steel, we might as well just put a gun to our foreheads.

I tell people, "If you don't have a grandmother or a grandfather, then go and adopt one. We cannot understand the cycles of life unless we have old people around us." The wisdom that comes with being an older person is wonderful. We need older people in our lives.

Reaching the age of sixty-five was not as traumatic as I thought it would be. . . . Age is relative anyway. You can find people in their thirties who are old. And that's sad, because there's so much to do in life. Life should not be wasted. Every day is precious.

— MATILDA CUOMO

Matilda Cuomo

The first thing that struck me about Matilda Cuomo was her radiance and her unrelenting positive disposition. This woman has lived a graced and privileged life, and no one is more aware of it than she. She exudes a kind of warmth that immediately puts a visitor at ease. As the wife of former Governor Mario Cuomo, Matilda spent twelve years as the First Lady of New York.

Not a woman to take such a responsibility lightly, she has been a tireless social activist and one of the nation's leading voices for the causes of children, women, and education. Matilda initiated and sponsored several programs for a variety of causes, and she was the chairperson of the New York State Mentoring Program (NYSMP), which she founded in 1987. The NYSMP was a unique, statewide elementary school–based intervention program linking adult volunteers on a one-to-one basis with children at risk of dropping out of school.

The Mentoring USA (MUSA) model, which replaced the NYSMP, is now site based as well as school based and has expanded to many states and is included in the continuum of care services provided by the Housing Enterprise for the Less Privileged (HELP), the nation's largest provider of transitional housing and comprehensive independent living programs for homeless families.

For more than thirty years, Matilda has been deeply involved with the fight to prevent breast cancer. After having personally lost twenty-one women friends to this dreaded disease, she has expanded her involvement to become a national spokesperson and inspiration in the crusade against breast cancer.

Matilda Raffa Cuomo was born and reared in Brooklyn, New York. She believes that her Catholic faith and her parents' encouragement to better herself through education equally influenced her passion for public service. At the time of her marriage in 1954 to the future governor of New York, Matilda had no idea just how far her and her husband's interest in public service would take him. She'd been a Spanish major at St. John's Teachers College, she taught in the elementary schools and eventually retired in order to become a full-time mother for her five children.

"We must reach young people *before* they attend high school," she told me with a sense of urgency. "Before it's too late." Her Mentoring USA program was the vehicle to assist thousands of children. "Youngs girls have choices I never had," she said. "In my day, you could only be a teacher, a secretary, or a nurse. If girls desire to go into the sciences or into politics, they should go for it. God gave us talents that we must use to achieve our potential."

Matilda and Mario's children have inherited their parents' humanity, and Matilda spoke proudly and admiringly of the contributions made by their two sons and three daughters. At the age of sixty-five, Matilda Cuomo shows no signs of easing her pace as social activist, and in her role as a grandmother to six grandchildren she continues her gift of mentoring.

The Gift of Mentoring

⁙

Aging can be traumatic when you hit fifty because you know that your life is more than half over. If you're an active person and involved in other people's lives, you never think about your own mortality. You're so active and excited about what you are doing that you almost become ageless. It's an amazing phenomenon! But then finally when you reach a certain age, you have to be realistic and say, "Oh, my gosh, it's like a bad dream. It will happen to me, too."

Reaching the age of sixty-five, though, was not as traumatic as I thought it would be, maybe because I have always been the type of person who sees the glass half-full rather than half-empty. I'm an optimist at heart. My family believes that

I'll never grow old because I look at the positive side and try to see what can be done better. Age is relative anyway. You can find people in their thirties who are old. And that's sad, because there's so much to do in life. Life should not be wasted. Every day is precious.

Too many people today are negative—the blamers and the critics. It's a dead-end street. How much can you hate? How much can you blame? There's always a way to solve a problem and make it better. I've always believed that prevention is the key. That's what Mentoring USA is about: prevention, helping children early on. Mentoring USA is a solution to prevent children from dropping out of school. By the time a child is in high school it's already too late because their paths are set.

In teaching methodology, we learned that children need three resources in their lives to do well—school, home, and community. If one of these resources is missing or not functioning—as in the case of an absent or abusive parent, a dysfunctional family, an overcrowded school, or a drug-torn neighborhood—the child surely suffers. For all these reasons, early prevention and Mentoring USA will encourage, motivate, and give hope to the child.

When my daughter Maria, who manages the HELP [Housing Enterprise for the Less Privileged] sites, and I met with Mayor Rudolph Giuliani last year, he suggested I establish Mentoring USA programs for the children in the New York City public housing sites. The children who live in these sites are now my constituency. With a mentor they can do better in school.

When the New York State Mentoring Program was first conceived in 1986, a bipartisan think tank was formed to address the problem of children dropping out of school. We all agreed that mentoring was a real solution to encourage children to understand the value of a good education. With the experience of raising my own five children, I knew that high-risk children needed a one-to-one relationship. To thrive, a child needs personal attention and care—someone who makes them feel special. The one-to-one relationship of mentor to mentee is truly effective.

Raymond Chambers, a humanitarian in every sense of the word, extended the one-to-one concept by establishing the National 1-1 Partnership, Inc., of which I am a member. Under his leadership, 1-1's goal is to engage two million young people in mentoring relationships by the year 2000.

From my own experience over the past four years as mentor to a young Albany girl named Ely, I know mentoring really works. I know that Ely was helped directly, and indirectly her mother benefited. Her mother's parenting and job skills improved, and her self-confidence grew.

The successful results of the New York State Mentoring Program and the current MUSA program are heartwarming. Children's grades go up, absenteeism goes down. Children are disposed to make better decisions for themselves, rejecting drug use and teenage pregnancies. That's why I say mentoring is a lifetime investment.

Mentoring USA is housed in the Genesis Robert F. Kennedy Center in Union Square, one of HELP's two permanent housing facilities for formerly homeless and low-income families. Genesis, with ninety-four apartments, is truly a haven for its residents. Child care and all kinds of services to help children flourish are provided, including Mentoring USA. Each eligible child living at Genesis has a mentor.

When Vice President Al Gore was here last Tuesday, I think he saw the resources that are available for the families. One of the residents, Stanley Karzwicki, spoke eloquently on behalf of the residents. Confined now by illness to a wheelchair, he said he came here looking for housing and "got a life" instead. He works directly with the children in the REACH program, a small public school at Genesis that serves students whose schooling has suffered because of frequent moves and low school attendance. Stan, in fact, is involved in every facet of community life at Genesis.

I take great pride in all my children. You can imagine the thrill I felt when Vice President Gore praised my son Andrew for establishing HELP. My husband also lauded Andrew, saying, "Some people have ideas; some people implement good ideas. Andrew did both." There are many sad stories of those who become homeless. We know that domestic violence is a very big cause for homeless women. HELP has eight sites now for these families, giving them the chance and support to rebuild their lives. I also give my daughter Maria a lot of credit. A mother of three little children and spouse of businessman Kenneth Cole, Maria manages to balance her family life with her volunteer work managing HELP.

From my parents, I learned to value education as a gift and the key to excellence. I believe that's what motivates me to expand Mentoring USA and try to reach every child in need. As my husband puts it, we must help others, if not out of compassion, then out of self-interest. Maybe it's a little of both that has spurred me on. How can we not be concerned for each child who can and should do better? It also gives me great satisfaction to know that my grandchildren will live in a better society.

At this point in my life, I am most thrilled to be with my grandchildren, who are teaching me so much. (My six granddaughters are delicious, but we're waiting for a little boy, too!) I see everything in the most positive light when I am with them. No matter how busy I am, I make myself available to baby-sit. When they need me, I drop everything because I feel close to them and love being with them. Here is a case in point: I went to Wyoming when Maria and Kenneth asked me, saying, "Please come, the kids want you to come so much." Even in Wyoming, it made me feel good that Maria and Kenneth could go out at night and enjoy themselves without having to worry. We went to the Grand Tetons in Jackson Hole, Wyoming, to see the refuge for the elks. I tell you, it's a trip we'll never forget, any of us.

Being a grandparent puts you in a whole different stratum. There's a lot of giving, but a lot of getting back, too. It's seeing your own children in a different way. No mother asks for rewards, but now that my children are parents, they see me in a new perspective, too, which is very gratifying.

Those are some of the benefits of aging. Many of the negative aspects occur in the physical realm. After sixty years, the physical side becomes a real consideration. If you don't keep yourself in fit condition, you can't work at your optimum. Good nutrition, which has to be learned and understood, is extremely important, as is exercise. I think you have to take genetics into consideration, too: arthritis, osteoporosis, and other predisposed conditions. There is a need to maintain and strengthen your immune system in the most efficient way possible. It's really common sense that you have to go for a routine physical examination.

I tell women, "Don't wait until you are sixty to think about osteoporosis. You have to think about it when you're in your forties." If you come from a line of mothers and sisters or aunts who had osteoporosis, you've got to be more aware of the preventive means. The deterioration of your bone structure can begin to happen, and it could be prevented.

In the case of most diseases and ailments, prevention is the key. I often tell the story of Dr. George Papanicolaou, who developed what we call the Pap smear, which can detect early signs of cervical cancer and, thus, save lives. Do you realize that initially, after it was first developed, doctors were not routinely offering this diagnostic test to women? Only when women pushed for it, passing the word from woman to woman, did this test become a standard part of gynecological care. Now, that's woman power!

There are so many issues for women that need to be a voiced. I focus a lot on the prevention of breast cancer because I've lost twenty-one friends to this dreaded disease. There is no cure for cancer. One out of every eight women is now getting breast cancer. This is very serious. And the older you are, the more prone you are to getting it.

I recently went up to Syracuse to meet Don Distasio, the director of the New York State division of the American Cancer Society [ACS], to implement an idea for a national campaign to encourage mammograms on National Mammogram Day in October. I want women to associate mammograms with an atmosphere of fun rather than pain. The plan is simple: via a voucher system, women who go for mammograms would have a free lunch or a beauty treatment. The idea met with great enthusiasm, and the ACS divisions in five states have already been designated to pilot this effort in October 1997. I hope that this national campaign will parallel the Great American Smokeout.

As First Lady of New York State, I felt a great sense of accomplishment in placing the issue of breast cancer prevention high on the agenda at a National Governors Association meeting of First Spouses in Boston. They united behind an extraordinary effort to promote the prevention of breast cancer to help all the women in our country. I believed then, as I do now, that this is a common cause where the leadership of First Spouses can have a major impact.

Aside from the health issues, having a good marriage or a good relationship in your life is extremely important. You have to have goals and know in your own mind that what you're doing with your life is worthwhile. A job that brings real fulfillment is essential for our well-being. Volunteerism brings great satisfaction. You give back to others and find, in the process, that your own life is richer.

I'll always be grateful for the wonderful opportunities I've had to get involved with issues of children and families as First Lady. At the very beginning, I recall my husband wanted me to chair the Council on Children and Families. He said that I had good credentials, being a teacher and mother of five children. I also remember well my youngest son Christopher's reaction when I asked him how he felt about my assuming new responsibilities that would take up more of my time. He was only twelve at the time, and he answered, "Listen, Mom, I didn't ask to be born. You are my mother. You had me, you're supposed to take care of me!" It's true—out of the mouths of babes. Totally honest about how they feel, and he was right! Fortunately, I was able to organize my schedule, chair the council, and still make Chris my priority.

Through my involvement with the Council on Children and Families, I developed wonderful relationships with the commissioners of education, health, and social services. With team effort and through some worthwhile initiatives that centered on prevention, we were able to help many families. We prepared two booklets, *You're Having a Baby* and *Welcome to Parenthood*, which were distributed free to the maternity units of all the hospitals in the state. The publications were a part of a comprehensive program for new mothers that included counseling. It was the best way to discern which mothers were more needy of learning parenting skills, which were suffering from domestic violence, and which had no support at home. Some mothers coped with all three problems. We would follow through with home aid to new mothers in an effort to prevent child abuse and neglect.

We also started a nutrition curriculum, again free, for all public and private schools, and we established a Parents' Information Line—a toll-free, statewide phone line giving families full access to needed services in their communities. The line continues today, handling two thousand calls every month.

The twelve years in Albany gave me a great sense of fulfillment. I have no regrets because I gave my best and could not have done more than I did in the areas of concern to families and children. Through it all, if I learned anything, it was that all the problems are interconnected and the solutions are interconnected, too.

My husband always says, "Help people up the ladder. You'll feel so much better about it." Everywhere he goes, my husband continues to inspire. It is a great God-given talent. He has in his heart the talent to express himself with the same feelings that other people have in common. And he says it for us. I think the big reason why he didn't want to be a Supreme Court judge was that he didn't want to be cut off from people. You cannot speak your mind publicly. As he would say kiddingly, "Under that robe, you don't know if they're even wearing pants." His words are lasting. His ideas linger in the minds and hearts of people. We still get letters from people who remember something he said years ago, and they write to tell us. That's really awesome. Mario has enriched my life, and he still amazes me.

For recreation, Mario still plays basketball every Saturday morning. Chistopher and Brian, my son-in-law, play with him in a pretty good league and they tell me that he competes with the young fellas and gives them a hard run for their money. He more than holds his own. Although he comes home with injuries, they say, "What are you worried about? He can outplay us!"

Now Mario and I are true Manhattanites, fully enjoying life in the Big Apple. We are both busy, I primarily with the Mentoring USA program and Mario with his law firm, speaking engagements, television appearances, travels, and writings. Besides being aware of our own mortality, I clearly understand that each of us has a destiny. Having been born in Brooklyn myself, I believe it was destiny just meeting my husband, who was also born in Brooklyn—"and never the twain shall meet." The fact that my husband and I were able to survive and thrive through twenty years of public service says a lot about our relationship. I still think of public service in a very positive light. My mother used to say that there's no perfect marriage, no perfect situation. If we involve ourselves with others and do not dwell too much on ourselves, our personal problems do not become magnified.

The fact is, though, we've been through a lot in the forty-three years of our marriage. Politics is not easy. It's a strain on any marriage and family. In fact, my compassion is for the children of politicians because it's a totally consuming kind of job and there are no set hours. Public service is everything to a politician, and it's understandable. The sense of responsibility and obligation is all-consuming. There needs to be a strong marriage in order for someone to go into politics in the first place. Through it all, our family has been together and is stronger than ever. We were able to work our lives out together, to be together.

Sometimes, when I walk by a mirror and catch my image, I see an older woman look-ing back. For a moment, I don't realize it is actually me. Inside, I always feel as though I am just beginning life. I am excited about what I'm doing now. . . .

— VIJALI HAMILTON

Vijali Hamilton

Bony Mountain, the highest point in the Santa Monica Mountains, is a rugged outcropping of granite and sagebrush northeast of Malibu. It is isolated, populated only by native fauna and flora. For millennia the range with the breathtaking view of the Pacific Ocean provided a peaceful home with abundant natural resources to members of the Chumash Indian tribe. For five years, with the same primitive facilities as the Chumash before her, Vijali Hamilton, an artist and sculptor, had lived as a solitary and celibate woman in a tiny abandoned trailer.

In 1986, when I first met Vijali, she was preparing her "return to the world," which is how she described her vision of the World Medicine Wheel that came to her in a dream. "My dreams have always showed me what was ahead for me through my dialogue with the dream images," she said as she recounted to me her experiences of traveling for seven years across the globe.

Vijali calls herself "an earth artist," in that her work combines elements of education, art, spirituality, and peace activism. It focuses attention on environmental, spiritual, and social problems and their solutions. In twelve countries she created and performed ceremonies involving the community, taught meditation, and carved images into stone outcroppings and in caves at the sites of the celebrations, all of which helped unite people in a shared experience of healing their communities.

Vijali is a diminutive woman, but in stature only; like the vast world she travels, her spirit is boundless. Her thick, golden, waist-length hair can be viewed as a metaphor for a mythic Rapunzel who, instead of using her hair to bring a man to her, uses her *life* to help others. Little more than five feet tall, Vijali bears, at once, an ageless, ethereal beauty and a childlike playfulness and enthusiasm. She seems all women in one: the youthful maiden, the nurturing mother, and the enlightened crone.

Vijali was a shy, introspective child growing up in Dallas and Los Angeles, and her earliest memories are of making circles of stone, "little shrines," in her backyard and sitting in them while drawing and painting. From the age of two she was the child of a broken home, so these first rituals provided "a kind of security, a grounding, a sense of the sacred." In hindsight, she now realizes that her "spiritual life" connected her to her inner world, and her art connected her to the outer world. In the early 1970s she met her first Native American medicine healer. In astonishment, she realized that on her own she had developed a similar philosophy to the Native tradition; and she undertook a several-years-long apprenticeship with a number of Native elders.

Her spiritual life has been as important to her as her artistic expression, and, indeed, they have fed and strengthened each other. Having been born into a Christian family, Vijali remembered, "As I grew older, my understanding of what divinity is or what God is changed." When she was nine, her father introduced her to the practice of Vedanta, the chief philosophy of Hinduism, and she met her first guru, Swami Prabhavananda. Through the Vedanta Society in Los Angeles, she met and remained lifelong friends with Aldous and Laura Huxley and Christopher Isherwood.

At the age of fourteen Vijali decided to become a monastic member and entered the Vedantic convent in Santa Barbara, where she remained for ten years. Around the same time, her father entered the Vedantic monastery, where he remained for forty years. Recently, at the age of eighty-four, he left the monastery and started a completely new life. After seeing each other an average of once a year during Vijali's childhood, they are at last becoming friends. "I think it's very important to know my father before he passes on," she said.

Vijali received her master's degree in fine arts from Goddard University. More than one thousand of her artworks are in private and public collections. Her work and life have been represented in two books: *The Once and Future*

Goddess by Elinor Gadon and *The Feminine Face of God* by Sherry Anderson and Patricia Hopkins. Vijali described to me the change in her "definition" of art when she said, "I kept expanding the borders of what sculpture was, what art was, integrating it more and more into life itself—the people around me: their problems, their hopes, their dreams of the future. I think as we get older it is easier to see life from the perspective of the whole."

Twice married and divorced, Vijali made the decision to "leave society, in a manner of speaking," and she withdrew to Bony Mountain. There she experienced the connectedness of everything and "literally saw the web of life, of energy, running through the whole of life. Going out and being with the mountains and the stones was like the healing I'd experienced in my childhood. It was a way to balance my life and gave me the opportunity to integrate that experience of connectedness into the cellular part of myself. It takes a long time, years, for the chemistry of our bodies to change, to learn how to walk in the world with a larger vision of who we are. During those five years, the mountain became my mother, my father, my lover. It became all that had never given me love, and I felt healed. I was never bored for a moment, never lonely, and never frightened."

Alone on Bony Mountain, Vijali wrote her autobiography, composed music, walked for hours each day, carved sculptural images into the boulders, and, at night, watched her "inner television." The World Wheel became the vehicle for her to return to society, but now she had her new vision of wholeness and connectedness, which the circle of the World Wheel represents.

To Vijali, the World Wheel is a vision of wholeness; it is a circle, and on this wheel are spokes that each represent a different culture. She began with the traditional Native American medicine wheel, then realized that she wanted to include more than a single culture, because her vision was global. "It is truly a World Wheel, and each culture has looked at it from its own viewpoint. Every point is different. The beauty of the wheel is that those differences make the circle, yet they are part of the whole."

She made a deliberate "physical wheel around the world" by staying on or near the thirty-fifth parallel. She remembered the day in Malibu, before the trip had any real form, when she was studying a global map. With her finger on Los Angeles, she spun the globe, keeping her finger at that same parallel. As the countries of Spain, Israel, China, and so on leapt out at her, she realized that they formed the wheel of her dream. They seemed appropriate to the upheaval of bloodshed and chaos in the Middle East, the Soviet Union, and China, places to which she hoped to bring a pattern of peace.

Vijali started the World Wheel in Malibu in 1987 because "I felt I needed to start in my birthplace." She then traveled to the Seneca Reservation in upstate New York; Alicante on the Mediterranean Sea of Spain; the Umbrian forest of Italy; the banks of the Dead Sea in Israel and Palestine; the island of Tenos in Greece; a Coptic monastery in Egypt; a tiny village in West Bengal, India; Shoto Terdrom, Tibet; the banks of Lake Baikal, Siberia; Xisan, a national park in Kunming, Southwestern China; and Tenkawo, an ancient Shinto shrine in Nara, Japan.

Last June Vijali tore the cartilage in her knee. In October of 1996 she underwent knee surgery. Because she is without health insurance, "it has been a jolt to realize that with a bill of ten thousand dollars ahead of me, it will be the first time in my life that I have been in debt." While most people would be frantic with worry, Vijali reasons, "I do feel that the universe takes care of me as long as I don't deviate from my truth, from the commitment of following my heart. When I take a step out of fear or a need for security, it is always a step off my real path. I have learned to totally trust this unknown, sometimes whimsical, hand of the infinite. And now the universe has responded in the form of friends helping me out with this pending bill."

On the cusp of sixty, Vijali spoke to me about her world travels and her concerns for the twenty-first century. Her observations are more about the well-being of the earth and its inhabitants than about herself as an individual. Aging in general, and being sixty in particular, feels to her like a natural progression of life and experience. Through the decades that remain to her she plans to continue with her travels and building bridges of peace throughout the world.

The World Visionary

ometimes, when I walk by a mirror and catch my image, I see an older woman looking back. For a moment, I don't realize it is actually me. Inside, I always feel as though I am just beginning life. I am excited about what I'm doing now: writing poems and books about my travels on the World Wheel and establishing the World Wheel Retreat Center on five acres of beautiful red earth, green piñon pine land in Castle Valley, Utah, along the Colorado River.

This center is a place to integrate intensive meditation retreats and creative expression through the sacred arts in order to deepen our connection with the earth and each other and bring back into our communities and countries a deeper awareness of our interconnectedness with all life.

For me, the World Wheel is connected to the twenty-first century because it signifies a time when I will begin another level of integration. Many of us have been working alone on our visionary paths, individually affecting people around us. Now is a time for us to join together and be able to do the work that will affect the world in a more direct way. It's a definite shift. We are becoming more visible, and we are affecting the globe.

We are witnessing the fragmentation of our world right in front of our eyes. Our social, economic, spiritual, and environmental systems are disintegrating, yet I hold a positive view of the future. In order to give birth, you have to let go of everything inside you. The old has to break up before the new can come through. So, what's happening right now is actually positive. But it's painful, because birth is not without pain. We are experiencing some pretty strong negativity in the world right now. People's dark sides are manifesting. It can't be hidden under a puritanical glaze. It's very visible. This is why I feel the importance of continuing with the World Wheel.

When I work in a new country, I try to address the problems of the world by addressing the individual problems of that country. The first thing I do when I enter a country is ask these questions: What is our essence, who are we? What is our sickness, our imbalance? Define it. Let's really look at it in ourselves, in our relationships, in our family, in our community, and how it is affecting the globe.

How does it affect the earth's problems? And finally, How can we heal that sickness and what can bring us into balance?

I show slides of my previous work in other countries beforehand, and I have a map of the locations of the World Wheel. I love to show the faces of the people of other countries. It is important to share the voice of the people, what they are doing in other parts of the world. Our discussion becomes not only a dialogue, but I feel that a new mythology is being developed. People get the sense of a family, that, really, we are all part of a global family.

Working together, we develop a ritual performance piece that I call "community theater." This piece becomes their answer to these initial questions. I create earth sculptures in the local natural environment. So the experience becomes a healing for that community because they look at the problem, and they leave with their own solution. A tremendous healing results from the process of the performance, which is really a ritual transformation.

The particular theme in every country is different each time. For example, in Greece the people identified their sickness as jealousy. When someone in Greece gets a break, people do everything they can to cut them down and diminish them. As in most of the countries, love was the solution.

Of course, the concept of love meant something different in China than it did in Greece. The Chinese people are programmed to think in a kind of group mentality. It's as if they have not been allowed to love in a personal way. Now on television they have some romantic stories. They even stop their work to be absorbed in these soap operas. So that kind of personal, romantic love is beginning to come through.

China is in the process of tremendous change. I'll have to describe what happened in order to explain what their "sickness" was. At first it was hard to get people to speak up, because basically they have to say what the government wants them to say. For the first time, I held a council. We made a talking stick and handed it to each individual, who then had a chance to speak. But first we had to make sure the room wasn't bugged, because I felt certain that I was being recorded. Slowly they began to speak out. The situation is very complex in China and my questions were very difficult for them. They were especially afraid to answer the question "What is the problem?" because they cannot *admit* a problem exists. It wasn't until the very end when I was ready to leave that they began to open up.

Allen Ginsberg had given me the name of a professor at the university in Kunming, and he arranged for me to give my slide show and talk there. The people loved the work. They were delightful. They advised me against choosing to do a ritual in a public place because they said it would take three years to sort through the bureaucracy. As it turned out, I received a call from the government and I thought, Oh, I said too much at the university and they're going to ask me to leave China. Instead they said, "We heard about the World Wheel, the world family you are creating, and we want to know which national park you'd like to do your work in."

So I chose a very beautiful Taoist park with ancient temples in southwest China that would now be revived because the priests were being allowed to return. The next day they sent a car to take me wherever I wanted to go. Every day, I would bicycle to the bus, which took one hour to get to the park; then, with my tools in a backpack, I would hike forty-five minutes to get to the site. Some of my friends from the Naxi, Bai, and other minority groups would model for me as I carved into the limestone cliffs overlooking a beautiful lake. Five images were carved in all. The faces peer out from the stone, and the natural twisting shapes of the limestone form their hair and bodies. They became the "Kuan Yin Bai" and "Kuan Yin Naxi," images of the divine goddess as ordinary people.

In every country I do research about their ecological problems and endangered species. I was amazed at how open the people were at exposing themselves. I met scientists and, with my interpreter, was able to do anything I wanted. I worked with the children and had them answer the questions through their drawings. It was the children who really started opening up first.

In Greece, I chose Tenos island as the place where I would do the work. My friends in Athens said, "Don't choose this island; it's so provincial. The Catholic and Orthodox churches are there, and the people only attend church activities. They aren't interested in art." But I loved that island and its inhabitants. They treated me like an ordinary person, not like a tourist. The governor and the priests and the teenagers all came to the ritual performance. The event united the two church factions. After the ritual, one of the village elders came to me and held my hand and wept. She said, "You have given something to the teenagers; they don't go to church. For the first time they can connect with something that has meaning for them." I found the women in Greece to be very strong, and in fact, their strength seems to increase with age.

Primarily, I travel by myself, although the year before I traveled to Japan, a friend went and made contacts with artists throughout Japan. That allowed us to accomplish a tremendous amount in a very short time. And an Israeli friend did a piece with me on the Dead Sea, where I lived with both Palestinian and Israeli people. For the ritual, their children planted a tree of peace in a stone circle on the Dead Sea, close to where the Dead Sea Scrolls were found. So those experiences had a different character from those that I did on my own.

Egypt was quite difficult for me traveling alone. I was attacked twice, but fortunately I was uninjured. At one point, I had been told about some Coptic monasteries somewhere in the middle of Egypt. I thought this was an environment that would possibly afford some protection for me in which to work. I very much wanted to go and meet the Coptic monks, who are still living the Augustinian tradition of the desert fathers there. I had read about the desert fathers, but I thought it was probably a dead tradition. I mean, there's nothing in literature that says, "Hey, there are saints living in these caves today!" So I took a bus along the Red Sea, and when the bus driver dropped me off he just pointed into the desert and said, "Three hours' hike." After a few hours there were a couple of times when I thought, Maybe I made a mistake. Did I really hear him right? I'd come around a hill and there was nothing and again there was nothing, nothing but desert, desert, desert. Eventually, I finally did make it to the monastery.

The monks were physically and intellectually beautiful. I fell in love with them. They were so present with me without any kind of manipulation that I experienced with other men. Many of them are Ph.D. scholars. They talked to their bishop and got special permission for me to go and live in one of the caves for a period of time. The location is kept secret, even from their lay members. In the cave I had a vision of a man who, I later found out, was someone who had previously lived in the cave, and they now considered him a saint. They were so alive, both the religion and the monks. I think they trusted me because I had shared with them the information about my ten years of being monastic and also my five years of being a hermit on Bony Mountain.

In India, I was on a train, going to Rabindranath Tagore's home. A group of very poor musicians came on the train and I kept giving them coins so they would stay in my compartment. Finally, they invited me to their very poor village, where I had the most luxurious evening of my life. They put a mat under a tree, and the full moon came up. The women made the most wonderful tea for me. The children made fresh flower garlands and put them around my neck. Musicians from other villages came when they heard there was a guest. It was the most beautiful evening of my life. It brings tears to my eyes when I realize that because of our consumer-oriented life in the West, we have lost the sweetness of these simple exchanges. We have lost *life*.

After about a week there, I kept thinking I should do a sculpture, but that didn't seem quite right because they already had beautiful sculptures. I discovered that the children had no schoolhouse, so I decided to build one for them. The funny thing is, when I made a circle on the ground, the children would sit in the circle even while I was building; this became their place. I hired a man to teach me the correct way to build the house. Structures have to be built in a certain way because of the harsh monsoons that can easily topple them if they aren't built properly.

The culture of these beautiful people is dying out—maybe it's because of television. They are a folk culture, and villages would support them to carry news or village stories—like minstrels. Their culture is what is needed in India. It reflects my own philosophy because it is about the whole. They have integrated Muslims, Hindus, and Buddhists living together. Their philosophy is very profound. They refuse to abide by the caste system. They do not worship statues in temples, but instead, their music and dance are their spiritual practice.

I enjoy having people come out to where I'm working and teaching them how to carve and having them help out. I usually do most of the work myself, but people will come out for one or two days and spend time with me. I use a hammer and chisel because I work in areas where there is no electricity, so I just keep the tools I can carry in a backpack. I have a global studio! When I travel, I carry only what I can carry on my back: my tools, a camera, a change of clothes, and a raincoat.

It's funny, I used to be a studio artist with a wonderful warehouse by the ocean and a huge mailing list with clients waiting to buy my art. I really changed. I felt very sad in the art scene, that it had moved away from what art is really about. I decided to stop that whole life, and I walked away from it—from the power tools and the sophisticated studio—to work out in life with people, to have my medium not just stone, but people and the interaction of life.

I feel that we all have visions. We all have insights and wisdom. But we don't give ourselves permission to act on them—most of us don't. That's what I did for myself; I gave myself permission to act. *That's* the hard part—giving ourselves permission to honor our vision. Also, our society is such that people want more and more visions or sensations. What we need is the *one* vision that we spend the rest of our lives working on in order to change ourselves, our family and society, and eventually the world.

Women are helping each other to do that now, but there's still the tendency to say, "Well, if my husband really understood or if I had enough money, I could do what I wanted to do." There's always some reason why we can't live our vision, but they are just excuses. Once we begin, our courage builds, then people understand why we are doing what we're doing. If we wait for people to understand first, we'll never do it.

As women grow older, we can shift our energies more into our life of vision. I think age can help with this focus. Our mate becomes the "whole": our relationship is with the whole of life. Instead of being bitter when our husbands leave us for younger women, we can take this moment of freedom to wake up and become divinely inspired.

Speaking of having enough money! I started the trip with virtually *no* money. I sold my car. I gave away or sold my belongings. Later I did receive some money through grants to complete the trip. The money isn't the problem because it comes if you take that first step; then you get what you need to take the second step. You don't have enough for the third step until you're ready for it.

I've thrown myself into a kind of void of not knowing. When I arrive in a country, I don't know anyone, I don't know the language. I purposely don't know what I'm going to do because the whole thing is about responding—to the people, the land, the situation. Of course, living in that void can be anxiety provoking. I've been in some *very* difficult situations: in India I lost my luggage when it fell off a bus in a storm; I had my passport and traveler's checks stolen; I always traveled in the cheapest way, which is by bus; I ate the food the common people ate. Under those circumstances, you are really vulnerable to having your belongings stolen or to getting sick. But it was a tremendous learning of trust and accepting whatever the situation brought.

After traveling for seven years, I feel that I have the resources within myself to meet whatever situation arises, but that doesn't mean I don't still get frightened sometimes. We have that illusion of the perfect person. Everyone in a body has a humanness—we carry that—which means at times we're vulnerable and at other times we're frightened. The difference is, although you have that pain, at the same time, you can still maintain a picture of the whole—your identity is not with this body that is Vijali, but with the whole of life.

However, I didn't want to be *stupid* about traveling alone. There were other periods when I avoided dangerous situations. I've learned to dress in a modest way to protect myself—similarly to how the women dress in each country. In a larger sense, though, I have no choice. I'm doing what my life is meant to do. This particular kind of blossom is formed out of childhood, out of my particular gifts that have been given to me as an artist and as a human being. Everyone has her own gifts. There is a wonderful feeling that comes when you're on your own path. I have a sense of freedom internally because I am walking on this path that has come out of my heart and my individual life.

And the truth is, I am aware of the possibility of my own death occurring during my travels. In Siberia I lived every moment with the feeling of death. A kind of courage came to me. I went into the Siberian virgin forests, where humans have never been before—Lake Baikal. The villagers warned me not to go, but it was almost like a spell. I fell so much in love with this forest. Wolves came to me, very gentle and curious. I knew I could meet a bear at any moment. People had been mauled and killed. I felt that if death came, I was prepared for it. The Siberian forests grow right to the banks of Lake Baikal, and that is where I chose to create the World Wheel Ceremony. I wanted to draw attention to the ecological problems of this very important lake, which holds almost a quarter of the world's fresh water. Now there are factories on the lake that are polluting the water and killing off the indigenous species.

I've had to step outside the cultural boundaries in order to walk my own path. I feel that's what we are all supposed to do. I don't think of myself as anyone special. We need to encourage each other to follow our own visions. Everyone's course is different; it would be wrong for anyone else to do a World Wheel—that came out of my own way of looking at life, out of my own experience and talents. Everyone has a shape of contribution to make that comes out of themselves.

But, I must admit, I find it difficult when I return to the United States from my travels on the World Wheel. In most of the countries in which I travel, age in women is honored. I see their place of respect in the family, in the community. Here in the States, I feel the great loss we have in our own lives and culture, where a young body is valued more than wisdom. I belong to a women's elders group that meets once a year. We are exploring the true value of age and the ways we can step more directly into the world as wisdom holders. We need to support each other, because who else will, in this sad American society?

At this time in my life, I feel playful with age. I am determined that I (we) set an example for all women who come after us to make it easier for them to move into this age of wisdom—in our sixties, our seventies, and beyond—with joy, excitement, and playfulness. I always tell people my age when I first meet them. I have no embarrassment about being nearly sixty.

Somewhere in the back of my mind, there is the notion that at sixty-five you are what Americans call "over the hill." Rather, I feel that I'm not even halfway up, and I'm going to keep climbing strong.

— RIANE EISLER

Riane Eisler

The time was November 1938; the place, Vienna, Austria. During this period of history, Vienna was commonly accepted as one of the most elegant, cultivated, highly literate centers of the world. But all of Europe and indeed the entire world was increasingly threatened daily by the lethal dominator political system of Adolf Hitler's Nazi Germany. Riane Eisler was seven years old at the time. Her protected life was abundant with love bestowed upon her by her parents and extended family members. Her pleasurable well-to-do environment was filled with the arts, music, and intellectual pursuits that stimulated the precocious little girl. That is, until the evening when a troop of Nazis invaded her home, beat and arrested her father, and carted him off to prison because he was Jewish.

This experience, Riane now understands, was a formative one in her young life. The cruelty, violence, and injustice she silently witnessed were seminal to the woman who would, decades later, develop the theory of a partnership model of cultural transformation as a solution to the dominator ethos that for five thousand years has ruled both kingdoms and individuals.

Today Riane Eisler lives in another seemingly idyllic atmosphere on the Monterey Peninsula in California. But as she spoke about the beauty and blessings in her current life, she was quick to knock wood. For the memory of fate's earlier maneuver still haunts her existence. The surroundings of her home are tastefully elegant, discriminating, and erudite. For a woman commended for her own scholarly brilliance by such luminaries as Ashley Montagu, Marija Gimbutas, Daniel Ellsberg, and Hazel Henderson, Riane seems almost effusive with her compliments to others. At times her charm and radiant smile can almost eclipse the seriousness of her research and her credentials, and one forgets one is discussing evolution and systems science or cultural transformation theory or economics "beyond capitalism and communism," with one of the most renowned women living today.

Fleeing from Nazi-overrun Europe, Riane, her mother—who had managed to secure her husband's release by sheer will and courage—and her father sailed from France on one of the last ocean liners that was allowed to dock in Cuba before the fatal *San Luis* was turned away by both the United States and Cuba and most of the passengers returned to certain death in German concentration camps. Riane and her family remained in Havana until she was a teenager. When she turned fourteen, they once again began a new life, in the land where dreams and the exploitation of women are big business: Los Angeles, California.

After an early marriage and eventual divorce, Riane raised her daughters, Loren and Andrea, on her own as a single mother. Becoming a world-celebrated thinker, futurist, and spokeswoman for evolutionary studies, human rights, and peace, Riane did not immediately become involved in feminist and environmental issues. She readily admits that she had "no consciousness whatsoever" until she was almost thirty-five years old in the mid-1960s, when she "woke up with a vengeance," quitting both her job and smoking and leaving her marriage all in the span of three months.

She then quickly "discovered the human potential movement, the era of group encounters. Then I discovered art and technology, the counterculture, politics, feminism, the struggle for justice, civil rights, human rights." One can feel her excitment as she recounts her exposure to the contemporary culture of the times and her inevitable blossoming.

As one of the early feminists in Los Angeles, Riane was cofounder of the second women's center to be established in the United States, the L.A. Women's Center. She now laughs in disbelief at the naiveté of the early feminists when she recalls, "We would go on marches in downtown Los Angeles. Now that we had seen how ludicrous the injustice and inequality was for women, we thought it would all be over in two years!" But thirty years later

Riane admits that the battle for women's, children's, and human rights in general is "far, far from complete." In the mid- to late 1970s she wrote the books *Dissolution: No Fault Divorce, Marriage, and the Future of Women* and *The Equal Rights Handbook.*

The following ten years were spent, along with a plethora of other activities, researching and writing the first volume of a projected trilogy on "power, sex, and money"—as she jokingly refers to this oversimplification of a meticulously documented and painstakingly researched body of work. The first book, *The Chalice and the Blade,* has, since its initial 1987 publication, had a staggering twenty-four printings and circled the world in fifteen foreign editions, among them Greek, Danish, Norwegian, Finnish, Czech, Japanese, and Chinese.

The Chalice and the Blade is a grand synthesis of multidisciplinary work from the fields of history, evolution, archaeology, anthropology, mythology, psychology, women's studies, and the arts. She is truly eclectic in her modus operandi. In *Chalice* Riane Eisler established her theory of the two models, dominator and partnership, exquisite in their clarity, which describe two fundamentally different ways of organizing human society. Her work (and Riane is the first to acknowledge her indebtedness to the work and vision of countless other women and men) has influenced numerous books as well as corporations and many of the arts.

I first met Riane briefly when this book was published. For the past nine years we have enjoyed intermittent contact, and in 1991, at my request, Riane was gracious enough to write the foreword to my first book, *On Women Turning 40: Coming into Our Fullness.*

In 1995, after seven years of research and writing by the author, Riane's second volume in her proposed trilogy was published. Titled *Sacred Pleasure: Sex, Myth, and the Politics of the Body—New Paths to Power and Love,* this book explores the premise that sexuality was at one period in human history held to be sacred. However, this emphasis was corrupted, and in its place came the erotization of domination and violence. There was a shift from pleasure as a way of holding human relations together to the fear of pain, which, as Riane explains, "is really what the dominator model is all about." As *The New York Times* commented in a review of the book: "*Sacred Pleasure* takes on cavemen and mullahs, the Pope, pornography, and Post-Modernism." More important, as her husband, psychologist, David Loye, explains, "It cuts through much of the sexual and social confusion of our time and offers grounded hope for a healthier, more balanced future."

I often find that people who are well-known display a reticence to expose personal aspects of their lives to an inquisitive interviewer on behalf of an eager reading public. At first Riane and I spoke mainly about her vast accomplishments and her accumulated awards, but when I began gently to nudge the persona, a very different woman emerged. The smile was the same, the warmth and humor equally familiar, but a new vulnerability emanated from her that made her somehow more human, less elite, more like Everywoman.

This is the woman to whom other women can relate: the mother who worries about her children, the wife who shows concern over her husband's health, the friend who encourages and consoles in times of need. In these latter qualities I found traces of the seven-year-old Riane who still bears deep anxiety and fear about losing what she has worked so hard to attain: her children, her rich partnership with her husband, David, good health, rewarding work, financial comfort, prominence, and the respect of many of the world's great minds.

But quickly the guard returns, and I hear the woman sitting before me refer to her recent scare by uterine cancer as "a small blip in my life." This woman will not yield, either to Nazism, patriarchy, *or* cancer! When someone once said, "You can't keep a good man down," they, as usual, had their genders confused. Riane Eisler is indeed a twentieth-century Renaissance woman.

Twentieth-Century Renaissance Woman

∴

I'm not a person who really thinks about age very much—either my own or that of others. I relate to people as people, and, I think to a large extent, I relate to myself that way. I have to admit, though, that sixty *loomed* for my entire fifty-ninth year because sixty is such a decisive age. Such a defining age. It is an age where one can legitimately look back and say, "Well, where am I? Where do I go from here?" These are questions I'm always asking in my work as well.

This summer, for my sixty-fifth birthday, David and my wonderful daughters got together and made me a book composed of perhaps fifty letters from people from all over the world. Letters for my sixty-fifth birthday from people who love me, who wanted to tell me how much they appreciate me. If I feel down, I can always go to that book. One of my closest friends—a sister, really—is a woman named Hilkka Pietila. She lives in Finland, and she came to visit as part of my birthday present, which was an incredible birthday gift.

Also, I received the Humanist Pioneer Award this year. I'm being given the Alice Paul ERA Education Award. Alice Paul began the work on the Equal Rights Amendment. The National Women's Party and National Women's Committee are giving me the award. Then I also got invited by the World Academy of Art and Science to become one of their fellows. (I hate "fellow"; we need to find another word.)

So, I have to say that this year, sixty-five, has been really memorable. I had my surgery, my grandchild, and a birthday that was an event of love, not only by my husband and my children, but by so many people.

Other than that, I don't really think much about age or birthdays. Sixty was a round number, a decisive figure. I might not have fussed much with sixty-five, except look what happened. My family was so relieved that I was alive and recovering so well. We had no idea how serious my sickness was. It was a real blow, and it scared all of us. It's scary; cancer is scary.

The surgery came about because there were some atypical cells in my Pap smear. I have had some physical problems here and there, but I never thought much about it because I really am healthy. I'm very active and vigorous. I may be slim, but I'm strong and healthy. I had a D&C and they said, "We don't like what we're seeing." I asked, "Is it cancer?" and they said, "No." So the D&C didn't even show anything. That's why I recovered so fast because it was very, very early. I really agonized about having a hysterectomy. But I am so grateful that I finally decided to do it, because that's how they found the cancer. We tend to think we can heal ourselves. I do believe in holistic, alternative medicine, but I know there are situations where you just have to cut. It was cancer in a very, very early stage, and my doctor says I'm now cured. But if we hadn't done the surgery, it would have spread, because that's the nature of cancer.

I was very shocked. I never thought I'd get cancer. I do have a lot of anxiety from my childhood that I carry, and I'm a worrier. But I'm also very positive. I'm really not a likely candidate for cancer. Nobody in my family I know of had cancer. The positive attitude issue certainly was in my favor: the will to live, my lifestyle is good, I eat well, get exercise. I asked my doctor, "How is it possible?" and he said, "Who knows? You just could have been in the wrong place at the wrong time. For some reason your immune system was lowered. It happens."

Between being sixty-five years old and having an encounter with cancer, one reflects on one's life; but I suspect I'd be doing that anyway because it is an age during which you do begin to understand reluctantly that you may not be here forever. I would like to have at least another twenty-five years, and I want to continue to live my life as I have lived it, no big changes. I'm entering a new phase now with my granddaughter. I really want to make more time so that I can enjoy her and so that she can enjoy me as a grandmother. Also I want to be able to help my daughter with the new baby and spend more time with both my daughters. But, other than that, I don't see any major changes for me in my life and my work. I may travel less, but I've been saying I'm going to travel less for years!

The point I try to remember is that just because I am sixty-five, I'm not going to start *de*volving my life. I still see my life *e*volving. I am excited about my life. Mind you, I'm very privileged. I'm privileged first of all because I'm healthy. I mean, I've got problems—my back goes out occasionally, for instance—but I've had them for years and I've learned to live with them.

I'm also very privileged for other reasons. I have work that I love. That's the main thing. I have that great pleasure of knowing that my work is making a contribution. One thing that *is* changing with my age is that I find myself more and more able to say things like "My work is important in the scheme of things." As women we are always saying "Well, I was lucky" or "Oh, it's nothing." It *is* something. The work that we do is major. And, as I say this, there is still something in me that says, "Oh, my goodness, how dare I say this about myself?"

But why not say it? I've had a great deal of evidence from so many quarters that attests to this fact. I was invited last year to be the only woman in a new book on macrohistory and macrohistorians. [Giovanni Battista] Vico, [Oswald] Spengler, [Arnold] Toynbee, and me. It makes me angry that I'm the only woman, because there have been other women who I am sure have thought in these grand systems theory terms, but they have always gotten disappeared. I will possibly get disappeared, too, but I'll work like hell to make sure that we *don't*— we, because it isn't just about me—again get disappeared. But the point is that, now, because of my age, I am able to sit here and say my work is a significant contribution.

I feel very much a vehicle for my work. I don't take dictation from some spirit. It's not channeled! That's not what I mean by being a vehicle. I believe that I am at my best in my ability to see patterns in history, in culture, in the sciences (which others have intuited but not painstakingly studied and supported with evidence). I'm at my best in my ability to express what I see—my cultural transformation theory—not only with clarity and scholarship, but with passion. And, yes, even love, as I am told by people who write to me and say that there is love in my books.

When I'm able to do these things, I feel that what I'm really accessing is, for lack of a better word, my higher self. I'm not too crazy about the terms "higher" and "lower," but there *is* such a thing as hierarchies of actualization, and there is such a thing as human development. There is also such a thing as ideals that we can aspire to and capacities in ourselves that we can begin to actualize at least to some extent. That's what I mean when I say that the work comes through me. If you will, it isn't my small self; it's something larger.

However, I still have my share of insecurities that come with the package of being a woman who is sixty-five, who was born into a time when if you didn't have a beard, you couldn't be an important person. I still carry that with me. It would be hubris to say that I don't. But hubris means challenging the gods, and I have literally challenged the gods in my work.

Of course, I'm not the only woman who is able to speak like this now. It is not only a function of age—although I think part of it is a function of age—it is also a function of our changing times. In fact, age or not, if the times hadn't changed, I couldn't be speaking this openly. It would even be harder because we live in a culture that still discards older women as superfluous. Men still marry trophy wives, looking for a younger model—quite literally. And it's ugly. I think the times have changed spectacularly, and it's very important for women to remember that, even though these are difficult times right now.

In terms of my conceptual framework, I call this period a time of dominator regression, which means that the accepted model of power and authority associated with white males is in decline. Precisely because the partnership thrust of equality between men and women is, on the grass-roots level, so strong, we are getting what is commonly called a backlash. But it's important for us to remember during this time how much we have accomplished. When I say we, I mean *we*. None of this was handed to women. If it were not for the feminist movement, a certain equilibrium and acceptance of women's differing roles would not have happened. And, of course, the struggle is far, far from complete.

In 1977, when I wrote the *Equal Rights Handbook,* the so-called Christian Right (people like Phyllis Schlafly) were not really mobilizing against an amendment; they were mobilizing against what I call a partnership way of living. The failure of the Equal Rights Amendment, as I predicted, was really a signal that there would be regressive times. Unfortunately my prediction was borne out.

Now these people would take us back to before the Enlightenment, to the good old days of the so-called Age of Faith, when there were witch burnings and drawings and quarterings. Unfortunately people know nothing of our real history because it's not taught in our schools.

That's one of the projects I've been working on in the last few years. I was invited to do some consulting for a private school, a very small girls' school. I was actually the only woman; all the others were men, which was rather strange. At that time, I wrote the beginning of something I've continued to work on, which is a completely new curriculum from kindergarten through twelfth grade. Our children need a whole new conceptual framework, a whole new way of seeing the world. Needless to say, it is gender balanced, gender fair, and gender holistic, which is part of what needs to be fundamentally changed. As I point out, much of the problem has been, for example, history. What does it teach children as important?

When I was a kid, I was so irritated that I had to memorize the dates of battles, of wars. Well, there was a reason for that. It was important to impress the children that that's what counts: Who kills who. Who conquers who. Who has power over other people—the power of the blade, to use the title of my book *The Chalice and the Blade*. Currently the most important aspect in modern history is what I write about in *Sacred Pleasure* in some detail: all the social movements one after another challenging entrenched traditions of domination, be it the so-called divinely ordained right of kings to rule over their "subjects" or the so-called divinely ordained right of men to rule over the women and children in the "castles" of their homes. The battle of social movements is fundamental; it is foundational. That's what children need to understand: the humanizing influences. That's what's important, not all the business as usual of conquering and killing and oppressing—that's not what we need to teach our children.

We need to teach them that these things happened, but not glorify them, and not exclude the so-called women's work: caring for children, for a family's health, caring that we have a clean and aesthetic environment. These are enormous contributions; where are they in what we teach children in school? No wonder little boys don't want to clean house—they want to do the stuff that's featured as important in what they learn. No wonder women who become homemakers have such a difficult time because of the double messages, the rhetoric, and the reality. We don't have pensions for homemakers, for people who are mothers—or fathers, for that matter—who care for life. We have pensions for soldiers, for people who are trained to *take* life. This is a truly pathological system. So this revised curriculum is one thing I'm working on now. I would like to at least contribute—there are other people doing *wonderful* work in that area, but as usual mine is a very ambitious project. It includes the whole picture from a systems theory approach.

On the back burner is my book on economics. You know, it's funny, someone pointed out to me that I dealt with power in *Chalice;* I dealt with sex in *Sacred Pleasure;* and now I'm going to deal with money. I said, "You got it." Of course, I deal with more than sex in *Sacred Pleasure,* but still those are the basics and that is my trilogy. There was a shift from pleasure as a way of holding human relations together to the fear of pain, which is really what the dominator model is all about. You can't maintain these hierarchies otherwise.

I'm also working on a project that amazes me: I am rewriting the "great love stories," old and new. I just finished with *Madame Butterfly* and *Scheherazade.* They are completely rewritten from a feminist perspective—no suicides. In fact, the last line in my *Madame Butterfly* is "How lucky I was that Pinkerton never came back." I've been wanting to do this for ten years. I've been trying to talk other people into it. I used to call it rewriting the classics, reframing, anything, because those old messages are so harmful.

Somewhere in the back of my mind, being a woman of sixty-five, there is the notion that at sixty-five you're what Americans call "over the hill." Rather, I feel that I'm not even halfway up, and I'm going to keep climbing strong. I almost have to not think of age. I remember that the hardest birthday for me actually was twenty-nine, but I had no damn consciousness at that time. It wasn't until my mid-thirties that I began to wake up. At twenty-nine I was lost in the land of suburbia.

I was a bright woman whom nobody had encouraged. I was a *brilliant* student. If I had been a man, I would have been encouraged to do a thousand and one things; and nobody ever thought of that. All they thought was, Yeah, you might as well go on to college because you'll meet somebody. And sure enough, I quit college to get married. I interrupted my graduate training. I was lost. The only identity I had at that time was the script that after thirty you run downhill. That was my hardest birthday. It's funny that becoming sixty was nothing in comparison.

I'm becoming me now. There was no way I could be me then. That's one of the subjects I deal with in the curriculum: How can a woman be herself, when most of what she still learns in school is about men, the things men do? And written by men. How can we find ourselves? Where are we in that scheme of things? We have no idea. Women have a relational identity, and that relational identity is very threatened by age. We don't acquire value, but men get more valuable as they get older—up to a point, of course, because we're also a very ageist society. Certainly no man turning twenty-nine would think it was a crisis in his life. That's ridiculous.

Along with all my writing, I also do a great deal of lecturing and consulting. Recently I was the general consultant helping to design and implement a project in Canada on the partnership creativity model. This was an outreach to the community, to get customers involved. I was invited by a group of people who had read my work, even though I said I'm not a management consultant. Of course, I've spoken at corporations such as Disney, Du Pont, and Volkswagen. But what's different is that they said, "We understand that, but we want to use the partnership model to frame this project, and you're the person."

So why is business so important? Business is where the power is, and that's where the transformation has to take place. Someone has to encourage and nurture the partnership model. Besides, I have to say, I love it and, as it turns out, I'm quite good at it. That's partly because I have a legal background, but, also, I was in the building business with my father for some years. I'm a very practical, grounded person. I don't think everything has to be cooperation. In fact, the partnership model is not all cooperation, as I tirelessly tell people. They say, "Oh, it's switching to cooperation," but the truth is there's cooperation in the dominator model, too. Look how often people cooperate to do some pretty rotten things. Certainly there's conflict in the partnership model, and yes, there's leadership, there's competition, there're hierarchies, but their power is conceptualized differently. There are hierarchies of actualization in which you can empower people.

Am I hopeful for our future? I would say this: I have realistically grounded hope, but I also realize that it's not a foregone conclusion. The struggle for our future is between these two very strong forces—the movement toward partnership against the incredibly strong dominator resistance and periodic regressions as experienced in Nazi Germany, Stalin's Soviet Union, and Khomeini's Iran. In fact, in much of the world we have been seeing dominator regressions. I mean

Bosnia, Rwanda. What's the ethnic cleansing about? It's the same old in-group vs. out-group dominator argument.

But, yes, I have hope, precisely because of the context I am in. Precisely because of the people I work with. I know so many wonderful feminists of all ages and colors and creeds, from Mormon women to African women to Chinese women. This is one of the reasons I became active in a new movement to change our mass media: the cultural environment movement. I sometimes think that if other people had access to the kind of information I do, they would be more hopeful, too. I know of people all over the world who are doing wonderful things, who are really making positive news—not what passes for news, which is always focused on either the inflicting or the suffering of pain.

Our commonly accepted standard of news maintains the dominator model because what becomes important is who can inflict pain and whom can you inflict it on, both of which cause suffering. But if people had an awareness of the many positive ventures that are going on, they would be much more hopeful and they would also be less apathetic. They would realize that we do have the capacity to influence consciously the course of history. We influence it unconsciously anyway; we might as well be conscious about our influence.

I get invited to speak by people who resonate to the partnership model, people who find in it support for what they're doing as well as a conceptual framework for their own work. So it isn't only that I know so many people; I know what so many people are doing. I know the work that's going on. I've spoken at many of the socially conscious business organizations.

I was invited to go to Prince Edward Island, the Canadian province, where they are trying to apply the partnership model on governmental, business, and community levels. They contacted me because of my work. One of the virtues of my approach is that it's not just deconstruction, it's reconstruction. We have to deconstruct the dominator model, but if all you do is deconstruct, then after a while you get to nihilistic postmodernism, which is okay, but it's very regressive and opens the door for the old paradigm. People need standards.

On a more personal note, I must mention my husband, David, who is an extraordinarily creative and brilliant man. He helps me so much in my work, and we often work together closely. His work is enormously important. Now he's working on the concept of morality. For example, in the dominator model you have to superimpose morality because the assumption is that human beings are bad. Men are innately violent, original sin exists, we have selfish genes—the whole bit. But suppose there were sort of a nudge of evolution toward a more evolved way of relating. Doesn't that change the picture a little? Suppose, then, that like everything else, morality is socially constructed and that, in a dominator-oriented society, it is what it is—coercive, punitive—and that in a more partnership-oriented society, morality is much more caring. So he's writing a fabulous series of books on this subject.

He also is a magnificent poet. He wrote me a whole book of poems for my sixty-fifth birthday. He's enormously supportive, and I'm supportive of him. It's a real partnership. I'm so lucky that I sometimes pinch myself to see if I'm awake. Because I had the childhood that I did—a good life and then everything was yanked away—I'm always afraid that fate will pull another rug out from under me. So I'm almost afraid to say out loud how blessed I am. But, look, I also want to say that David and I fight, and we are sick sometimes, and we worry about our children, and we worry about friends, and there are setbacks and disappointments. There are things that I would like that I don't get; there are things that he would like that he doesn't get. So it isn't as if I have a perfect life.

However, I do struggle with my unfortunate perfectionism, which can be a wonderful quality within limits. There are things I'm still working on, and one of them is my anxiety and my perfectionism; the two go together. I mean, if you're an anxious person, you have to be perfect, right? Not that I'm *ever* perfect, but my standards for myself and my judgmental quality are severe. It's funny, though, I'm not particularly judgmental of others. But that comes out of anxiety. In a way it serves me well, because it makes me try to do good work. So there are things that one always has to struggle with in life, but I'm very lucky in so many ways.

In January 1997 it will be twenty years since David and I met. And it is wonderful, it's a comfort. I've never really felt this comfortable with another human being as I do with David. I didn't think it was possible. Probably because I was on my own with two little children for ten years between marriages, I had the time to sort of find myself. I think it was infinitely harder being alone. When I was writing *Sacred Pleasure*, I realized that, whether it's with a man or with a woman, we need contact with other human beings. It gives us so much pleasure to share and to be touched and to touch and not just, as I write, to be loved, but to love. I think that's why people who live alone very often have pets. It's very important; we need someone to love. Humans have that yearning for connection. So I'm incredibly blessed to have my relationship with David.

I was without a partner for ten years, and I have good friends who are without partners, and they do just fine. It can be done. You can have a very rich, fulfilled life. It's important that there be some kinds of relationships in your life with friends and relatives. Independence is part of the macho creed. The delusion that we don't need anybody. Well, we do. I believe it's worth searching for some support, some love, some caring, in one's life. Find people to validate you.

It wasn't until my late forties that I actually realized how much my childhood had shaped me. I began to understand that since I had been a little girl, I'd had a sense of wanting to "do something important" in my life. That came from my feeling of having been saved by a hair. But little girls really aren't supposed to think like that because what we *do* is not supposed to be important. Of course, this is crazy. What women have traditionally been assigned is the *most* important work, when you come right down to it. I became properly socialized in Cuba. I had no clue, no clue of the socialization process that was operative for girls.

I just got brainwashed. It was such a strange thing, because even then I was always first in my class. There were three of us girls vying for that prize. I was at a private school where they gave prizes for excellence. That's something that I have a great deal of anger about. I have to tell you that. I am angry about the fact that here were brilliant students, *brilliant* girls, and they were not nurtured, they were not encouraged, they were not given the vista of possibilities to do something with their brains, to do something with their energy, to do something with their talent. It wouldn't be so bad if what they were slotted to do was really valued, but it wasn't, of course. That's what I realized in the suburbs in the 1950s. That's where women began to consume tranquilizers and drink heavily, because we'd go to parties and women would be asked, "What do you do?" and they'd say, "I'm just a housewife." Anyway, that's what happened to me. I had this sense of wanting to do something important as a child, and then it truly just went away.

Charm was my survival. I saw my father and mother surviving because he was handsome and she was beautiful, and they were charming. It was that simple. For me that was survival. I saw it in Vienna. Later, in Cuba, it was still very clear. My father would take me with him as he went to explore business opportunities. It was wonderful and still is one of my favorite memories. He charmed these people—ooh, this handsome man with the gentle humor. So I learned that I had to be charming, too. It's more pleasant to be around somebody like that than somebody rude and abrasive. I have a really hot temper, but I also have great passion. I have very intense relationships and a great need to love and be loved, a need for closeness and for intimacy.

Even with all the wonderful people and the meaningful work in my life, I do get depressed. When that happens, I try to remind myself that it usually passes. And if I don't, my husband will remind me. But I get depressed about the world. I get depressed about all the unnecessary pain that goes on in the world. I get depressed when my children are hurting. I get depressed and frightened when David isn't well. I get quite depressed if I am ill myself. Depression lurks in me.

This is an effect of my childhood. When children have gone through very painful experiences, those experiences remain in us, especially for sensitive children, and I was a very sensitive child. Depression lurks in me. I sometimes say, "That silver cloud has a dark lining."

There probably isn't much I need to say to women my age, because they've really lived these years. When women get to be this age, they know many things. I suppose the one thing I would say is, "Value yourself," and try to change the society so that it will value women like us.

Find out what you want to do and do it! Don't worry about image. . . . Take care of yourself. And that means not doing a lot of the things that you're told will make you feel and look younger. It means not using chemicals, not dying your hair . . . because they are really hazardous to your health. And it means kicking up your heels sometimes and saying, "I'm outta here."

— VIRGINIA R. HARRIS

Virginia R. Harris

A friend had told me about the exquisite and powerful art quilts on exhibit at a gallery in Palo Alto. When my friend also mentioned that the artist was sixty, I decided to make the short trip up to Silicon Valley. *Piecing It Together,* as the exhibit was wryly titled, was a mixture of quilts containing both beautifully abstract images and figurative narratives. In one of the latter, called "One Nation Under God," the picture plane consists of a church with stained-glass windows enveloped by flames, a large burning cross, several white-hooded figures (unmistakably representing the Ku Klux Klan), and, most chillingly, an African American military man hanging by his neck from a tree. The juxtaposition of the luxurious and colorful fabrics with the stark and unforgiving message makes the quilt at once difficult to look at and riveting.

On the title card, Virginia R. Harris, the quilt maker, explained the inspiration for the quilt: "I woke up one morning with that quilt in my head after hearing Janet Reno say there was no indication that the recent church burnings had been racially motivated. That's the same thing that was said about lynchings: they were not racially motivated. I just woke up with that entire image in my head. So I decided I would put it in my quilt."

I called Virginia and asked to meet with her at the exhibit. When I arrived, I found a woman emotionally guarded because (as she later revealed) of the decades of betrayal and prejudice she had repeatedly experienced in her life. She eventually warmed to me and the process of our interview.

Virginia described to me in detail several of her quilts, including "Self-Portrait," which has four windows. "Each window represents a period in my life.

All the windows have boxes—tight little ones that we are supposed to fit into. After I made the first window, I realized that those were the colors of my bedroom when I was ten years old. The valances were that same shade of pink, the shades were white, the walls were blue. The second window is all silk. Everything in that window is about buying the best, having the best; the boxes are still there, but jazzier. In the third window all this stuff is vomiting out of the boxes. Then in the last window, the symmetry is different, the boxes are disappearing, and it's not finished."

For years Virginia had searched for a creative outlet "that engendered the passion of which artists speak." After professional careers as a chemist and an organizational consultant, she tried photography in the 1970s and wrote two novels in the 1980s. In 1991 a friend asked every woman in her circle to make a quilt square for her fiftieth birthday. After checking out six books on the subject from the library, and redoing her quilt square several times, Virginia bought enough fabric to make a full quilt. She felt that she had "come home," and she explained to me how her view of quilt making as a metaphor for life has changed how she relates to the world.

During the creative process, Virginia asks herself questions such as "What does it look like to be fully in one's humanity?" She is convinced that "quilt making offers opportunities to search for the many answers, to use creative energy in constructive, life-giving ways, to use differences as the starting point to make a cohesive whole." The creative spirits in quilting allow her "to create from a personal aesthetic, a new, truthful tradition."

Virginia spent most of her childhood in Maryland and Virginia, where she attended segregated schools. The first time she was in a situation in which, as an African American, she was a minority was when she went to graduate school at the age of twenty-one at Ohio University in Athens, Ohio. She majored in chemistry but decided not to go on for her Ph.D. because "it had nothing to do with anything other than how much I was willing to endure, and I felt that I had endured enough: academically, socially, emotionally, spiritually, physically." She was the only graduate in chemistry—both graduate and undergraduate in 1961—who left without a job. She was also the only black woman in the group. After getting a master's degree in chemistry, she still could not get a job.

When the campus recruiter was interviewing for positions in her field, she was told to get a Ph.D. When she asked one recruiter what they would want after she got a Ph.D., he said, "Two." "At least he was willing to say it," she told me, still quietly enraged thirty years later. Eventually she found a job. "People were very enthusiastic until they saw me. It was quite a difficult time, quite a difficult time."

She has done a lot of work around the topic of diversity and conducted workshops on unlearning racism and dealing with issues of oppression. "I still see racism and prejudice all over the place all the time," Virginia revealed. "People still want two Ph.D.'s from me."

Virginia was married in her thirties for ten years and then divorced. She never had children and admits, "I never wanted children. I got a lot of flak for that in the sixties. 'Why would you get married if you're not gonna have kids?' It is the one decision I made that I have never regretted. And I am fine with that 'never.' I made good choices in not becoming a parent; I really did. I think more people should do that."

A week from the day of our meeting, Virginia was scheduled to move from Palo Alto to Albuquerque, New Mexico. Due to her finances, she could no longer afford to live in California. She and her friends were celebrating Thanksgiving a month early, so that she could join them. "I want to say thanks to all my friends," she said, "and I want us to sit down at a traditional Thanksgiving dinner together. Don't ask me why, but that came up in one of my novels I was writing in 1992: the woman was moving, so she had Thanksgiving in June and invited all of her kids and her grandkids for Thanksgiving dinner." As Diane Johnson wrote in *Dashiell Hammett: A Life*, there is an "odd way life catches up with things that you write, after you have written them."

An American Quilter

.·.

When I was a teenager, I remember thinking that my aunts should act their age. They were in their forties and having a great time. "They should act their age." What did that mean? That they should go sit on a porch somewhere and rock in a chair? They certainly weren't acting their age, whatever that was. I know when I was forty, I was not acting my age. When I was forty-two, I gave myself a motorcycle for my birthday present and I loved it. It was the only *thing* I had wanted that I'd never had. So I said, "Well, this is as good a time as any." I still like riding motorcycles, although I haven't ridden since 1988. I was rear-ended and I didn't get enough money from the insurance to buy another bike. When I recently went to renew my license, the guy said, "You don't want to renew the motorcycle license, do you?" I said, "Absolutely." I haven't ridden, but I don't see any reason to give up my motorcycle license. One day I will get another motorcycle.

Now you've got all these movie stars who ride Harleys, but in the seventies you didn't see that. You saw the biker broads, and even they were usually riding behind somebody. Women have ridden motorcycles since forever, but did we ever hear about them? No. I saw a film called *Harley Women*. There was an eighty-year-old woman who used to do the Harley rallies when she was in her twenties. She has a pink Harley and rides around with her name on it: Dot. She's been rid-ing Harleys for more than fifty years. She gets on her Harley and goes to play golf with her other eighty-year-old friends. I wanted a Harley-Davidson, but I couldn't afford it (God, they are expensive).

In the last few years, I have been struggling just to keep my head above water and to buy fabric. It hasn't been easy because I refuse to go to a nine-to-five job, even if I could find one. Given my background and experience, I am unwilling to work for eight dollars an hour. I will do freelance organizational development consulting, but I have found that I am doing fewer and fewer consulting jobs. Now you can get a master's degree in organizational development. Oh, my good-ness, I wonder what they teach!

I've been doing it for a long time. Not quite thirty years, but a long time. I think this decrease in offers absolutely has to do with my age. I may interview for a consulting job that I could do in a walk, and they will hire someone with a few years' experience who is usually young and white. I say, "Okay, they don't want experience, they don't want know-how, or they are unable to believe that I can bring them any expertise." In that way, nothing has changed in terms of prejudice.

I don't feel "bitter," I feel outraged. Bitter is one of those words that white people use: "Oh, you must not be bitter. You must bear up under anything that we hand you, in any way that we hand it to you, and never react to it." Pulleez! When I told someone in graduate school that my grandfather hated white people, they just couldn't understand why. He had been born a slave; why should he hate white people?!

I'm moving to Albuquerque because I can't find an apartment I can afford in the Bay Area. My basic living expenses have to come out of my retirement income—the income that does not depend on consulting or selling quilts. I took early retirement in order to have time to quilt. By taking it at fifty-five, I got forty-eight percent of what I would have gotten at sixty-five. But who knows if I will survive to sixty-five? I wanted to make quilts now. All the pieces in this exhibit are since 1992, but mostly 1995 and 1996.

I don't necessarily spend eight hours a day quilting. I can spend one hour a day or twenty-three. It varies. It depends on what I'm doing and how I'm feeling. Once I started "One Nation," I couldn't stop. I think I made that quilt in a couple of weeks. I worked on it all day, every day. There were a lot of things I had to do for it: make the doll, the shirt, and the pants. I decided to put medals on the shirt, but I wanted them to be accurate, so I had to find out the colors by reading military sources, and I had to embroider each one of those little ribbons on that shirt. As the quilt was building, I worked on these little things, too. My process varies on just about every quilt.

I never know what the quilt is going to look like when it's complete. That's part of the fun and also the tension. The first block I made with a particular pattern—there are sixteen pieces in each block—I got depressed when I started sewing piece one to piece two. I finally understood what the depression was about: I wanted to know what the entire quilt was going to look like from the very beginning. Now, project that into life. We're getting started here with something that we're doing, and we want to know what it's going to look like in the future. That's what we're supposed to do all the time, predict what this project is going to look like twenty years from now. "What are your plans for five years from now? Where do you see yourself ten years from now? And what are your career goals for the next forty years?" We ask those kinds of dumb questions in interviews with kids just coming out of college, and they're supposed to be able to give us an answer. Well, I did give answers forty years ago, and I had not a clue. If anybody had told me that I would not be going to a nine-to-five job, that I would be making quilts, that I would live on poverty wages, I would have said they were crazy. There is no way I could have seen myself doing this, but here I am.

Do I have health insurance? Surely you jest. It would take all of my money to have health insurance. I can't afford it. So I cannot afford to get sick. Period. I refuse to get sick, so I have to take care of myself, which is not cheap. Eating properly and getting the correct exercise is very important. Another reason that I'm moving is because it's so polluted where I live. Right now I live three blocks downwind of a chemical waste reprocessing plant. I can't continue to do that. I *will* get sick. When I was in New Mexico I didn't have anywhere near as many problems with my allergies as I do living in East Palo Alto. I have chemical sensitivity, and I am living downwind of a chemical waste reprocessing plant! Am I stark, raving out of my mind? Yes. So I'm going to load my belongings into a truck, and my brother and I are going to drive it to New Mexico. I'm going somewhere hopefully where the cost of living is less. But I don't expect racism, ageism, and sexism to be any less in New Mexico.

For a number of my friends who have turned sixty-five, this is the first time they have had medical care in a long time. They just couldn't afford it. So I do the minimum, pay for it, get it done. I have a mammogram and a Pap smear every year. Every three to four years I will have the sigmoidoscopy since I have a history of colon cancer in my family. I have to pay for that. Yes, there are clinics, but the dehumanization you have to endure isn't worth it to me. The idea that no one in this country is denied medical care may be true, but because of what you have to go through to get it, you could die before anything is done. It took me six months through the county system the last time I had a sigmoid done. And every visit I had to pay for. If anything had been wrong, after six months I could have been dead.

Yes, I was married. I got married because I couldn't think of anything else to do. I got out of school, got a job, and worked every day. I said, "Is this what the rest of my life is going to be like?" I hated it. I hated getting up in the morning. I hated my job. Yech. So, what to do? You look around at your options, and getting married seemed the only one. If I got married, then I would have two salaries that I could work with and I could acquire the American dream. Well, I did. I was solidly upper middle class. I had the house, the boat, the cars, the clothes, the vacations—and I was dying. I was in the upper percentiles of everybody, and I was in the high upper percentiles of black folks. I said, "Oh no!" and gave it up. I realized I was working at trying to make myself "better" by buying things. The American dream didn't *become* a nightmare. It *is* a nightmare.

Everything in this society has to be quantified: it is worth so much only if it takes this much time, and if it takes that much time, it's worth that much. Everything is equated to the amount of time it takes, how much material it takes, how much, how much, how much. That's how I lived my life for years. If I buy this kind of fur coat, it makes this statement. If I buy this kind of car, it makes that statement. Quantifying is about external statements. I can tell you it doesn't make my quilt less beautiful if I say, "It took me three weeks to make." Is it less beautiful than if it took me three years? See what I mean?

That's what's fucked up about this society: you get paid to do what you don't want to do. And you can get paid well to do what kills you. Most people don't even get paid well for what kills them; it just kills them. Think about it: you get paid to do what you don't want to do but have to struggle to do what you want. It's so screwed up that I want no part of it anymore. It's virtually impossible not be a part of it, but you can refuse to allow it to run your life.

Yes, I want to sell my work. Yes, I want to get paid for what I do. But when I start a quilt I don't want to say, "Okay, I have got to have it done in *x* amount of time or dah, dah, dah." I consider myself a beginner, but a professional beginner.

I had a lot of trouble trying to come up with prices, and then a curator suggested that as a beginner and as a maker of art quilts (and I consider each one of my quilts a work of art), I start pricing at fifty dollars a square foot. So I take the square feet in a quilt and multiply them by fifty dollars and ask myself, "Does that feel okay to me?" Some do, some don't. Some need more, some need less. But that's where I start. I think my technique is good; it's not perfect and I don't care. It will improve, but it'll never be perfect. I went to an exhibit and the Best of Show quilt hung like a board, and I said, "This is fabric, it should *hang*." It was totally dead.

I will say one thing: none of my quilts is dead. Some of them have more life than others, but they're not dead.

By the time you get to be this age, if you still give a flying fuck what anybody thinks about you, you're absolutely crazy. It took forty-five years to realize that. It took going to China, realizing that I could drop off the face of the earth and nobody would give a damn. Nobody in the world cared what a black woman did, and I mean *nobody* cared. So why did I care so much what *they* thought? Older women have to really get it that nobody gives a damn about them. So we have got to give a damn about ourselves. I wanted passion in my life. On my thirty-fifth birthday I woke up enraged because I had spent half my life (my life expectancy is only about seventy) doing what other people told me to do. I said, "I'm not going to do this anymore." Not that I stopped immediately. At forty-five I was still struggling with having the *right* to do what I wanted to. I always said, "Nobody's gonna tell me what to do. I do what I want to." The China trip made that lie very clear, so clear it was absolutely devastating.

I went to China because I couldn't think of a valid reason not to. I tried to convince myself I couldn't afford it. But I worked every day, and if I couldn't afford three thousand dollars, something was very wrong. I had never seen so many people before—rivers of people. I knew that the goal of business in the United States is to get them to consume in the same way that we do in this country. It blew me away. I knew I had to change. When I went back to work, I told my supervisor that I wanted to work three days a week, get paid for four, and I would give them the same level of work I'd previously done in five. And that is exactly what I did. Six months later I said, "Lay my butt off." I collected unemployment. I lived in a studio apartment that I could afford on my unemployment check. Every day I sat at my typewriter and I wrote. I wrote first drafts of a couple of novels and started an anthology about women over forty who were living on their own—by choice. I didn't like the material I was getting, which mostly fell into two categories: "Poor me" or "There's nothing to it"—the old bootstrap theory. Living it, I knew there was more to autonomy than just those two options. But when you're in the middle of a brand-new process, it is hard to articulate it. I discontinued the anthology. That was in my early forties, after I was divorced.

I don't have a fantasy of aging. Aging is one of the most foreign things ever presented to me. I have not a clue. I cannot visualize myself as an eighty-year-old woman. I cannot even visualize myself as a sixty-year-old woman! What does that mean? It means that I have spent sixty years on this planet, doing what? And that's exactly what it comes down to: doing what? Well, I spent forty years doing that, and I spent twenty years doing this. What am I going to spend the next twenty doing? I have no idea. Maybe I'll be making quilts, maybe I won't. I don't know. But what I need to be is open to whatever the next twenty years brings moment by moment and hopefully it will be healthy; that's the main thing. A friend of mine said, "How dare anyone tell me that I don't have the right to decide when I have had enough of this life?" If I am no longer enjoying it—I haven't had too many years of enjoying it out of sixty because I was too busy doing what other people wanted me to do—I don't want to be here. Who knows what's gonna happen? I may get really rich in my old age; that would be a trip, wouldn't it?

One of the gifts of age is learning not to worry about the future. If you're too concerned about tomorrow, you never live today. I don't regret my choices. Now I ask, What is absolutely necessary for my life? Food, shelter, health, friends, love . . . and fabric. I know my life isn't over if I never make another quilt. But it won't be as much fun until I find the next fun thing to do. I deserve some fun. We all deserve some fun.

Quilting is a metaphor for life. In every quilt I make I learn something about myself. I learn things like where I'm hesitant in taking a step. I learn where I hide.

I learn all the places and things that we set up to make life look like something that it's not. When I was working on my quilt "The More Things Change," the piecing got so tedious. I realized that I was trying to do the impossible, and the impossible is to make *other* people change. That was not what I was doing with the fabric, but what was going on with me at that point in my life: I was trying to make other people change. I thought I had given that piece up. Hey, been there, done that. That's why I named the quilt "The More Things Change" . . . the more they stay the same; that's how it's a metaphor for life.

Menopause affected my sex drive for a long time. Celibacy is so easy. In my thirties and forties I felt guilty about being celibate. I would go out and find a man, sleep with him, and be totally frustrated. Why did I do that? Because I was supposed to want it. And if it wasn't working, there was something wrong with me. There is something wrong with the whole idea of having to want sex. It's nice to snuggle, and it's great to have fireworks with sex. But when I found out that I could make my own fireworks, I had to sit back and think about that. I decided not to sleep with men anymore. Another revelation from China. A few months after I returned I had my first sexual relationship with a woman. Sexually it was great, but relationships with women carried the same baggage my relationships with men had. I decided that my most intimate relationship had to be with myself.

Menopause came in, my interest in sex left. Lots of women experience that, but after a while it comes back. Now when I want sex, I have it with myself. It's a lot easier. Women need to know that they can take care of their sexual needs, too. I'm not going to say I will never have sex with a man again—or with a woman, for that matter. Who knows? Right now I want companions. I want people in my life. And that's people, not person. My friends all work at doing what they want to do, to find what it is they want in life. They are very, very important to me.

I still want to shoot the Colorado River rapids down through the Grand Canyon. I keep saying, "Virginia, you're getting old; you better hurry up and do this." So now that I'm moving to New Mexico, maybe I will finally do it. That's my advice to other women: find out what you want to do and do it! Don't worry about image—not that you're ever going to stop worrying about image. But if you don't let it drive your life, you can say, "Oops, oh, that's all about image, isn't it?" and then make choices about it. Take care of yourself. And that means not doing a lot of the things that you're told will make you feel and look younger. It means not using chemicals, not dying your hair, not doing these things because they are really hazardous to your health. And it can mean kicking up your heels sometimes and saying, "I'm outta here."

Aging is a trip with an unknown destination, but at the same time very known, because the destination is death. It's important when you get scared or sick to remember to stay where you are, that it will all get better. Life changes. If you run away from a problem, you will run into it again, but if you stay where you are, it'll change. When you're forty-eight, stay there. Don't worry about being sixty. When you get to sixty, stay there. When you get to eighty, stay there. Don't worry about what you didn't do; don't worry about what you're gonna do. Think about what you are doing—stay there. And that's what I'm gonna do.

People say, "Oh, aren't you excited about going to New Mexico?" No, I'm not. I'm here. I'm trying to get through today. When I'm done with it, I'm outta here. I'll go get set up someplace else so I can take my sewing machine out and get back to work. But right now, I have to stay here.

It's all a surprise, and I hope the surprises continue. I lived the life of no surprises. You make sure there are no surprises. You take care of everything so there are no surprises. That's how quilting is a metaphor for life. It's full of surprises, you never know what's going to come out. You can try to control it. If you've gotta control your quilts, then you're trying to control your life. And I was trying to control my quilts, and my quilts would just say, "Heh, you think so? Watch this! Un-unh, that's not what we're about; that may be what you're about, but that's not what we're about." So I'm learning from the quilts that I don't have to be in control all the time, that if I'm not in control all the time, I may get some surprises.

You learn when something unexpected happens that it's not a mistake; it can be turned into a different experience. When I get critiques that say, "Your points don't match," well, so what? It would be nice if all the points matched, but when you cut one piece of fabric, it is different from another piece of fabric—they move, they shift. But the quilt Nazis say, "They must be all the same."

I get asked to do shows in February—Black History Month. Thanks a lot. I will not do another show in February. If my work is so great, or whatever you want to say about it, then you will exhibit it in a show that is not focused on me as a black person. In the quilt world, white men have defined what an African American quilt is. By their definition, I do not make African American quilts. It's all about who gets to define, and in every endeavor that I pursue, someone else tries to define what I am, who I am, and what I should be doing. They did it in chemistry; they did it in personnel; it was done in photography; it was done in everything that I have tried to do. I decided in quilting I was going to do what I wanted to do, not try to prove them wrong, as I have done so much of my life. I do what *I* do, and that's got to be enough.

When I hit sixty . . . I thought I would be old . . . and therefore [unacceptable]. I thought, I'm just going to go through this anyway and make it the best thing I can possibly do. So I just went for it! Now I'm proud of my age.

— JUNE CANOLES S.N.D.

June Canoles S.N.D.

June Canoles is a woman of many facets—some of them more unusual than others—but she has successfully woven them into a seamless whole: businesswoman, teacher, administrator, corporate consultant, graphoanalyst, and member of the religious congregation the Sisters of Notre Dame de Namur.

From her home office in a residential section of Cupertino, California, in the heart of Silicon Valley, "Sister June"—as she is often called—does handwriting analysis and motivational consulting for individuals and corporations across the United States and Canada. She is founder and president of Insyte, Inc., her graphology business, and recently, at the age of sixty-seven, she launched the Insyte CHALLENGE Correspondence Handwriting Course. She returns the profits from these endeavors to her religious community, whose provincial offices are located in Saratoga, only minutes from June's office. June lives with another nun, Sister Harriet Dow, a Franciscan, who helps with the organization and running of Insyte.

According to June, graphology is now considered a behavioral science rather than "a mystical theory or metaphysical science." In fact, the Library of Congress reclassified graphology from the occult to individual psychology. Sixty percent of corporate hiring in Europe involves the use of graphology. According to Michael J. McCarthy, writing in *The Wall Street Journal,* "Handwriting analysis is quietly spreading through corporate America." And Sister June is one of its main proponents.

Graphology is the scientific system of identifying and assessing the character, personality, and aptitudes of an individual through the study of his or her handwriting. June is committed to bringing out the best in people: "I'm in a position to give people the good news that they are better off than they think. They always have more positive qualities, and their flaws are far below their strengths and talents."

June's work offers individuals and corporations insight into the personalities of current and potential employees. This insight allows managers to place employees in positions that will encourage and maximize their potential. She is on-line and communicates with 900 men and women from seven nations, as well as 175 handwriting analysts. Every morning after rising at 4:30 A.M. and spending time in prayers, she looks forward to receiving her e-mail and faxes.

When I first met June, I was immediately taken in by her infectious ebullience, good humor, and genuine kindliness and hospitality. Earlier that morning, at her request, I had faxed a sample of my handwriting to her and she began our interview with its analysis. Her description fit me to a T. I mean that literally, for with her positive and glowing report came two suggestions: one, to cross my *t*'s rather than just float the cross above the vertical line, which was my habit ("This will help you to better realize your dreams"); and two, to open my capital *C*'s rather than make them so convoluted ("This will help you to be more open to life"). Her interpretation was fascinating, and I must say, I have since followed her advice, with positive results.

"I will touch the hearts of people who come to my business, and then they can build their own reality," June said with enthusiasm. She admits that initially, when she tried to sell her service of handwriting analysis to the corporate world, being a woman *and* a nun was not an eagerly received combination: "It wasn't a big winner." June admitted that she often "came home wounded," but believing that she had "a gift to share," she felt responsible to offer it to help make the lives of others more fulfilling. "It just shows you *can* realize your dream, if every day you are positive and hopeful about your future," she said in reference to the success of her business. "You must believe in yourself."

June was reared in Carmel, California. Her first memory is of her mother kneeling by her bed and saying, "There's faith, hope, and love, and the greatest of these is love." "That has become my theme," June acknowledged. June's mother enrolled her in a Catholic school, even though her family was Methodist. At first the nuns wearing habits frightened the young girl, but "I learned to love them," June reminisced. "They were so kind. I idolized them."

In high school she met "a little old, bent-over nun" named Sister Berchman, who told June, "I'm going to pray that you become a Catholic." June tried to convince the sister that she was "fine, thank you," as a Protestant. Within a year, however, she had been received into the Catholic Church. When June next saw Sister Berchman, the nun said, "Now I'm going to pray you become a nun." June's pleas to be left alone went unheard, and a year later, thinking that she had to make a choice to either "get married or enter the religious life," she chose the Congregation of the Sisters of Notre Dame. "There are so many more people you can serve as a nun," June told me. "Besides, I think I would have been married two or three times, to tell you the truth. I couldn't stick with one person that long!" she said, laughing.

Eventually June became an elementary school teacher and administrator working on the West Coast, where she trained children to sing in four-voice choirs. "I'm always trying new things, always stretching," she said. "It has been great. I'm not the traditional nun, as you can picture. Here I am starting something new at my age. I know I will bring it to full bloom. It will be an asset for the sisters' retirement. Then I'll sell it and somebody else can continue the process, give a little bit back. Then I'll know I've done something to say 'thank you,'" June said, smiling.

The Nun's Story

⁖

How did I get started in handwriting analysis? About thirty years ago I was in Oregon, teaching. One of the students left a handwriting book in my classroom. I picked it up, and I was *fascinated* by it. When I was in Seattle, I met a sister who put me in touch with some people who told me about a school in Chicago. I started by taking a correspondence course from them—that's where I got the idea for the correspondence course that I have now. I studied with the Chicago school for twenty-five years. Then I left them to develop my own comprehensive course, which includes the knowledge from noted graphologists in Europe, Israel, and the United States.

In the meantime, I had made many friends in graphology across the United States, Canada, and England. They are supportive of me and encouraged me to create a comprehensive course in graphology. So I did! We hope to expand our output and employ more retired sisters to work with us. The average age of sisters working at Insyte is seventy-four: I'm sixty-seven, two sisters working with me are in their seventies, and one is eighty-two. This makes our staff one of the oldest in Silicon Valley! All of us who work here at Insyte have spent many years teaching children and young adults; so we have come full circle—back to teaching and correcting papers again!

What I like most about doing graphology is that it's creative. It not only helps people who need help, but it also helps our sisters—the money from Insyte goes to them. It's not mine; I can't use it. In fact, I don't care about using it. I still have lots of fun. Then, of course, I want to keep learning and urging others to learn. I love my work because it's different all the time. In the morning, corporations from all over the United States fax or Federal Express an individual's handwriting to Insyte. It takes me an hour and a half to two hours to analyze it. Within a twenty-four- or forty-eight-hour period, I have written out a page or two in phrases about this person. I take the whole character of the subject and condense it into a page.

Then the company makes its decision about whom to hire, promote, or whatever. One of my sayings is "We help you make even better decisions for your business." So my mornings are taken up with corporate work; in the afternoons I work with individuals. I also give presentations.

When I meet or talk with people who have really serious problems, I send them to a counselor. I make it a point to tell people the truth, usually starting by telling them what is best about themselves and gradually showing them what in their personality needs to be improved. As I watch people, I know when they are ready to hear about the difficult parts of their personality. Then I move in and give them the skills to work out of the difficult places, always with supportive help. Most of the people I see have been in counseling before they come to me. I try to add the touch that will get them "up and flying." It isn't unusual for me to spend an entire day with someone who needs extra help, and they often come from great distances to get the lift they need.

For several years I worked with three gambling casinos in New Jersey, helping with management, hiring, and outplacing. I would stay three or four days at a time, two or three times a year, working only with upper management and the hiring department. I was there to motivate and encourage them and their families. It gave me an insight into the high quality of the employees at that level. One manager said, "The Mafia doesn't really run us; there's a little nun in California and she *really* runs us! Her name is June." I still keep in contact with them.

I worked hard in the casinos. I would get up to say my prayers and be in the upper level of the casino at about seven A.M. After eating some breakfast, I would go into the offices of the upper management and work from eight o'clock all the way, many times, to eleven o'clock at night. After that, I'd have a glass of wine with one of the bosses, go have dinner, and retire late at night. After about four days, I was zonked. Some employees would invite me to come home with them to see their family and talk over difficulties.

Meeting them in their homes with their families was difficult but rewarding. Most of them were not practicing Catholics, but I don't talk about religion unless somebody wants to talk about it. My belief is that all of us are good people, God's people, and I don't have to preach. I just have to be who I am, and if God chooses to use me as an instrument, all the better. They recognize my goodness, and they talk to me. Of course, I have to maintain confidentiality.

Through someone's handwriting, I can see into his or her soul. I really can. That's the insight—their history, their anxieties, their joys, their passions—everything is transparent. Most people are very honest and vulnerable; they want to know that they are okay. And, you know, people *are* okay. But home, school, and church have combined to make them feel inadequate—and they have bought that fallacy. I did, too, when I was young. We may have to work on ourselves, but we're okay. People need buoying up.

When people are really having problems, they will often come to me as a couple. I know when the love is still there, and I know when the love is gone. It's the same with the members of religious orders—I may tell them, "It's time." If you can revive your calling or marriage, fine, but often it has gone too far and there's too much anger and hate; too much water has passed under the bridge, and it can't flow back. But I can tell, almost immediately. I am blessed with a wonderful intuition. I know things about people the minute I see them. It's a gift I've always had.

For instance, on occasion I work with a couple who are very angry with each other. When I know they are coming to see me, I do a lot of praying to help me know what to say to them. When I see them, I can tell when there is a spark of love left; so I work with them to give them the skills they need to make a marriage work.

There are a lot of wounded souls out there, far across the United States. I often call them to let them know I care. I support them. That is how I do my charity work. I call them, give them time, energy, and hope. Corporate businessmen don't have many people to talk to, and often they will say to me, "June, can I tell you about this relationship I'm having?" or "How do I get out of this problem?" or "I'm starting to pray. Can you tell me what I should do about prayer?" or "I can't talk about this to many people; what do you think?" Sometimes they will fly out from the East Coast to have a day with me.

Mine has been a wonderful life. I look back and thank God for everything I've been given. I've had a lot of good times. There was one time that I realized I was getting old. When I hit sixty, it scared me. No problems healthwise—I have a bit of rheumatism, but nothing major. I had always been aware of my image, concerned with looking good and the other vain ideas that women have. So now I thought I would be old. I think that's what hit me. I would be old, and therefore would I be acceptable? I thought, I'm just going to go through this anyway and make it the best thing I can possibly do. So I just went for it! Now I'm proud of my age.

My hairdresser is forever trying to make my hair dark. One time he did, and I came home and washed the whole thing out. I called him up and said, "There goes all my money down the drain!" I've got facial lines (I love my lines), but I say, "I earned these." I'm very at peace with my age now. I have many older people around me. I love older people because they are full of wisdom.

Now this correspondence course is taking so much of my time. I do find that people change as they are taking the course. Naturally, you can change only so much. Just like going to charm school: you can beautify yourself a little bit, but you are still *you*. You can't get away from that. What I *do* see, which I think is beautiful, is if people see something they don't like about themselves and their attitude changes, then their handwriting changes. There are handwriting analysts who want to change their clients' handwriting, and I say, "I don't like that idea because the person may need the stubbornness or sarcasm or whatever." Once in a while we can say, "Change something in your writing that will help you because you're thinking of it," like crossing your *t*'s. People want to make their dreams a reality, so it doesn't work if they don't do that little part of completing their letters. You can do those small things, but you can't change your basic personality.

My friend and housemate, Harriet, and I also work with teenagers: children who seem so hopeless that nobody will take them. We turn them around. I would take a child who was just impossible and work with him or her every week until he or she changed. I would give them certain exercises for control, self-discipline, and motivation. I loved them, listened to them; we did things together, and I had little skills they would have to do to learn to express themselves. I've worked with kids who go out and slam the door, say they hate me, and then come back, and so we start again. If they like working with you, seem to love you, then they'll change because they want to be like you. And you slowly indoctrinate them. Instead of violence and hate, I indoctrinate them with love of self and fairness. The joy of seeing them change and grow is the reward for the work of helping them.

Where do I think my work is going? At my age, many sisters are retiring. I do not know where it's going, but I believe in Joseph Campbell's advice: "Follow your bliss." I just follow God, follow my bliss. I believe that when it's time to happen, it will happen. So I don't worry about it. I think I'll still be doing the correspondence ten or fifteen years from now. I'll never retire. I'll drop dead first! Let the other women retire. I have too much fun to retire. Work is my fun.

I expect to live to my eighties, but that's about it. My father lived to eighty-two, my mother to seventy-seven. But I'll always make things fun, make things happen. I can live in a little hole and I'll have more things going on in that little hole . . . I think dying will be wonderful when the time comes. I believe in life-after-death experiences. At this time, I'm not a bit afraid. I try my best; I'm not perfect, but I try my best. I believe there is a heaven. I don't know where it is. I think that hell is what we make for ourselves and each other. The demons, the good and the bad, exist in our present lives, but I believe that there is life beyond this one that will be filled with happiness and peace.

The most important virtue I've learned is compassion. My motto is you never heal if you hurt. And the greatest joy we can give ourselves is to show others their own gift. It comes right back to us. It's the most joyful thing for us to see that the other has recognized and become what they could become in life. A man just called me yesterday and said, "You did an analysis for me in the 1970s; I still have it. I'd like to come see you and get updated." You can't buy those feelings of satisfaction. So the greatest joy I have is to see that others try, arrive at, and realize their own giftedness.

The most difficult thing for me is to have been unable to do everything that I wanted to do in life. It hasn't been difficult for me to give up an intimate relationship and children of my own. I have *wonderful, dear, dear* friends who couldn't be more supportive and loving. No, it's not anything that I gave up; it's that I don't have time to do even *more*. I want to do more for my sisters, and time is running out on me. I've got to get this business really coming in good for them. That is my big thrust.

Is my order dying out? Quite the contrary. In this respect, there's a great rebirth, and it's not the birth of women in these parish convents, all running around and teaching school. We are receiving women who have been married and people who want to share the last of their lives as associates with us. Second-vocation people come in now, and older women who are now free to try something new. We find that we are growing again, out of the ashes, but growing differently. It's so much richer—not this caricature of the good little nun who goes on the Ferris wheel in the nun movies—but real women of faith, strong women in the world. It's a whole new growth, an exciting time to be alive. Women are not joining us in droves, but they are joining us in quality. There's a tremendous rebirth of creative activity that is encouraged in our lives, and we experience the genuine love of the people we serve.

There are several sisters in our order who have homes for battered women; we have established homes for the very poor who have no livelihood; we work with disturbed children; we work as lawyers. Within the entire congregation, Sisters of Notre Dame work for peace and justice. It makes me so proud to be a part of this effort. My companions in the congregation are very kind; we really are a community of highly educated women who are *focused* on the poor, *focused* on social justice. We are active, calling on our congresspersons to represent us promoting social justice.

This is a ministry of people who build community wherever we go, because that is what we are: community builders.

In your sixties you realize that this is your only life and you'd better make it just what you want it to be. And you realize that you can. You can still escape, still look to the next horizon and fly there, still traverse or inhabit lands only imagined, beyond.

— ROSE STYRON

Rose Styron

DEATH AND A WILDERNESS OF DREAMS PURSUE MY WAKING.
— ROSE STYRON

"Death and a Wilderness of Dreams,"

from *By Vineyard Light*

I first met Rose Styron in July1993, when she invited me to interview her at her home on Martha's Vineyard, where, since 1959, she and her husband, novelist and essayist William Styron, have summered with a variety of visitors, including family and friends. A great beauty is rendered even more beautiful if she is oblivious (even naively) of her effect on others. Rose, beautiful, breathless, and flushed from her morning workout of tennis ("I'm always late wherever I go because I'm doing one thing too many—but it's still one thing too few as far as I'm concerned!"), came to pick me up from the ferry. She was still outfitted in her tennis gear—her standard apparel, along with a bathing suit, I later learned. Seeing her this way gave me more of the sense of an active, carefree, exuberant schoolgirl (who is "much too devoted to pleasure and adventure") than a sixty-year-old socially prominent human rights activist, poet, journalist, wife, and mother.

When we arrived at her domain in Vineyard Haven, we were greeted by a playful menagerie of dogs and cats and a not so playful, but hungry, husband. Rose insisted that I go for a swim in the estuary behind their property, provided me with a swimsuit, and went in to prepare lunch for us. Thirty minutes later I returned refreshed, as she had promised. We took our meal outside on the veranda and left Bill to visit with his Vineyard neighbor Art Buchwald. While dining, Rose gave me a mini-tracing of the trajectory that had brought her here, to heaven's door.

Raised in Baltimore ("I'm just a Southern girl"), Rose attended Wellesley, which she entered with the intention of becoming a doctor. Having written poetry since she was eight, she discovered in less than a year that what she "really wanted was always to be outside and always to be writing." In the Department of Writing, Speech and Drama at Johns Hopkins, Rose received her master's degree in the field of aesthetics. Her thesis was on Wallace Stevens.

A contract to complete a book of poems then took Rose to Rome, where, as fate would have it, she met, fell madly in love with, and soon married Bill Styron. Eventually she published two books of her own poetry, *From Summer to Summer* and *Thieves' Afternoon*. Her interest in Russian history and culture prompted her to learn enough Russian to translate poems for a third book, *Modern Russian Poetry*.

In 1968 the Styrons were invited to attend a writers' conference in Moscow, at which they would represent North American writers. After a turbulent visit to Frankfurt, which coincided with the Soviet Union's invasion of Czechoslovakia, they finally reached Moscow and were met by the Russian poet Yevgeny Yevtushenko. Protesting the invasion, the writers were sent to Tashkent, where, without surveillance, they could walk around the walls of old shrines and through the melon markets and talk to each other privately about their countries' systems of political imprisonment throughout North Africa, the Middle and Far East, and South Africa. Rose admits that it was "an eye-opening experience" for her.

Back in the United States and looking for a conduit for the disturbing information with which she had been entrusted, and finding the newly ensconced Nixon administration uninterested, Rose connected with a friend who introduced her to the British-based organization Amnesty International. She joined the first U.S. chapter, in New York.

In her words, "The human rights movement and I grew up together."

Amnesty International was only the beginning. In the years following that first trip to Moscow, Rose was a delegate to the first Abolition of Torture conference in Paris; she was sent to Chile in the aftermath of Pinochet's coup; she went to Czechoslovakia as Charter '77 was getting under way, then to Hungary, back to Russia, through South Africa to Botswana, to Nicaragua and El

Salvador, to Poland and East Germany, ad infinitum. Her missions were for PEN and the National Council of Churches, as well as for Amnesty and other human rights organizations. More recently she has made human rights–related trips to Ireland and South Africa.

Early in the 1970s Rose began writing articles for such magazines as *Ms., New Republic, New York Review of Books,* and *The Nation* about the repression and torture she found and the political prisoners she met on her travels.

For more than twenty years Rose put the welfare of her own family first: "My children always come first, and will when *they're* sixty. Someone said, aptly, 'You are only as happy as your unhappiest child.' When they were sixteen, I took each of the four on at least one mission abroad. They preserved my sanity." From then on, human rights activity became an important focus of her efforts. Simultaneously she became more and more focused on trying to integrate the human rights movement with the environmental movement and, more recently, much to her surprise, with the women's movement. "I pretty much put poetry in the drawer for twenty years," Rose said with a shade of melancholy. But since the fall of Communism and other significant changes in the world, it has occurred to her that "as the century is ending and I'm not getting any younger, what I really need to do before I face the rest of my life is to take a lot of time off to write again and see where I am now, which is very different from where I was twenty years ago. But I will never be far from the world of political activity."

In the autumn of 1996 Rose and I met again for an update at her "winter" home in Roxbury, Connecticut. Always a generous hostess, she saw to it that for this visit she had apple pie, with vanilla ice cream *and* cheddar cheese, warm and waiting for my consumption. Her beloved animals, a golden retriever and black and yellow labs, were equally welcoming. Even Bill was chipper. In the three years since our first meeting, Rose's fourth book, *By Vineyard Light,* which combines her poetry with photographs of Martha's Vineyard by Craig Dripps, had been published and was selling well. With pleasure and adventure she is rediscovering once again the poet who has lived inside her since she was an eight-year-old girl in Baltimore—"I want to concentrate now on retrieving my eight-year-old self, the self that knew exactly who she was and where she was going."

After a poetry reading Rose had given a few days earlier, someone from the audience approached her and told her that she was driven by beauty. "That pleased me enormously," she relayed to me, "because part of my vision has to do with the beauty of wilderness and gardens, the beauty of people and ideas. If I'd been asked what I was driven by, I might have said love, accompanied by certain notions of art and justice, but beauty encompasses these."

A Poetic Passion for Justice

✧

I've recently started a book on human rights. It's about people whom I have met or corresponded with through my work with Amnesty International, including those who were once political prisoners and now have emerged as great humanitarians and leaders in their own societies. They are among the profoundly thoughtful, creatively active, and inspiring people who, whether they're in politics, the arts, the sciences, or education, make a real difference and enhance the lives of their fellow citizens, thus our own. I've traveled a *great* deal in my sixties, which I've always loved doing, but since I started planning this book, I've done it with more specific aims. For instance, I interviewed Václav Havel in Prague, in his Castle office, where he kindly allowed me to come for an hour visit in the midst of a troubled, hectic day just before Czechoslovakia split in two.

Last year I did a monthly series for the Voice of America: conversations with prominent writers like Carlos Fuentes, Kenzaburo Oe, Breyten Breytenbach, Gabriel García Márquez, Robert Hass, and Czeslaw Milosz—writers who have involved themselves with all manner of current public issues and events.

This has been very enjoyable for me, something brand new in my sixties. Before that I was just too shy to ask anybody personal questions. I always felt it was a complete invasion of their privacy, especially if they were friends—although somehow I didn't feel that as strongly with strangers. All the subjects for the

Voice of America conversations were people I knew. I had a personal investment in them, and that makes me very, very inhibited because I was brought up never to pry, never to confess; there were borders between your person and their person. You took people at face value as they wished to be taken, and that was also the way you were to be taken. And it was not a bad way to be reared; it worked very well for friendships. But as long as I had a mission like a book to do or a TV series, then I felt okay about asking questions; I actually had a good time.

What childhood experiences expanded my imagination? Well, I started reading at three or four. I was the youngest child in my family by many years, and therefore by the time I was through first grade, my older brothers and sisters had gone off to college and further. After I was six, I was the only child in the house. There were books everywhere. My father, who was a former investment banker, at that point worked in Washington, D.C., in a department store on Pennsylvania Avenue, which he'd taken over from my mother's father. This store had a book department, so he would bring home a book for me every night. I'd read it and he'd take it back the next day. It was *glorious* and really expanded my horizons.

Being outdoors has also been very important to me. When I was very small, I had a wonderful black nanny from South Carolina; she had raised my brothers and sister. She spoke Gullah, the African American Creole dialect of the Carolina islands. We took walks every day, all day; you didn't go to nursery school in those days. I went to kindergarten when I was five, but for the first four years I have the most vivid memories of the walks I took with her, picking dandelions for the dandelion wine she made in my closet so my mother couldn't smell it. I could smell it, but I never got to taste any. We picked four-leaf clovers endlessly for good luck. So I have this child's-eye view of walking. Finally I was old enough to go to kindergarten. I was so in love with flowers, and grass, and trees by that time. We had a lovely garden that my mother tended. I always hated being indoors and was constantly escaping. If I was told to come in, I'd climb a tree or go hide somewhere. I realize that has been the pattern of my life, escaping to the out-of-doors to be a part of nature and feeling totally claustrophobic indoors. I write outside as much as I can, whether sitting still or being peripatetic; that's where I get my inspiration.

When I turned sixty I decided that if I was ever going back to poetry, I'd better start doing it soon. I had been working in human rights solidly for twenty years, I missed the poetry, but I just didn't think it was as important to me as the fact that I could do something out there in the world. Now I was becoming obsessed with getting back to my poetry, either to find my muse again or to admit that she had fled permanently. I forced myself to sit still, and gradually, miraculously, the poetry habit of old returned. Because the place I write best is Martha's Vineyard, I would stay there longer and longer after each summer. The book is based in Martha's Vineyard and it's called *By Vineyard Light*. It has a few old, vineyard-based poems and a few poems from a child's point of view, because I'd done two books before that: one from a child's point of view and one from a grownup's point of view. Both of them had some pieces of the Vineyard in. A great bulk of the poems for this book were new and written in the last three or four years. It was really rewarding, and it made me realize that I will never stop writing poetry again.

My experience changed from writing poetry in my forties to the time I started writing again in my sixties. I guess that's inevitable. I'd written since I was eight until I was forty, and it was always lyric verse, personal and not thematic, rarely narrative. My work came out of just the moment's inspiration, inspired perhaps by what I was reading or a painting or seasonal changes or who I was looking at or parting from or wished I were with again—the usual youthful stuff. When I started up again in my sixties, I didn't have any plan at all. I started first doing the kind of lyric and rhyme I'd done before, but I found a lot of other things creeping in, like my twenty years of human rights activity. Even though I wasn't specifically writing about that, there was no way I could block out my travels, and not only those for human rights. I've gone birding for years and years, and I've been on marvelous jaunts with my husband. I found that I was writing much more free verse; it just came from some other place.

It's been very interesting to do poetry readings for this book. It made me take my four books and look at them all again and realize how this book is the only one that's eclectic. The others are all of a piece, whereas this is back and forth, up and down, as if all the tracks of my life were beginning to come together now.

Before this, the tracks that were family or poetry or international affairs or nature or journalism may or may not have run parallel, but they never seemed to meet. Somehow, in this book of poems, I can detect an underlying place where they're beginning to join, so it makes me think I will soon try to do some linear, autobiographical poetry. It's a bit daunting. Who knows what affection or rage may surface at the next station!

I don't know if this weaving together is an inevitability of being in my sixties; it may be. I haven't gone into analysis or tried to write my memoirs or to recapture specific pieces of my life. In fact, when the University of Colorado came to ask for all my human rights papers, I just took them to the attic and happily gave them twenty years of stuff, keeping only a tiny bit from the last five or six years where I might want to use something for my book. But I didn't look at it, reread it, and think, Ah, I'll just do my memoirs. I just wanted to be done with it. I always want to go forward; I don't have a real taste for my own past. I like *other* people's pasts a lot, though. I've had a very good life, but there's always something around the corner I want to see or something at the top of the next tree or over the next horizon. There are just never enough hours in the day for what's coming next, so I never really want to dwell on what's past. But inevitably it all comes in when you sit down to write poetry.

Yes, I've had bouts of being depressed—who hasn't who has any brains or sensitivity or any feel for poetry or an awareness of what's going on in the world? I've had very sad, depressed times in my life, but I've never had a clinical depression. I've never for one second wanted to kill myself. Whatever bouts of melancholy I may have had about myself, my work, they cannot compare to Bill's real clinical depression. From my view at sixty, perhaps fifty percent of the reasons for any difficulties between us may have been centered on his incipient depression and neither of us understanding what was happening. Certainly I, from a calm, cheerful, quiet-voiced suportive family, was not prepared for such volatility. And two people who had not isolated themselves in the country, writing, might have had the sense to seek therapy, to talk with someone who could help them talk to each other.

Still, I think it's been an incredibly good marriage. We still love and value each other. We talk more easily now, are more companionable, even when we're reading our separate books after our traditional late dinners à deux in Connecticut. Since Bill's crisis, I try to stay home more, and even abandon planned trips for my work abroad if he seems "down" (though I've been known to curse myself for my decisions later!). This is probably why sixty seems calmer than fifty or forty and why we consult and accommodate each other more now.

Every decade of our marriage has been different. I could have been married to four different people. We've been married over forty years, and we've both changed so, repeatedly. The dynamic of how each of us feels about the other and everyone else alters and yet is basically the same. Bill's relationship to the world has changed, publicly and privately, being "up" or "down"—and I react to his changes and he reacts to mine.

I'm more gregarious than I would be if Bill weren't such a dedicated loner. One of my missions is to bring him together more often with our good friends—after all, the glue of our marriage since the children left home is not only our common history and the values and private and public passions we share, or views on events from movies to politics, on crime and punishment, on food (Bill is a great gourmet cook), or daily walks with the dogs: it's friendship. We've shared a number of long-term friendships with remarkable individuals and couples.

To backtrack a bit, the easiest thing in the world would have been for us to separate, and I'm sure we both thought of it many times. You decide again every decade or every morning, are you going to go on with this or are you going to run away and do something else? But if you don't separate, then you tend to go deeper, to know each other better, to know your own needs and his. You make your compromises, and I guess you're glad the other person is still around. You develop a lot more compassion for the other person. You wake up forty years later and find you are with someone who is familiar, no matter how difficult it might have been at times. The skies may be different, but you look around and the house has survived and its transients are dear and recognizable, even if their sizes and hair colors are different from what they used to be.

But in my sixties, the freshest component of my life is true friendship with a number of amazing women, and that number seems to increase by one, and by another, almost every year. Most of these friendships, which I didn't have enough time to build on in my thirties and forties, had their foundations laid a decade or two or three ago. From different places and a diversity of careers, we meet on Martha's Vineyard or other territory and talk, and play, and expand our outer and inner lives with mutual affection.

Something that has begun to interest me for the first time in my life is women's rights, the quality of women's lives, and their leadership potential for the next century. In the human rights movement, I felt I did not want to spend time in gender-specific work, that rights were human. It was fine to start or to join auxiliary human rights groups that were professionally oriented, so that in addition to the original Amnesty International with its broad mandate, there would be a human rights group of artists, one of physicians, one of writers, one of lawyers. But I never wanted to separate it out in gender or age. Now I've become quite interested in women's rights and women's potential.

I was grateful to be asked by the Women's Commission on Refugee Women and Children to go to Bosnia this spring, and I have willy-nilly become involved in trying to get the women of Bosnia all the money appropriate from the U.S. government and from private sources that I can find, because they're the ones who are going to save the former Yugoslavia. They're the *only* ones who want a united country, who want to live next door to their former neighbors who are of a different ethnic background, who see the family and culture as the important thing to hold together, and who are willing to work in the smallest or the largest possible way to get it done. They will get rape victims to The Hague to testify and then protect them when they get back and find a way to get treatment for the children of Croatia who are casualties of a leukemia epidemic, and training for the doctors who know that four years of war have deprived them of the latest medical skills. They keep makeshift schools and centers for the elderly, the displaced, and the traumatized going somehow. These women are confident, spirited, full of goodwill; they make us proud to be their sisters.

When I was aproaching sixty, I was in total denial about aging. I just did not want to face it. That round number 6-0 meant "over the hill," "youth gone," "out to pasture." I thought my lively mother, who is about to turn one hundred, was dying when she turned fifty. I felt *young*, and I wanted everyone to think I was. My fear was that once I admitted I was sixty I would no longer be sexy, no longer a writer on the way up, no longer eligible for a foreign affairs adventure. I would have to think about decline and about reordering my life and changing my priorities and staying home, and I don't want to do any of those things.

So when my sixtieth birthday was coming up, I swore my kids to secrecy, I made my husband promise he would not give me a party, and I went to a spa to be alone and get renewed. I got to the spa, and wouldn't you know, my friend Ann Buchwald was there also and knew it was my birthday, so of course she and her group toasted my birthday at dinner. I was furious yet totally amused at myself, and I just laughed all night. I thought, How silly can you be?

The next morning I hired a hot-air balloon and I went up as my birthday celebration. It was *fabulous*. So there I was, escaping into the stratosphere. I'd always wanted to levitate. "Oh, well," I said, "here we are, I'm sixty." You cannot expect certain things of yourself that you did when you were forty, but on the other hand, I haven't found anything I have to give up.

I feel lighter, freer, almost at home with myself (not quite, yet). Family responsibilities are not a burden, because my children, who are much smarter and more disciplined than I, are all well and launched in their chosen fields, are close to each other and mutually supportive, and come home to share their loves with us, and the tennis court, often. Sixty is full of unexpected pleasures. In your sixties you realize this is your only life and that you'd better make it just what you want it to be. And you realize that you can. You can still escape, still look to the next horizon and fly there, still traverse or inhabit lands only imagined, beyond.

Perhaps the most perfect day of my sixties, so far, totally within myself, for myself, occurred in January 1993. I was trekking across a mountaintop in Bhutan during a blizzard with three sixtyish friends: Peter Matthiessen, George Plimpton, and Inge Morath. We had spent several grand weeks in India with Bill (who rarely wants to come on extended trips) and other pals. Some, including Bill, had gone home to the States. Those of us who stayed got stuck in our van halfway up the Himalayan ridge in a snowdrift. We four had opted to continue walking till they could rescue the van.

Now, in this glorious high place in remote Bhutan, unable to see anything but the person ahead or behind through the soft white pelting snow, we walked, each in his own silence, the only occasional sound a crane's cry from far down the valley. Or a child's high-pitched voice wafting up from somewhere. Or a bell chiming, far away. The rest of the time, hours, absolute silence. I thought, By nightfall, we'll find a monastery or a place to camp. But if we don't, I'll die here, inspired, content, eternal.

I never feel that way when I'm at sea level or at normal-life level. I don't take big physical risks; I don't want anything to incapacitate me or kill me because I want to participate actively in what comes next. At great heights (and I feel this on planes over the ocean) one doesn't care. The present is very clear, and one is totally oneself. At least I am. I think lots of people are totally themselves all the time, but I'm not, when I'm in motion. Unless all the external stimuli are removed. I'm still in motion mostly, not completely myself. I need to learn, again, to be alone, to sit still, to meditate.

I feel very earthbound these days. I am definitely not prepared for death. I'm not afraid of it—I can't imagine it—I just want life as is to be extended as long as possible, as long as my *health* lasts. There's so much more to see and do, to think and love and write. In my sixties I contemplate not death, but the beautifully lit theater of life I am sure is still awaiting me. Yet when I pass the little cemetery under whose greensward we Vineyard pals will one day lie as neighbors—no doubt still talking—I wonder what my tombstone will say: DRIVEN BY BEAUTY AND A PASSION FOR JUSTICE? Or, I STILL WANT IT ALL?

I'm now as content with solitude as I have been since I was twenty-one. I was *very, very* content to be alone when I was growing up; in fact, I preferred it most of the time because it meant I could read, write, paint, or sing. I've found myself, in the last few years, singing again. Then, I like being alone at the Vineyard, with its *light,* its vast horizons, beaches, sky (though I miss Bill and my Connecticut family when I stay too long). I *don't* like being alone in Connecticut. I get claustrophobic, lost, haunted by a house once full of children, now dark under its high trees. I'm not as comfortable in myself in Connecticut as I am when I'm by the ocean. I like those horizons and the sense of eternity, so it's being alone in the landscape or on the the water where I feel I could go forever, as in Bhutan, I guess.

There is one thing I *don't* like about being in my sixties. I really think my brain is slower to process standard things like people's names. Boy, is it tough. I hate to admit it! We all excuse it by saying, "Well, we've known *so* many people, our brains are so overfull that of course we lose pieces of our memory." I don't lose today and yesterday, I'll lose five or twenty-five years ago—a whole piece of it I won't remember—and it's just shocking to me. Often I'll have to reach for a word. I always find it, but it's not there immediately, and it's very bothersome. It's not true when I write or think—that's between me and myself—only when I'm talking to someone. Maybe the distraction of talking and seeing so many things at once and trying to explain affects me. Every now and then I find that I'll instinctively say the wrong word and have to correct myself right away. I find that *very* scary—a lot of people my age find that scary. James Merrill wrote a wonderful funny poem on this subject. All we can do is laugh about it together.

But I know that the world is a wonderful place, filled with extraordinary human beings and incredible opportunities. I'd like to tell young people to seize the day. To stop, look, listen, pay attention to where we are, what we are doing, who we love, who's in front of us. It's best not to be judgmental; being judgmental closes out so much that we might learn and enjoy, so many people we might enjoy and learn from. We need to project into other people's frames of mind and reference and see where they're coming from. We should look before we leap, but not too hard or we'll never leap. Be impulsive, be spontaneous. That's the most important thing. And to trust. Yourself. Every day.

I believe, not from my mouth but from my heart, that life is beautiful. Live it, if you can, and don't begrudge it. . . . If you grow to be an old age, expect to tell yourself, every year, "I didn't know anything last year." . . . And whatever opportunity comes before you, take it. Don't think it's too small. Life has a lot to offer.

— NABEELA GEORGE

Nabeela George

I arrived in Port Chester, New York, on the eight A.M. train from Manhattan. A taxi took me through a working-class town in which the streets were colorfully camouflaged by autumn leaves. I had been told of Nabeela George by her friend Oh Shinnah Fast Wolf, another participant in this book. Nabeela was an artist who had been disabled by polio in her early childhood. She lived with her closest friend, Dolores Krieger, the great proponent of hands-on healing and author of *Therapeutic Touch.* Nabeela's paintings hang in the king's palace in Jordan and the UNICEF Center in Lebanon.

When I knocked on the screen door, a voice called faintly, "The door's open," from a back room. Within moments Myrtle, Nabeela's full-time caretaker, met me in a room with walls covered in both oil and acrylic paintings of portraits and landscapes. Myrtle took me into Nabeela's bedroom, where she was sitting up in a bed surrounded with as many items as could fit on her single bed, windowsill, and reading table: telephone, water, books, a mirror, eye makeup and lipstick, magazines, writing implements and pads of paper, a pair of glasses, Kleenex, personal telephone and address book, and the unmistakable pile of bills demanding attention.

Nabeela, in her mid-sixties, seemed radiant and soulful. Her diminutive size and the fact that her hands and fingers with their well-manicured and painted nails were somewhat twisted and misshapen reminded me instantly of "the Little Sparrow" herself, Edith Piaf, who had suffered terribly from degenerative arthritis. When I mentioned Edith Piaf, she smiled brightly, as if this was not the first time the comparison had been made, and said, "I love her voice."

During the next two hours we spoke about art, painters, living with a physical disability, her forty-year friendship with Dolores Krieger, whom she calls "a real sister," her life in Beirut before she came to the United States at the age of twenty-four, and how living life with a positive outlook has helped her survive an often difficult and an unceasingly physically painful existence. The opposite of self-pitying, she spoke of the gratitude and wonder she felt toward her life experiences.

Nabeela has undergone twenty-six corrective operations because of her polio and is essentially bedridden. It seemed natural to mention another artist, Frida Kahlo, who, because of an accident in her teenage years, also lived with enormous physical anguish. "Oh, yes," Nabeela replied, "I feel a real connection to her, too." Only two weeks prior to our meeting, she had had a general checkup. "I was wondering why my voice was so gravelly," she explained, "because I was always a soprano. I used to sing solo in the church." On examination of her left breast the doctor found a lump and said, "Something is cooking." He sent her for a biopsy immediately. "I thought he wasn't in his right mind," Nabeela said, still visibly shaken by the experience. "They took a specimen and told me right away, 'It's a malignancy.'" Ordinarily the doctor would not have recommended surgery, he said, but would have prescribed chemotherapy. Because of Nabeela's lack of mobility, it would be difficult for her to travel back and forth to the hospital, however, so he recommended a mastectomy.

As a result of her polio, Nabeela has only one lung and therefore cannot be put under anesthesia. "They have to perform it while I'm awake. I'm scared," she told me, her dark eyes wide and liquid. "I feel anxious and frightened about the mastectomy. When they did the biopsy, I felt everything; I screamed. I hope it will be different this time. It has to be done." At first she resisted it and told Dolores that she would not undergo yet another surgery. "I'll tell you why I'm resenting it," Nabeela said. "After twenty-six operations, enough is enough. I feel I have seen life and enjoyed it. What difference is one more year going to make? In that one year they add to my life, I'm going to suffer while recuperating from the operation. So why not leave me alone? I accept having one more year left because now I know what's after. Life is a continuum. I came, I was, I am to come again. That's what I believe, and that makes sense to me."

Two weeks later Nabeela underwent her mastectomy. We spoke several times by telephone during the following three months. When I called on New Year's Eve, I was stunned when Dolores informed me that Nabeela had peacefully and painlessly passed away the week before, on Christmas Eve. "She had a beautiful attitude," said Dolores. "Nabeela always endured what came her way during her life. And because she believed that life is a continuum, she graciously accepted her death."

Nabeela's determination and bravery remain vividly impressed in my memory, and I believe the way she lived will continue to inspire all who hear her story.

A Courageous Life

❖

My father was born and raised in Africa. My mother is Lebanese. I was born in the Holy Land, Nazareth, which was Palestine at that time. I am as old as Methuselah! My family went to Tiberius when I was ten years old, and we lived in Jerusalem. When we lived in Jerusalem, we lived near the garden tomb, which is the tomb of Christ. I remember how my cousin and I used to go and sleep and play in it. We didn't realize at that time how important it was. By the time I was eighteen, because of the partition between the Jews and the Arabs, we were considered neither/nor. My father had a British citizenship, so we all had British citizenships. From there, we went to the American University of Beirut. Some of my siblings continued education, but I wasn't accepted because of my disability.

Polio visited me when I was eleven months old. It affected my neck and spine. I wasn't able to walk until I was seven years old. No school would accept me. That year we heard of a German Jewish doctor who was an expert in polio. He said, "I can operate on one leg" (because it was getting too long), but he was honest and said, "More than that, I would not attempt." I used to walk leaning against an available wall. I remember once, coming out of class, the kids stepped on me without knowing it. A nun was near me and pushed them aside, saying, "Can't you see where you're stepping?" They didn't, of course. But this was the sorry part of it. I haven't walked for almost forty years. I sit in the wheelchair now because it makes life easier. Much easier.

As a little girl, I started painting when I realized all schools refused to allow me to attend them. I got so discouraged, and I went myself to the headmistress and cried, "Please give me a chance." I was then given a chance at the orphanage. I couldn't imagine why my sisters were in very expensive schools and I was in an orphanage. It didn't sit right with me. Anyway, soon after that, I came home.

In order to distract me, my father bought all the best editions of books on artists in Italy and France, and I came home to a studio that he had furnished with everything I needed so that I could paint. And you know what? I hated that. I knew what he was trying to do, and I didn't want to see any of it. Now I love it. But this was the beginning of my painting. The first person to instruct me was one of the czar of Russia's horsemen. He went every day to inspect all the soldiers and horses of the czar, and his wife was the lady-in-waiting. Unfortunately the czar was killed, but my instructor was spared. This I say, because I went to his house, I saw the pictures with him and the czar and czarina. These memories I cannot forget.

For my first big show, before I came to America, I was invited by King Hussein and Queen Dina, his first wife, to exhibit my paintings in the palace. I remember very well when I went there. I was the guest of the palace in Jordan for a week, and then a friend of my father's, who was an M.D., invited me to his house. There is still one of my paintings on display at the palace. There is a second one at the UNICEF Center in Lebanon.

One day in 1957 when I was twenty-five years old, somebody from America who was connected with New York University came to Lebanon while I was having a one-person show. He said, "Would you like to go to America?" I said, "Sure, who wouldn't?" I was happy that I was offered this opportunity to come to this country. I didn't know a single person here, but I wanted to see America. My other brothers and sisters chose England. I thought America. I came on a scholarship from the American University of Beirut to study occupational therapy. I was working for the dean of the medical school as a medical artist, someone who draws human anatomy. I used to go into the operating theater—you have to be fast before, during, and after an operation. For instance, we had a boy who was born with his fingers connected together like a web. So I drew a sketch showing the boy's hand before the surgery, while the doctor was doing the incision, and one after the surgery.

I'll never forget the day a taxi brought me to First Avenue to the institute connected with NYU where I was to work. I saw eight million people! Beirut had had one million, so it was really strange. I was one of the foreign student therapists, and we had a dorm for ourselves. And then I used to commute from First Avenue down to Washington Square to the New School of Social Research. It was very interesting.

I had all my clothes stolen the first New Year's Eve I was in New York City. Afterward, somebody I'd never met before came to the Art Students' League, where I was taking classes, and said, "May I take you out for lunch?" I consented to go. On the way he says, "This is Third Street." I told him, "But you said we were going to lunch." He said, "Little friend, somebody told me that all your clothes were stolen, and I'm going to replace every one." I couldn't believe it. I told him, "I can't accept this." He said, "Not to worry." We went to every department in Macy's. If I flipped the tag on a sweater or whatever, he would slap me on my arm and tell the salesgirl to wrap it up. Every dress or a jacket I wanted! There haven't been many people like that in my life. He was one I can never forget.

There was another outstanding incident around that time. I used to live at the YWCA on Eighth Avenue then. One evening I came home from school smelling of turpentine, my hands colored with paint. There were cabs and policemen all around. I asked what was going on and they said, "It's the dedication of the YWCA by Mayor Wagner and Governor Rockefeller." A girl who was seating people said, "We have a place for you, right in the front so you can see everything." I didn't even look presentable; I was so embarrassed. So after they served the refreshments, I tried to leave. But before I could, wouldn't you know it?

Governor Rockefeller came up to me and said, "I'll help you." He came and gave me a hand. It was memorable.

One day I also went to see the UN. I speak five languages: Arabic, English, German, Hebrew, and French. I thought it might be a good idea to do some translating. I was sitting in a small room waiting to be interviewed. In walked a most elegant black lady. The woman who was with me said, "I bet this is Marion Anderson." By golly, she said, "Yes, I am Marion Anderson." She came and sat beside me, and she noticed I was Oriental. "Who are you?" she asked. I told her and we became friends. She was so charming.

I also met Mrs. Eleanor Roosevelt. I sat at the same table where she was having dinner in New York at the Institute of Physical Medicine and Rehabilitation, which is now the Rusk Institute. All the therapists were invited. I met Margaret Bourke-White, the photographer. She lived there and was receiving treatment. Because she had Parkinson's disease, she had lost her hair. I asked her, "You don't mind going without your wig?" She said, "No, I look just as nice without it." She was remarkable.

Six months after I came to America, they discovered my left hand was withering. The doctors said, "We can operate on your arm and save it." I said, "I have no money. Whatever money I have is for my scholarship." "Don't worry," they said, "we'll do something about it." So I had to be in a cast for a year. While I was in the cast, I was a patient at the Rusk Institute. One evening—it was Christmas Eve—I heard the supervisor of nurses listening to Handel's *Messiah* and she asked me to come in. I said, "No, patients don't go into the nurses' stations." She said, "I'm the supervisor, I invite you to come in." That nurse was Dolores. Right away we had a very strong connection, and the next day she asked me if I'd like to see New York decorated for Christmas. I said, "I'd love to."

Shortly after that it was discovered that I had only five grams of hemoglobin in my body and the normal is fourteen grams. People usually don't live with less than five grams. I was really anemic. Dolores said, "My mother will nurse you to health. Would you like to come and live with us?" That was the beginning of our lifelong friendship. Then, wherever she moved, she said, "I'm to have an apartment. Would you like to share it with me?" She's a remarkable lady. She has not only been my closest friend, she has been a sister—in the true sense of the word. Every time I wake up from an operation, I find her sitting day and night by my bedside while they're giving me blood transfusions. I literally did not have one person in America until Dolores. We have been friends for almost forty years. The one who really gave me the most insight and enlightenment has been Dolores. She is magnificent.

When I first met Dolores, she asked me if I'd like to tour by car with her and see twenty states in America. We also had with us a man who was born without hands. He had been a thalidomide child. Nothing bothered him really except when children stared at him. We camped at Grand Canyon, Oak Creek Canyon, and all the famous places. We went to Kentucky (near the university), and they gave us an elaborate welcome. All the singers really pampered us. So we had a good time.

What keeps me so positive? Friends. I discovered that friends, and really whoever you come into contact with, have more than three-quarters to do with how you live, with your perspective on life. I grew up in a house in which there were two disabled children: my brother and myself. My younger brother passed away when he was eighteen. He died of degenerative arthritis. He started getting crippled when he was eleven years old, so he and I developed a special bond.

When we were living at the American University campus in Beirut, we decided to start a cultural group for music, painting, and poetry. We would invite all the poets of the country and let them argue and debate among themselves. And for music, we would read about the piece first, then put out the lights and let people listen to the music. We loved those times. I remember, when I was about to leave Lebanon, he said to me, "Nabeela, there is a special event tomorrow evening for you." I asked, "What are you doing?" He said, "You'll see." He had invited all the musicians he knew—we had a beautiful piano—and we had a beautiful recital at our house. Not a huge amount of people, but at least fifty, and we listened to the music. Then he said, "This is for my sister's good-bye." About six months later, he died. I loved that brother so much. It's not love only; it's respect. If he ever saw me come to his room and I was not in my usual mood, "Out," he would say. "When you smile, you can come back."

I said "three-quarters" of what makes me positive is having wonderful friends. The other quarter would pertain to my mother, who had two disabled children. "What am I to do? How am I to keep them?" she would complain. She dwelled on the sad part. My father didn't, but Mother did. So that made me feel I wanted to be more positive. I wanted to live. Her mother was like that, and her sisters still are like that. I never understood that. I mean, it's happened; so let's do something about it. Go ahead with our lives.

Success to me means that in spite of my disabilities, I have managed to reach my goal, I've been able to do what I wanted to do. Not only in art, but in myself, to be a person like others, to be respected like any other person—that was my aim. I could have achieved more, perhaps. Financially I am poor, but I'm content. What I have, I am grateful for. And I believe, not from my mouth but from my heart, that life is beautiful. Live it, if you can, and don't begrudge it. Other people might be denied it. If you grow to be an old age, expect to tell yourself, every year, "I didn't know anything last year." That's what I did. "Where was I last year? How little I knew." How true it is. And whatever opportunity comes before you, take it. Don't think it's too small. Life has a lot to offer. I don't understand how people can go and do away with their lives when there's so much in life.

At this age, I love being a single woman. When I divorced some years ago, after thirty years of marriage, I looked on it as a failure because I had all the old tapes in my head. I still mourn the loss of that institution in my own life, but it's more out of romanticism about the notion of marriage than it is about reality. I enjoy being single.

— ANN RICHARDS

Ann Richards

For her sixtieth birthday present to herself, Ann Richards, former Democratic governor of the Lone Star State of Texas, learned how to ride a motorcycle and got her special license. This unconventional display illustrates her feeling that at sixty "we don't have to pretend anymore, and we can be exactly who we are." At sixty-three she remains colorfully unhomogenized. For a woman with a reputation for bold and brassy rhetoric, Ann is surprisingly cautious in her speech, thinking through her responses and choosing her answers with care. Her throaty, (ex-)smoker's, throw-back-your-head kind of laugh punctuates her often exuberant, funny, and sensible observations, which are spoken in a playful country-girl drawl that belies her oratorical gifts.

This is a woman who works hard ("probably too hard," she admits) and plays just as hard. Clearly intelligent and an impressive raconteuse, she is also a great deal of fun to spend time with. Slightly puzzled that I hadn't asked her what kind of music she listens to and if she likes to dance (country, yes), she chided me with, "Your questions are mighty lofty." Aside from her obvious command as a politician, and behind her practiced smile, Ann Richards is about as authentic as they come. She is *exactly* who she is without apology. Still relishing a more-than-full schedule, Ann was not only generous with her time with me ("As much as you need"), but equally liberal with her personal reflections and anecdotes.

While governor of Texas (1991–1995), Ann became a celebrity with old-fashioned star power; television viewers saw her profiled on *60 Minutes* and as a guest on just about every network talk show. Her keynote address at the

Democratic National Convention in 1988 was studded with barbed wit and had the audience riveted. As a way of accounting for her audience's direct and complete grasp of her speeches, a year later Ann wrote in her autobiography, *Straight from the Heart,* "If my mama in Waco can't understand what I'm talking about, no one else can."

The hard living that shows on her still pretty face reminded me of something the Italian actress Anna Magnani is quoted as having said to her director, Federico Fellini: "Don't retouch my wrinkles, it took me so long to get them." In a time of the easy fix of cosmetic surgery, four children, six grandchildren, a thirty-year marriage and painful divorce, politics, alcoholism, decades of sun, chronic laughter, hunting, fishing, winning, and losing are all etched on her face and linger in her forget-me-not blue eyes. Her supercoiffed, gravity-defying helmet of upswept white hair ("I rat the tar out of it," revealed Ann's hairdresser, Gail, in an interview, "then I spray the hell out of it") gives off an aureole of light that makes her easy to spot in any full room.

She admits to being "driven" and attributes it to the fact that her mother, who was "and *is*" also ambitious, instilled in Ann, her only child, the ethics of constant hard work, high standards, and perfectionism. Perfectionism comes with a high price, however: the perfectionist internalizes the fear of never quite living up to one's own (and one's parents') standards.

Ann was born just outside Waco, Texas, and "raised in a community that was probably poor, although I never felt poor." She attended Baylor University on scholarship and graduated with a B.A. in 1954. At the University of Texas at Austin she earned her teaching certificate. Married at nineteen and the mother of two girls and two boys, she became active in the civil rights movement and Texas politics. As governor she was the champion of the poor, the elderly, children, and pregnant women; and early on she became a heroine to the women's movement.

The week I met Ann in her Austin office, where, now, she is a senior adviser at and lobbyist for Verner, Liipfert, Bernhard, McPherson and Hand, a Washington, D.C.–based law firm, she had just recently settled her eighty-six-year-old mother, whom she calls Mama, into a local retirement home. This clearly had left her in a reflective frame of mind about her own aging process. "Mama has a hard time dealing with it," said Ann. And she charges this difficulty to the fact that her mother no longer has any responsibility. "There's nothing she *has* to do, and there are a lot of things she can't do. She doesn't have to cook meals or do laundry or water plants—and she had to give up her dog." Ann is trying to "figure out a project" she can give her mother but also realizes her own tendency to be "a fixer and controller." In the middle between her eighty-six-year-old mother and her four children and six grandchildren, Ann Richards talked about what it feels like to be in her early sixties.

The Personal Is the Political

I t feels absolutely great to be this age. It feels as good as slipping into an old bathrobe or an old sweater that always hangs on the hook. I tell people when they have birthdays: "When you turn fifty, you don't have to pretend anymore. And when you turn sixty, you are at ease with it—if you're lucky." If we're fortunate enough, I think sixty is an age at which we come to terms with who we are. We don't think we have to be something else. That doesn't mean we don't think we have to be better, because usually we do. I'm the best person to tell you where I need to improve. But I'm content with who I am. Of course, that doesn't mean I still will not always feel driven—I will. But I am *content* with the fact that I will probably always feel driven. So now I can accept the negative aspects of myself as well as the positive.

I've been talking with my friends about the fact that I may need a counselor, maybe a career counselor, for lack of a better term, to help me learn how not to work so hard. Since work has been the driving factor in my life, I would like now not to strive so hard. I'd like to learn to enjoy leisure, to have some serenity without so many responsibilities. I don't know how to do that. I think it's a skill I could learn, but I need someone to teach me.

A friend of mine is approaching retirement and easing into more down time.

To begin, he is taking Mondays off from going to his office, and then in six months he'll start taking Fridays off, too. That way retirement will be a gradual process. Well, that won't work for me because I *also* work weekends. I am in my office only about ten days a month. I spend about ten more days in Washington for lobbying. Often I'm on the road Saturday and Sunday going to board meetings or giving speeches and attending events for people running for Congress (principally women). So I don't have any routine. There is no predictability about any week. And I love it that I don't have a rigid routine! The work I do involves so many different aspects that the variety keeps me from being bored or impatient with it.

Work is such an integral and crucial part of our lives. That old business about thanking God every morning I get up because I have something to do is true. That means something I *have* to do, and that's what I think has been removed from my mother's life. When work has driven you for so many years, some other force has to take its place—I don't care what the age is, whether it's sixty-five or seventy-five. Volunteering, of course, is one alternative, and I know a lot of people who do that. I can understand that people would like to work longer, but let's face it, we've got too many people and too few jobs. And as long as we are in there hanging on, there's no place for the young people coming up.

My friends and I have been talking about this for a long time. We always said we were going to build a place called Curtains, and Curtains was where we were all going to live when we got older. It wasn't so much that we want an exclusive place to live. It's that we want to choose the people we live with. In most retirement homes you don't have a choice.

Women see their lives in a circular fashion; one period of life connects to another, and that period connects to the next. Men see their lives in a more linear fashion, in which they start at A and go to Z. Women are constantly reinventing themselves. Particularly for women my age, who were born in the 1930s and who went through the women's movement and self-realization, there was absolutely no predictability whatsoever other than marriage and parenthood. And that's not predictable at all anymore. The only role model I had was a very hardworking mother who, when I left home, had a difficult time with her reinvention. In fact, she never quite got there, and her life—at least what was communicated to me—became one of waiting for me (the only child) to return home on holidays.

I remember writing a speech once in which I said something about empty, unlived days, waiting until the children came for Christmas. I was determined from early on in my own motherhood that, although my children were really important to me, I would not make them feel it was their job to entertain me. So now, at my age, I look at the business of women's reinvention and I realize that most women never had the opportunity to make enough money to feel secure. And every woman's greatest fear is being old and poor.

Years ago, when I heard Gloria Steinem say that, I thought, Man, if Gloria Steinem is worried about that, it really *is* everybody's fear. It is my greatest fear. Absolutely. Most women do not have a level of financial security that allows them to feel comfortable about getting older. Men know they need to put money away for their retirement; and I'm telling you that very few women of my age have had the opportunity to do that. We don't have that pattern. We're still trying to figure out how to live our lives: as young women, as parents, and certainly as we get older. Thank God the opportunity is there for us to do something unpredictable.

At this age, I love being a single woman. When I divorced some years ago, after thirty years of marriage, I looked on it as a failure because I had all the old tapes in my head. I still mourn the loss of that institution in my own life, but it's more out of romanticism about the notion of marriage than it is about reality. I enjoy being single. Perhaps my situation is unique in that I have a particular male friend who also loves being single, so I have male companionship in the sense that we go to movies together when I'm in town, but there is a total freedom in the relationship. I can be gone for weeks at a time and we may not even talk, and there is no guilt on either side. So I have the best of both worlds, an interesting, charming, kind man who asks absolutely nothing of me, which is great.

Our tendency, whether it is a man or someone else close to us, is to mirror and reflect back what stands in front of us. Women are acculturated to think of themselves as the glue that holds society together, that we are the peacemakers, the community builders, the caretakers. We work so hard at trying to be whatever we think the other person wants us to be that we either don't take the time to be us or don't know how. I can't tell you how many widows I've seen who suddenly became the world's best mom; they transfer their role from being the world's best wife to the world's best mother or mother-in-law or grandmother.

Now, in my talking to women, I encourage them to be responsible for their financial well-being. That it is absolutely essential for them to recognize that they must make money. I don't care how they do it: if they have a job in the workplace or are paid for the job of being a housewife. I had twenty-plus years as a housewife that were very satisfying, but I didn't get paid for it. Women should have their own bank accounts and manage their own money. Until that financial security exists, the freedom to be who you want to be is simply not there. It's fundamental. You just cannot have good mental health; there is no feeling of ease and comfort without financial independence.

I don't know exactly when I came to feminism. Somewhere I knew that women ought to be able to do anything the men could do. My mother-in-law had an impact on me. She was the state president of the League of Women Voters. Although she was intellectually adventurous and very bright, she was not a feminist—she would never have called herself that—but I got some of that message from her. And I have to say that my husband was very sympathetic and encouraging.

We were crusaders, we were fighters for civil rights, for equal justice. It would have been hypocritical to suggest that the equality you desired for minorities, you would deny to women. I became involved in Sarah Weddington's political campaign in the early 1970s. Sarah argued *Roe* v. *Wade* before the Supreme Court two decades ago, and I was impressed by her. So when Sarah asked me, I was intrigued by the idea of being in charge of her campaign (as it turned out, I really wasn't).

Through that campaign I met a group of young women who were probably ten to fifteen years younger than me. I really liked these women. I liked their energy and their drive. I liked their in-your-face attitude. That core of women has held together now since 1972. It has been an incredible support system and camaraderie. I think it was that association with those women more than anything else I could name, other than this seed in me that said women ought to have a chance to do anything a man can do, that brought me to feminism. Some of them were in my cabinet when I was governor. I know that should I ever be in trouble or need anything, I could call on any of those women and they could call on me. They are a very interesting group.

Politically speaking, we women have not yet come into our own. One of the reasons is that the political system is still, by and large, run by white men. It isn't out of meanness or unkindness that it is difficult for them to make the changes. It's simply that they grew up as little boys and we grew up as little girls; it's just an instinctive thing. (I can talk to you a lot about the differences between men and women!)

The second reason is that men—white men I'm talking about here—have some kind of informal communication system that we don't have. We still lead pretty isolated lives, and we are terribly consumed by the demands on our lives. Young women have got to get up, feed kids, get them to day care, go to work, pick up the kids, and come home; then they are expected to have shopped for and prepared food, and often they have work to do from the office and help to give to their kids with their homework; then they have to check in on Mama and make sure everything is okay in the parent-care area. You know, the whole litany. Because of the paucity of personal time, they have very little opportunity to share and reassure each other that it's okay to think the way they think and have the fears they have. Men have established a communication system we simply don't have. And politically it makes an enormous difference.

Women really don't trust anyone in politics, female or male candidates—they think it doesn't make any difference—and they are the first group not to vote. That's because they don't see any effect or change or improvement in their daily lives. Men love to talk about issues like Bosnia, the impact of Chinese policy on trade. Women want to know: What will you do about my retirement? What about health care, parent care, child care? Despite the rhetoric, they don't see much improvement.

What about politics in my future? I have none. Absolutely. I just think there is a time for every season. "Turn, turn, turn . . . ," like the song says. I feel extraordinarily fortunate and rewarded for having been a public servant. I loved doing it and being part of that life. But it's time for me to step aside and do something else. As long as the older generations are always in the forefront, it doesn't leave room for young people to stretch their wings and emerge. And that's very important to me. I just think when public leaders hang on too long, it has a tendency to stifle the process. It's not that our ideas aren't good, but they probably hinge too much on what *was* rather than what ought to be.

I'm definitely thinking more and more about the time I have left. I look at Mama and see that she is beginning to lose some of her short-term memory. I think I have at least twenty good years left, and I've been thinking about how to plan those years. It's not that I want to predetermine what's going to happen in them, but I would like to expand my leisure time and do the things I want to do. I'd like to make more time to go to the beach. I always said that what I was gonna do when I grew up was to own a combination bait stand and breakfast bar and lending library at South Padre Island on the Gulf, and it's still very much in my mind. But there is still a lot I want to learn. That's the best part about what I'm doing now: I'm learning so much.

Since I left the governorship I've wanted to manufacture a women's purse. I'd like for women to start thinking in practical ways about breaking really bad habits. One of them is carrying a purse full of junk. It's really unnecessary and troublesome. If that is successful, and I think it will be, I'd like to develop a line of travel goods. Because I travel constantly, I know exactly what it is like to need things a certain way when you are packing and unpacking all the time. I think it would be fun. I want to do everything that comes next. And you see, that flies directly in the face of what I say I want, and that is to take time off. If I wanted to do that—take time off—I'd probably do it. But since I don't do it . . . I'm working at it.

When I left the governorship I made up a list of what I wanted from life. Financial independence was number one on the list. Number two was being able to work with people I like. I wanted to be able to travel and to learn new things. With those four items at the top of my list, it made decision making easier for me, to check invitations of things to do against that list. It just helps you decide to say, "No, I don't want to go and do that activity," and "No, I cannot make that speech," or whatever may *seem* like a good idea. But I have to pay my debts. I owe a lot of loyalty to friends all over the country, and I try to accommodate where I can. But if it doesn't meet those criteria, pretty much I don't do it.

That list is not occupational at all. It is much more about what is both emotionally and intellectually satisfying. The greatest satisfaction I have—and I could cry talking about it—is that I own the place in which I live. I own it outright, I don't owe anything on it. I own my automobile. I don't have to worry about the future. Very soon I will own a house at the beach. I've wanted a place down there since I was twenty years old, so here we are forty-some years later and I will actually *own* a spot on one of my favorite places on earth; it's not something I will have to keep working to get.

So tomorrow if I fall off the face of the earth, with Alzheimer's or something, I have enough creature comforts so that I can live—not in any grand style, I don't have any desire for that. My apartment is probably not much bigger than this whole office, but it gives me enormous satisfaction that I can live there and that I can afford it until I die. It's a huge thing. It also gives me great satisfaction to know that my children have interesting, meaningful lives and that they are not dependent on me to do anything but love them. And I do not depend on them to do anything for me but love me. You can't ask for more than that.

Probably the most important lesson I've learned in my life is to quit planning and let it happen. Our tendency—and I'm the world's worst—is to plan what's going to happen tomorrow, what's going to happen next week, next vacation, next trip, next year. And it never arrives, because you are already planning for what comes next. John Lennon said it so well: "Life is what happens while you're making other plans."

Of all the experiences I've had in my life, the most significant is my treatment for alcoholism. It was really, really important. I learned more in that month than I had learned in all the years that came before it. Much of what I have done and thought and acted upon is a consequence of what I learned there. This is my sixteenth year of sobriety; I went into treatment in 1980. That's when I began to see the fragility of life, how tenuous it is, how unbalanced it can become. It forced me to do an inventory, which I'd never even thought of doing before. The

Serenity Prayer is a very powerful message: "God, grant me the serenity to accept the things I cannot change, the courage to change the things I can, and the wisdom to know the difference." I still go to AA meetings, though not as often as I would like, because I simply don't have the time.

I have a regular group here in Austin. I've learned so much from those meetings. People think you talk about being drunk under a bridge or something—it really isn't that way at all. The meetings are very lighthearted, they're fun; it's a sharing of human problems. Many women my age go in there and talk about their problems with their aging parents, their problems with their kids. It helps so much to see yourself in those people and to realize that your problems are not unique—not to trivialize them, but to see them in a wider perspective.

I wouldn't trade anything in the world for having done that. I tell my friends who get put out with me if I have any anxieties and worries, "Well, I can walk out of here and go to a meeting, anywhere, anytime." It's an enormous support system and reassurance. My friends say, "I wish I had someplace like that to go," and I say, "It's a wonderful thing, but it's not worth becoming an alcoholic to do it."

After I finished my treatment I never had any desire to drink, but I know that can be a pitfall—the feeling that you don't have to worry. I saw too many people and I talk to too many people in meetings or in treatment who just, out of the blue, suddenly reached over and picked up a drink. Alcoholism is a disease that is so pervasive. It is not only the genetic makeup of the person who has it, but it is intrusive in the relationships of families. Even after we're sober, we still have behavioral characteristics of drunks. The disease is transgenerational. My mother was not an alcoholic, nor was my father; both my grandfathers were, and some of my uncles were, but the behavior patterns of the family system that was set up in my mother's childhood household (I don't know before that) all transfer down to my household and my children. I tried very hard, and I still do, to break that pattern. I can't do anything about my children's and my grandchildren's chemistry, but I can do something about our behavioral patterns and relationships.

One day in 1980 I walked into a room in my home and there were twelve of my friends and family sitting in a circle. They each had a prepared statement they had written. It is so hard to confront someone you love with their behavior. What courage it takes. They read their statements rather than trying to say them, and they ended with, "I know you would not have done that if you had not been drinking," so that I could see my behavior. Of course I was hurt, I was offended, I was angry, because most of them had drunk with me. I had a case of "Why don't you fix yourself instead of pointing a finger at me?" I was on the plane that afternoon to a Minnesota treatment center. It was a very low point in my life.

In truth it was an enormous relief. Even though I was angry and frightened and all those terrible emotions, I was so relieved that someone had taken charge. I'd felt out of control and miserable. Really miserable. For the first week I think I still felt that anger, but then I realized what a courageous act it had been for them to do that. And how much they must have loved me. It was a life-changing, incredibly valuable experience.

We laugh in AA circles and say if you take a drunk SOB and sober him up, you get a sober SOB, so I'm not so sure that your personality changes for the better. But your feelings about how you are going to live your life, your ability to take anything that comes your way, your resoluteness in the face of adversity, are so strengthened because you really do feel that if you can come through that, you can come through anything. I feel *so* grateful to those people, just enormously grateful. All my kids, in one way or another, have been affected by alcoholism—mine and those the generations that went into making mine.

If you think of a family as a mobile where all the pieces hang in some harmony with each other and some balance, and then you take one piece of that mobile and jerk it awry, all the other pieces dance and shake, and they try to get into balance with the most out-of-balance piece of that mobile. That dysfunctionalism is based partially on denial—we call it the elephant in the living room; everyone knows that the elephant is lying there in the living room, but no one acknowledges its presence. They nudge at it or kick at it, but no one says, "Hey, there is an elephant here in the living room and we oughta get it outta here." We still think it's bad behavior, and if this person would just pull up their bootstraps, they could do something about it; but it isn't that way at all.

Lately I've gotten on a new program, and I hope I can keep this up. I've started going to a personal trainer, and I'm really excited about it. I feel physically better than I've felt in years. We go to the gym and she's very sensitive and kind and encouraging and says things like "Oh, you could only do six of those when we started and now you're doing twenty." She doesn't push me too far, because I told her that if I got too sore, I'd get discouraged. So I was willing to take it easy and take my time at it. The best thing it does is to make me aware of how I feel. I have a very high pain threshold, and when people say to me, "How do you feel?" I have to stop and really think about it. I'm so in my head that my body is just there to hold my head up. I'm very excited about feeling strong and physically fit.

One of the other great things about being single is that I don't have to think about what anybody else wants to eat and I can buy whatever I want when I want it; I really love that. The number one thing I do, other than work, is read. I give myself permission every night before I go to bed to read. I'm burning late-night oil when I should be asleep, but I love to read.

If I could have any impact on our culture, it would be for women to have self-confidence, to have self-esteem, to see their value and then act on it—whatever their value or talent is. It need not necessarily be women's rights or politics, but to act on their own initiative of what that self-worth has produced is so important. That would be a very valuable impact.

Workshop and Lecture Announcement

If you would like to sponsor a workshop or lecture
with Cathleen Rountree on the following subjects:

Women's Studies and Issues

In Full Flower: Embracing Women's Widsom
Celebrating Midlife Discoveries
Changing the Face of Age: A Cultural Perspective
The Heroine's Journey: The Pivotal Years Between 30 and 65
The Third Act: Age as an Adventure

Creativity and the Creative Process

The Spirit of Aliveness: Cultivating Spirituality and
Creativity in Your Daily Life
Documenting the Soul's Journey Through Art and Writing
Body and Soul—A Soul Portrait, A Body Poem: Healing Our Self-Image

Love, Relationship, and Marriage

The Heart of Marriage: Discovering the Secrets of Enduring Love
50 Ways to Meet Your Lover

please send requests to:

Cathleen Rountree
P.O. Box 552
Aptos, CA 95001